NDARD

Conversational Routines in English

CHICHESTER INSTITUTE OF
HIGHER EDUCATION

WS 2110247 3

AUTHOR
AIJMER

TITLE
CONVERSATIONAL

CLASS No.
421.52

MAY97 ENG

Studies in language and linguistics

General editors: GEOFFREY LEECH & MICK SHORT
Lancaster University

Already published:

CONVERSATIONAL ROUTINES IN ENGLISH:
Convention and Creativity

KARIN AIJMER

Longman
London & New York

Addison Wesley Longman Limited
Edinburgh Gate
Harlow, Essex CM20 2JE
and Associated Companies throughout the world

Published in the United States of America
by Addison Wesley Longman, New York

© Addison Wesley Longman Limited 1996

The right of Karin Aijmer to be identified as the author of
this Work has been asserted by her in accordance with the
Copyright, Designs and Patents Act 1988.

All rights reserved; no part of this publication may be
reproduced, stored in a retrieval system, or transmitted
in any form or by any means, electronic, mechanical,
photocopying, recording, or otherwise without either the
prior written permission of the Publishers or a licence
permitting restricted copying in the United Kingdom issued
by the Copyright Licensing Agency Ltd.,
90 Tottenham Court Road, London W1P 9HE

First published 1996

ISBN 0 582 08212-9 Csd
ISBN 0 582 08211-0 Ppr

British Library Cataloguing-in-Publication Data
A catalogue record for this book is
available from the British Library

Library of Congress Cataloging-in-Publication Data
Aijmer, Karin.
    Conversational routines in English : convention and creativity /
Karin Aijmer.
        p.   cm. — (Studies in language and linguistics)
    Includes bibliographical references and index.
    ISBN 0–582–08211–0 (paper). — ISBN 0–582–08212–9 (cased)
    1. English language—Spoken English.   2. English language—
Discourse analysis.   3. English language—Prosodic analysis.
    4. Computational linguistics.   5. Conversation.   6. Semiotics.
    I. Title.   II. Series: Studies in language and linguistics (London,
England)
PE1074.8.A37   1996
420'.141—dc20   96–17540
                                                                          CIP

Set by 8 in 9/11 pt Palatino
Produced by Longman Singapore Publishers (Pte) Ltd.
Printed in Singapore

To Celia, Kristofer, Paula and Lovisa

Contents

CONTENTS

Preface

The aim of the present work is to study the range and frequency of conversational routines in the London-Lund Corpus of Spoken English. The number of spoken texts which have been collected and transcribed make up almost half a million words. The original recordings on which the texts are based were made mainly during the 1960s and 1970s at University College, London, as a part of the project Survey of English Usage (SEU).

The samples represent various text types such as face-to-face conversations, radio discussions and telephone conversations, described in more detail in Chapter 1. The telephone conversations and many of the face-to-face conversations were recorded surreptitiously, i.e. one or several of the participants did not know that the recording took place. All the surreptitiously recorded face-to-face conversations have been published (Svartvik and Quirk 1980) but the major part of the corpus is only available in computerized form.

The examples of written British English in my analysis come from the written part of the SEU corpus and are mainly taken from business letters.

The prosodic transcription of the examples

When one analyses spoken language, the prosodic transcription is important. As Du Bois et al. (1989) emphasize, there will always be more than one way of transcribing spoken discourse and the choice of what prosodic features are useful depends on the needs of the user and the topic studied.

The transcription of the London-Lund Corpus is based on the prosodic system in Crystal (1969) and includes a large number of prosodic features. In the present work, a reduced transcription of the system in the London-Lund Corpus has been used. Tone units are fundamental since it is clear that speakers organize their messages into 'chunks' of different length. In addition, the following prosodic features have been marked: location of the nucleus, pitch direction (falls, rises, etc), two types of stress, short and long pauses and onset (the first prominent syllable of the tone unit). Moreover, boosters (i.e. relative pitch levels) have been indicated since they were frequent in conversational routines expressing thanks or apologies as reinforcing devices.

Speaker identity has been indicated by upper-case letters at the beginning of the turn (A, B, C, etc). When a speaker is identified by a lower-case letter, the reason may be that he or she knows about the recording and acts as a prompter in the conversation. In such cases the speaker contributions have usually not been transcribed prosodically.[1] In addition, I have indicated simultaneous talk, contexual comments (laughs, etc), and incomprehensible speech, i.e. parts of the text which were difficult to interpret. For each example, the location in the spoken corpus is indicated (e.g. S.1 1–3).

Key to prosodic symbols used in the transcriptions[2]

Type	Explanation
#	tone unit boundary
{ }	subordinate tone unit
' "	degrees of stress
∧	onset
`	fall
´	rise
=	level
˅	fall-rise
∧	rise-fall
ˎ´	fall+rise
´ˋ	rise+fall
_ : !	degrees of booster
.	brief silent pause
-	unit silent pause
--(-)	longer than unit pause
* yes* + yes +	overlapping speech
(( ))	incomprehensible speech
> A (A	current speaker continues where he left off
A,B	A and B
A/B	A or B
VAR	various speakers
?	speaker identity unknown

Sociolinguistic information about the corpus

The basic information on the spoken texts includes 'speaker category' (e.g. university lecturer, undergraduate), sex and speaker age. The texts have been subcategorized with regard to the social distance between the speakers (see Greenbaum and Svartvik 1990 for more information about the individual texts).

The generalizations which are made are restricted to the data in the corpus. As a result, many text types are absent where social routines for thanking, apologizing and requesting can be assumed to be frequent, such as service encounters. Moreover, only educated British English has been studied and routines which have come into existence recently have not been included.

The London-Lund Corpus of Spoken English (LLC) has been the basis for a number of empirical studies of spoken English (Greenbaum and Svartvik 1990: Appendix 2), research projects (e.g. Altenberg and Eeg-Olofsson 1990 on collocations, Tottie and Bäcklund 1987 on English in speech and writing) and for textbooks of spoken interaction (cf. Aijmer and Olsson 1990, Stenström 1994). A discussion of corpus methodology and additional information about the London-Lund Corpus is found in Chapter 1 of this book. Other useful sources of information about the London-Lund Corpus are Svartvik (1990) and Aijmer and Altenberg (1991).

Notes

1 Lower-case letters are, however, used in some texts even when the examples have been transcribed. Combinations of upper-case letters are used in some texts (9.3).
2 The principles underlying the rendering of the examples are the same as those in Stenström (1994).

Acknowledgements

For this book I have had the privilege of using material from many sources. I am grateful to the late Professor Sidney Greenbaum for allowing me access to the transcriptions of the London-Lund Corpus and for the use of the written part of the corpus. Professor John Sinclair and Antoinette Renouf kindly provided me with additional examples from the Birmingham Corpus of Spoken English. I wish to thank Professor Anna-Brita Stenström for reading and commenting on Chapters 2 and 3 and Bengt Altenberg for some general comments in connection with Chapter 1. I am particularly indebted to Professor Göran Kjellmer who has read a large part of the book and provided suggestions and useful criticism. Special thanks go to the postgraduate students for encouragement, interesting discussions on pragmatic issues and good company. The book was written in the congenial atmosphere of the English Department, Lund University.

CHAPTER ONE

Introduction

1.1 Aim and scope of the present study

Many grammatical structures have a stable form in all the contexts in which they occur. One of the first scholars to draw attention to this was Jespersen:

> Some things in language – in any language – are of the formula character; that is to say, no one can change anything in them. A phrase like 'How do you do?' is entirely different from such a phrase as 'I gave the boy a lump of sugar.' In the former everything is fixed: you cannot even change the stress saying 'How *do* you do?' or make a pause between the words. ... It is the same with 'Good morning!,' 'Thank you,' 'Beg your pardon,' and other similar expressions. One may indeed analyze such a formula and show that it consists of several words, but it is felt and handled as a unit, which may often mean something quite different from the meaning of the component words taken separately.
> (Jespersen 1968 (1924): 18)

Lately a great deal of attention has been paid to expressions such as *how do you do, I am sorry, hello*, etc which are closely bound to a special function or communication situation (see also Carter 1987: 59).[1] They are variously called 'bound utterances' (Fónagy 1982: 4 – 'énoncés liés'), 'situation formulas' (Yorio 1980: 436), 'discoursal expressions' (Alexander 1984; see Figure 1.1) or 'conversational routines' (Coulmas 1981a: 2). The aim of the investigation undertaken in this work is to examine the properties of such expressions, which will here be called conversational routines.

In the past, fixed or formulaic expressions have, above all, been studied because of their importance for language acquisition (see section 1.4). Recently, there has been a greater interest in studying formulas in their own right from a linguistic and pragmatic perspective (see Bahns et al. 1986). This group is not homogeneous, but classes of fixed expressions can be distinguished on the basis of the degree of fixedness, institutionalization, situational dependence, syntactic form, etc (see Coulmas 1979; Lüger 1983). As a result there are idioms, clichés, proverbs, allusions, routines, etc (see Figure 1.1).

I	Idioms	(*to smell a rat*)
II	Proverbs	(*A watched pot never boils.*)
III	Stock phrases	(*a vicious circle*)
IV	Catchphrases	(*What do you think of it so far?*)
V	Allusions/Quotations	(*You've never had it so good.*)
VI	Idiomatic similes	(*as sober as a judge*)
VII	Discoursal expressions	(*How do you do?*)

Figure 1.1 Types of fixed expressions
(Simplified after Alexander 1984: 129; see Carter 1987: 60)

Conversational routines or discoursal expressions include a variety of phrases which are frequent in spoken language such as swear words (*bloody hell*), exclamations (*oh dear*), greetings (*good morning*), polite responses (*thank you, I'm sorry*), discourse-organizing formulas of different kinds (*frankly speaking, to be brief*) and 'small talk' (*what a nice day*).[2]

Conversational routines are analysed semantically in terms of the situation in which they are used. They can be grouped into several classes. One group consists of formulaic speech acts such as thanking, apologizing, requesting, offering, greeting, complimenting, which serve as more or less automatic responses to recurrent features of the communication situation. This class comprises both direct and indirect speech acts, simple speech acts and (routinized) patterns of speech acts.

A second large group of routines is characterized by their discourse-organizing functions rather than by their association with the social context. They are either 'connectives' contributing to the cohesion of the discourse or 'conversational gambits' with the function of opening the conversation (Alexander 1984: 129). They can, for example, facilitate the transition to something new in the discourse, signal a digression and organize different aspects of the topic. As will be shown in Chapter 5, an account of discourse markers could be given in terms of whether they point backwards or forwards in the discourse context, are oriented to the speaker or hearer, etc.

A third group of conversational routines, which will not be dealt with in this work, consists of routines which express the speaker's attitudes or emotions ('attitudinal routines').

In the linguistic literature the discussion has mainly concerned idioms, i.e. phrases whose meaning is not identical with the sum of their constituent parts (e.g. *red herring, kick the bucket*) (see, for example, Makkai 1972), although also proverbs and clichés have been the subject of interesting studies (see Norrick 1985 on proverbs). The current interest in conversational routines can be seen as an outcome of their idiomatic nature and their importance for communicative competence. They have become a major area of pragmatic research and have had an effect on our views on language acquisition, language performance and foreign language teaching.

When Uriel Weinreich delivered a number of lectures on the problems in the analysis of idioms in the middle of the 1960s (published in

Weinreich 1980), he began by apologizing for taking up so unfashionable a topic. Since then, the pendulum has swung in the direction of making the study of idiomaticity fashionable, and bold claims have been made with regard to the overall importance of idiomaticity and formulaicity in language. One can distinguish two trends in this development. On the one hand, lexicographers have started to compile special dictionaries of fixed expressions (see, for example, *The Oxford dictionary of current idiomatic English*, *The BBI combinatory dictionary of English*). On the other hand, large-scale investigations of collocational phenomena have been undertaken which indicate that lexical patterning is indeed pervasive in both speech and writing (see Altenberg and Eeg-Olofsson 1990; Kennedy 1990; Kjellmer 1991; Sinclair 1987).

As I see it, there is no definite cut-off point between fixed or completely conventionalized ways of expressing functions and the use of less stable or 'free' utterances although the emphasis in my presentation will be on devices which are fixed according to some or several criteria. The approach in this work is similar to that in communicative language teaching, as the starting-point is functional, and I am interested in the realization of certain common and useful communicative functions. Conversational routines can, however, be multi-functional, and the derived functions will also be considered in this work. *Thank you* will, for example, be analysed both as a gratitude expression and as a closing signal.

The study is organized as follows. Chapter 1 discusses the theoretical framework within which conversational routines will be described formally and pragmatically. Within this theory a psychological and social explanation for conversational routines is proposed, conversational routines are defined, and aspects of their use and linguistic realization are discussed (frequency, fixedness, function, grammatical and semantic analysis, etc). Finally, a model for describing conversational routines grammatically, semantically and pragmatically is suggested. In Chapters 2 and 3, I describe different types of routinized speech acts in the London-Lund Corpus of Spoken English. Chapter 2 deals with speech acts with the function of thanking, and Chapter 3 with apologizing. Chapter 4 discusses routinized requests and offers which are usually expressed indirectly. Chapter 5 is concerned with routines which have a discourse-strategic and cohesive function.

1.2 Material and method

The present study is based primarily on the London-Lund Corpus of Spoken English. The use of a corpus is a fairly new method for studying speech acts and other routines, although a number of studies of spoken English have been carried out on the basis of the London-Lund Corpus (see Svartvik 1990). The corpus approach needs to be discussed and related to other approaches.

The usual method of collecting spoken data, consisting of speech acts and other routines, is role plays enacted by native speakers (e.g. House and Kasper 1981; Cohen and Olshtain 1981; Eisenstein and Bodman 1986). The advantages of this method are that the analyst can choose what situations he wants to study, and that larger quantities of data can be collected. Many sociolinguists, on the other hand, have emphasized the importance of authentic data and ethnographic observation and have collected their own data (e.g. Manes and Wolfson 1981; Ervin-Tripp 1976; Holmes 1990).

The most extensive study of speech acts so far is the Cross-Cultural Speech Act Realization Project (CCSARP) (Blum-Kulka 1989: 47). In this project requests and apologies were examined in a large number of languages by testing a number of informants. The cross-linguistic data were elicited by means of a written discourse-completion test consisting of scripted dialogues representing different situations in which the informants were expected either to apologize or ask for something. It is obvious that data which have been extracted experimentally have certain methodological advantages, as these can be contrasted in different situations, media, cultures and languages. As stressed by Rintell and Mitchell (1989), elicited data must, however, be analysed with care. When they compared different methods, they found that the speech acts extracted by means of the discourse-completion test used in the CCSARP project tended to be quite long in comparison with role-play data.

Perhaps it is a sign of the novelty of the study of spoken language that there has been much discussion of methodological issues such as the authenticity of the spoken data collected by role play (see Holmes 1990: 164; Haggo and Kuiper 1983: 536). Another issue is the use of corpora as a methodology for pursuing linguistic research on spoken English. Text corpora are especially valuable because they provide information about facts which are difficult to study by means of introspection, such as the frequencies of linguistic elements in different genres and subgenres and their social and contextual constraints (see Leech 1992: 110; Svartvik 1992: 9).

The investigation of frequencies can also throw some light on language competence. As Weinreich points out, 'for an arbitrary sentence, it is clearly not part of a speaker's competence to know whether he has heard it before or to know how frequent it is' (1980: 255). On the other hand, it can be argued that the frequencies of linguistic routines are as important as their syntactic, semantic and pragmatic properties and that it is part of the speaker's competence to know how frequent they are.

In a wider perspective, the methods of corpus linguistics can be combined with different linguistic theories and approaches. Quantitative methods and corpora have been successful in studying phenomena like gradience and 'stereotypes' in the area of modality (Leech and Coates 1980; see also Karlsson 1983a on prototypes in grammatical description) as well as grammaticalization (see Mair 1994; Thompson and Mulac 1991).

Several methods can be used together, and introspection may well be the first step in a corpus study. As Kennedy (1990) has shown, introspection can be of help when one makes an inventory of the types which are available to express a particular function. In addition, introspection (besides the reading of secondary sources) is needed to suggest the factors or dimensions of the pragmatic situation determining the form that routines of a particular function can have. Some examples of contextual factors which are intuitively likely to have a determining influence on the form of speech acts are setting, social distance and power relations between the participants. Experimental methods, however, may be necessary to test the results of a corpus investigation.

The number of spoken corpora is limited, and the spoken corpora which are available are considerably smaller than the written ones. The (original) London-Lund Corpus of Spoken English (LLC), which provides the spoken material for this study,[3] consists of some 435,000 words divided into text samples of approximately 5,000 words.[4] Most of the recordings were made in the 1970s, mainly in an academic setting, and have been subsequently transcribed by means of a prosodic system which marks tone unit boundaries and the direction of the nuclear tone.

A variety of topics and settings is represented in the texts which are taken from several genres such as face-to-face conversation (surreptitious and non-surreptitious), telephone conversation, public speeches, news broadcasts, interviews, etc (see Table 1.1). The speakers are males and females of different ages with a professional background as university lecturers, students, secretaries, estate agents, etc.

The textual categories are 'fuzzy', and each text needs to be further described with regard to the social situation, setting, topic, goal, etc (see Levinson 1979: 368 – 'discourse activity types'). In the London-Lund Corpus, information is given about the setting, social roles, the power relations between the participants and the topics of the different texts (see further Greenbaum and Svartvik 1990). A variety of additional sources (informants, other corpora and previous studies) has been consulted when I have wanted more or newer material. The Birmingham Corpus (BIR), which is the basis for *Collins COBUILD English language dictionary* (see Renouf 1984), has been especially useful because it also contains spoken language.

Speech acts, like thanking, apologizing, requesting, are characteristic of spoken language but also occur in some written text types. I have therefore included some texts from the written part of the Survey of English Usage (mainly personal and business letters). (See Preface and Greenbaum and Svartvik 1990: 13.)

Table 1.1: Types of text in the London–Lund Corpus

Type	Texts	Number of texts
FACE (surreptitious)	s.1.1–14, s.2.1–14, s.3.1–6	34
FACE (non-surreptitious)	s.4.1–7, s.5.8–11, s.6.2	12
TELEPHONE	s.7.1–3, s.8.1–4, s.9.1–3	10
DISCUSSION	s.5.1–7, s.6.1, s.6.3–5, s.10.8	12
PUBLIC	s.10.1–7, s.6.6, s.11.1, s.11.3–5	12
PREPARED	s.11.2, s.12.1–6	7
Total		87

Comments:
FACE = face-to-face conversations; s.1–3 are surreptitiously recorded; s.4, 5.8–11, s.6.2 are non-surreptitious
DISCUSSION = public discussions and interviews
TELEPHONE = telephone calls including messages on the answering machine (s.9.3)
PUBLIC = public unprepared commentary (e.g. commentaries on sports events and state occasions)
PREPARED = public prepared oration (e.g. sermons, lectures, addresses by lawyers and judges and political speeches)

(Cf. Svartvik et al. (1982) and Greenbaum and Svartvik (1990) for additional information on the texts.)

1.3 Frequency of conversational routines in spoken language

Phrases which are fixed to varying degrees are extremely common in spoken English. Sorhus (1976: 217) arrived at the figure 'one fixed expression per five words' in a spoken corpus of about 130,000 words of Canadian English, and an investigation by Fillmore of 'fixed expressions' in English (referred to by Tannen and Öztek 1981: 37) resulted in 'at least 2,500 (phrases), including idioms, clichés, stock phrases, aphorisms and proverbs'.

Investigations of collocations, taken in the broad sense of recurrent word combinations, show even higher numbers. Altenberg's inventory of recurrent phrases in the London-Lund Corpus resulted in some 200,000 tokens corresponding to over 68,000 different combinations (types). Thus 'roughly 70% of the running words in the London-Lund Corpus form part of recurrent word combinations of some kind' (Altenberg 1990a: 134f), and other researchers have arrived at similar high figures.[5] It is obvious that the amount of elements which are lexicalized (i.e. which are recurrent only) is far greater than the number of elements which have (also) been idiomatized (Lamb 1992, unpublished). The high figures established by Altenberg and other researchers should be viewed in this light.

Recurrent phrases in speech are, for example, *you know, I think, sort of, thank you* which are extremely frequent (see Svartvik 1992). Similar inventories of written English indicate that writing is characterized by fewer tokens but a larger number of types. Thus Kjellmer (1987: 134) found 336,103 collocations (tokens) in the one-million-word Brown corpus of written American English (i.e. 34 per cent of the word combinations were recurrent) and as many as 84,708 combinations when he counted types. We can conclude that recurrent phrases are, above all, typical of spoken language, at least if we count tokens.

If conversational routines are a characteristic feature of spoken language, this raises several questions. What criteria or procedures are used to identify them? What is their role in speech performance and language acquisition? How should they be described? After a general discussion of psychological and social explanations of routines and other formulas I shall turn to criteria and discovery procedures for conversational routines. As Haggo and Kuiper stress (1983: 535), conversational routines involve a complex array of interacting criteria which are functional (social, pragmatic) and formal (grammatical, positional, prosodic, etc).

1.4 Psychological aspects of conversational routines

Expressions which have a fixed form are probably best known for their central role in (first) language acquisition and the learning of a second language under natural conditions. In a study by Hakuta (1974) of second language acquisition, it was found that the young Japanese learner first used the strategy of memorizing a sequence of words. As his mastery of the language progressed, the boy learnt to assign grammatical structure to the previously unanalysed elements and to create new sentences. In fact, 'chunks' were used even after the child had acquired the grammatical system, which suggests that they have additional functions.[6] Similarly, Peters (1983) has discussed how new forms are created on the basis of the syntactic 'frame' as the child's linguistic competence develops.[7]

From a different perspective, routines can be viewed as a response to performance constraints. This has been proposed in highly interesting work by Kuiper and Haggo (1984) on the formulaic speech of New Zealand stock auctioneers (see also Kuiper and Austin 1990 on race-calling speech). According to Kuiper and Haggo, the auctioneer's speech has a number of interesting linguistic features. The auctioneer speaks at a rapid rate of articulation, using short chunks and varying the prosody less than in normal speech. The syntax is formulaic, i.e. there is little grammatical or lexical variation, and sentences follow each other in a fixed order. Kuiper and Haggo claim that the linguistic features of auction speech can be explained as the result of memory constraints and the organization of the memory into a short-term and long-term memory. In the case of stock auctions, the need for the auctioneer to be fluent and to concentrate on the audience puts a heavy load on the short-term memory. However, the capacity of the short-term memory is small, and the information stored there decays quickly. On the other hand, the long-term memory can hold enormous quantities of information (Peters 1983: 86; Kuiper and Haggo 1984). In order to minimize the load on the short-term memory the auctioneer therefore internalizes completely or partly lexicalized units in the long-term memory which can be retrieved when needed. According to Kuiper and Haggo, the auctioneer's speech is almost completely made up of such routinized units which are serially ordered and generated by discourse structure rules (Kuiper and Haggo 1984: 227).[8] The units serve as a short-cut in planning and processing, enabling the auctioneer to speak rapidly and fluently and leaving him time to attend to the audience.

Kuiper and Haggo have proposed a theory of language performance shedding light on what Pawley and Syder refer to as 'the two puzzles for linguistic theory'. How do speakers produce speech which is fluent and coherent and select expressions which are natural or idiomatic (Pawley and Syder 1983: 209)?

On the other hand, generative linguists have not been interested in explaining features of naturally occurring verbal behaviour and performance. The focus has been on competence although formal structures are sometimes explained in terms of performance constraints. Thus, in *Aspects of the theory of syntax*, Chomsky (1965: 10ff) discussed some formal structures generated by the grammar which are unacceptable because of constraints caused by the organization of memory. As Leech suggests, the study of language performance must however be regarded as primary since performance is observable:

> It can also be argued that the putative gulf between competence and performance has been over-emphasised, and that the affinity between (say) the grammar of a language as a mental construct and the grammar of a language as manifested in performance by the native speaker must be close, since the latter is a product of the former. ... It can be argued that language performance is abundantly observable, that its study is more obviously useful than that of competence to most applications of linguistics (e.g. in education, in translation and in material language processing).
> (Leech 1992: 108)

The main reason for discussing Kuiper and Haggo's theory of language performance at some length is that it can explain linguistic and extra-linguistic features of ordinary conversation (cf. Altenberg and Eeg-Olofsson 1990; Pawley and Syder 1983). The most striking thing about informal conversation is that it has to be planned under very tight temporal constraints.

This follows both from the lack of pre-planning in spoken communication and from the orientation towards the hearer's needs and wants in spoken language. The speaker selects his conversational contribution so that it fits that of the previous speaker at the same time as he is planning 'locally' how to present the message. As pointed out by Pawley and Syder, there are many simultaneous demands on the speaker, all of which have an effect on his production:

> A speaker is expected to make contributions to conversation that are coherent, take into consideration what has gone on before and what might happen later, and are sensitive to audience knowledge and other features of the social situation; this talk should be nativelike in an appropriate register and meet other general and specific requirements (e.g. of accuracy or vagueness, as the situation demands, of logic, wit, modesty and the like). He is by no means free to concentrate on the grammatical content of his productions.
> (Pawley and Syder 1983: 204)

Experiments have shown that speakers are capable of encoding fluent units of considerable length without internal breaks and hesitations (Pawley and Syder 1983: 202). On a deeper level, units are 'chunks' in the long-term memory, which can be retrieved at short notice, making it possible for speakers to speak without hesitation or pauses. By combining chunks or tone units into larger units in a fragmentary or chainlike fashion the speaker is able to produce long stretches of speech at a high speed which do not impose a load on the short-term memory (Chafe 1979; Pawley and Syder 1983: 218).

1.5 Conversational routines and ritualization

The ritualization of certain polite speech acts is almost taken for granted (Ferguson 1981). One of the first linguists to describe the ritual character of human interaction is the American anthropologist Erving Goffman (1971). According to Goffman (1971), thanking, apologizing and requesting correspond to 'everyday rituals' strengthening the social bonds between the interactants. Goffman (1971) distinguishes between two kinds of ritual interchange: the first is a positive, supportive ritual which is caused by the need for mutual support. The acceptance of an offer may, for instance, be responded to by a gratitude phrase (Owen 1983: 12; see also section 4.20). The second is a negative, remedial ritual which can be illustrated by strategies of apologizing. This ritual occurs when an offence has been committed, and the speaker ('offender') attempts to remedy the offence and restore harmony (Goffman 1971: 140; see also Chapter 3). Another major function of routines, which is not accounted for within this model, is that they add to the structural coherence of the discourse (Keller 1981). In Chapter 5, I account for the cohesive function of discourse markers in terms of the principle of relevance (see Sperber and Wilson 1986).

1.6 Lexicalization, grammaticalization and idiomatization

We can shed some light on conversational routines by regarding them as the result of lexicalization, grammaticalization or idiomatization. It is well known that many prepositional phrases (*in any case*) and compound noun phrases (*headache*) are the result of lexicalization (see Pawley and Syder 1983: 209). Lexicalization presupposes a linguistic process which makes it possible to create new wholes or 'gestalts' from the combination of single words.

For example, *headache* is not simply understood as the combination of the meaning of *head* and *ache*, but has a new meaning which is to some extent arbitrary. For lexicalization to take place the new concept must also be culturally recognized and be familiar to the users. This explains why there is no corresponding compound *footache*.

When we have sequences of words which have syntactic structure, it is more difficult to decide when a form has been lexicalized, and we have to recognize degrees of lexicalization on a scale of frozenness (cf. Bauer 1978: 10). An expression may be more or less fixed in form, more or less institutionalized or culturally recognizable, more or less close to having its literal meaning, more or less easy to analyse into its constituents (Pawley and Syder 1983: 212). There is no fixed cut-off point between different types of phrase in the language, only a number of tests which may give different results. The fixedness of conversational routines will be further discussed in section 1.8.

One can expect constraints on the grammatical structure of routines to be similar to restrictions on the process of word-formation. Thus there is a parallel between non-occurring compounds and complex words on the one hand and, on the other hand, 'grammatical gaps', i.e. constructions which are not current or not used although they would be generated by the grammar.

A vexed question is whether the fixedness of routines involves grammaticalization (Thompson and Mulac 1991 – 'grammaticization') rather than, or in addition to, lexicalization. Grammaticalization is clearly involved when the category which is created by 'decategorialization' (Hopper 1991: 30) is a secondary category such as an adverb. Thompson and Mulac (1991) claim, for example, that the epistemic phrase ('parenthetical clause') *I think* has been reanalysed as an adverb through a process of grammaticalization, and it is clear that multi-word discourse-organizing routines or 'gambits' (*to tell you the truth, after all*) can be regarded as secondary adverbs with constrained conditions of use. Other phrases such as *thank you* or *sorry*, which can hardly be analysed as secondary adverbs, are more problematic.

A distinction can also be made between lexicalization or grammaticalization and idiomatization. Not all sequences of words which are lexicalized become idiomatized (in the sense of receiving a meaning which is different from the combination of the meanings of the parts), and idiomatization can be strong or weak.

1.7 Conversational routines and meaning

Conversational routines are phrases which, as a result of recurrence, have become specialized or 'entrenched' for a discourse function which predominates over or replaces the literal referential meaning (Leech 1983: 28 – 'pragmatic specialization'; Cowie 1988: 132; Nattinger and DeCarrico 1989: 128; Fillmore et al. 1988: 506 – 'idioms with a pragmatic point').

A piece of evidence that conversational routines cannot be defined semantically in terms of compositional rules is that conversational routines from different semantic sources can be functionally equivalent:

> let's face it
> to put it mildly (putting it mildly)
> to tell you the truth
> frankly
> honestly
> forgive me if I say that ...
> I don't want to be personal but ...
> (Aijmer and Olsson 1990: 190)

The common pragmatic function of these phrases, which occur at the beginning of an utterance or a larger discourse unit, is to warn the hearer that the message may be experienced as indiscreet, embarrassing or too blunt. The referential meaning does not completely disappear, however, but is 'overlaid' with a pragmatic function, which may be more or less dominant. The relationship between literal meaning and pragmatic function is nevertheless complex and is best explained in a model where linguistic elements can have several different functions simultaneously and have more or less referential meaning. The cooccurrence of different functions can be indicated on scales perhaps in the manner suggested by Holmes (1990: 158).[9] In Holmes's interactional model, any utterance can be placed on parallel scales, indicating the degree of propositional meaning as well as the degree and type of interactional (interpersonal or textual) function.

To describe different types of semantic function and elucidate the pragmatic role of conversational routines we can use Halliday and Hasan's interactional model of language (1976) or the modified version of it proposed by Traugott (1982).[10] According to Traugott, each utterance is described in three functional semantic components: the propositional, the textual and the expressive. The propositional component deals with the resources in language which make it possible to talk about things in the world. It has, above all, to do with meanings which can be described in truth-functional terms and can be analysed on the basis of the syntactic structure by means of semantic compositional rules.

Conversational routines are mainly accounted for in the other two functional components. This means that they are not interpreted by semantic, compositional rules, but that they are defined functionally and pragmatically (see section 1.14). The textual component involves linguistic devices which create textual coherence such as discourse markers. The expressive component deals with elements expressing personal attitudes to the message but also with routinized speech acts which have a social or polite meaning such as thanking and apologizing.[11]

It would be too optimistic to expect that all conversational routines have some common formal features since there is so much formal variation. The formal features which will be discussed have to do with fixedness, position, syntactic integration, grammaticality, and textual distribution. Routinized speech acts can also be described on different textual levels as single speech acts or as parts of larger discourse structures.

1.8 Criteria of fixedness

Carter (1987: 59) mentions fixedness as a criterion of conversational routines, although most are said to exhibit 'lesser degrees of structural fixity' than (semantic) idioms. Fixedness can be described as non-substitutability or in terms of collocational restrictions (see Carter 1987: 63). It is also a prosodic notion (see section 1.8.2).

How do you do illustrates a speech act which is fixed by several criteria (see Quirk et al. 1985: 11.54 note; Jespersen 1968 (1924): 18). The phrase cannot be made a constituent in a larger construction (**I wonder how you do*) or be modified (**How do you do today*?); the present tense cannot be replaced by the past tense without a change of meaning (**How did you do*) and the person of the subject cannot be changed (**How does he do*).

Besides, diachronic considerations can be involved in defining the fixedness of an expression. A criterion is the use of forms which are archaic or synchronically irregular or forms which can only be explained in the light of diachronic processes such as phonological weakening (Ferguson 1981: 31). Consider, for example, the use of the present tense rather than the expected present progressive in *how do you do* (cf. the less fixed phrase *how're you doing*). Phonological weakening or attrition is illustrated in the diachronic shift:

how do you do → *howdy*

Finally, the phrase is fixed in the sense that the idiomatic function (= a greeting) is associated directly and unambiguously with the linguistic form. A high degree of fixedness is also indicated by the fact that, in a discourse perspective, *how do you do* must be followed by another greeting, usually a copy of the same phrase (A: *How do you do?* – B: *How do you do?*). (See section 1.10.)

According to the same tests, the greeting *how are you* is less fixed. It can either be interpreted literally or have an idiomatized pragmatic function. The idiomatic meaning is illustrated by the following exchange:

How are you?
Fine how are you?

However, the phrase can be understood literally as a question if it is asked by one's doctor and answered by a specification of one's health (Makkai 1972: 175). Grammatically, it is also less fixed. The form of the verb can be changed (*How have you been?*); the subject can be the third person (*How is he?*). The phrase can be embedded in another structure (*He wondered how I was*) and it can be expanded (*How are you today?*).[12]

The majority of routines are like *how are you*, which is fixed according to some criteria but not others. *Thank you* is another example of how each phrase needs to be described on the basis of several different criteria. The phrase cannot be passivized (**you are thanked*), and the verb cannot be replaced by a (near-)synonym (**appreciate you*). However, *thank you* can be modified (*thank you very much*), embedded (*I wish to thank you*), etc in ways which will be further discussed in Chapter 2.

Haggo and Kuiper (1983: 541) account for the grammatical and semantic restrictions on formulas and their potential variability in a finite state grammar without loops (see section 1.12). Another model is provided by lexicalized sentence stems, an alternative I explore in section 1.12.

1.8.1 *Repetitive phrases and pragmatic idioms*

Conversational routines can also be fixed because they always appear in a certain form. Manes and Wolfson's work on compliments (1981) is of special interest here. To begin with, Manes and Wolfson noticed that there is an almost infinite number of (indirect) realizations of a compliment. However, some variants are never chosen, although they are grammatical and would be functionally appropriate. Manes and Wolfson found, for example, that as many as 85 per cent (out of 686 compliments) fell into one of only three syntactic patterns such as *I (really) like NP* (Manes and Wolfson 1981: 123). Furthermore, just two verbs (*like* and *love*) occurred in 86 per cent of all the compliments containing verbs expressing a positive evaluation (Manes and Wolfson 1981: 117). Of the compliments with an adjective, 22.9 per cent contained *nice* (Manes and Wolfson 1981: 117). (See Figure 1.2.)

Manes and Wolfson concluded that compliments were formulas (routines), just as much as greetings or thanks, because speakers used only a restricted set of expressions. As a result, compliments are

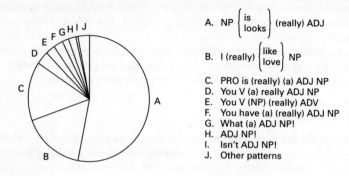

A. NP $\begin{Bmatrix} \text{is} \\ \text{looks} \end{Bmatrix}$ (really) ADJ

B. I (really) $\begin{Bmatrix} \text{like} \\ \text{love} \end{Bmatrix}$ NP

C. PRO is (really) (a) ADJ NP
D. You V (a) really ADJ NP
E. You V (NP) (really) ADV
F. You have (a) (really) ADJ NP
G. What (a) ADJ NP!
H. ADJ NP!
I. Isn't ADJ NP!
J. Other patterns

Figure 1.2   The distribution of syntactic patterns in compliments (after Manes and Wolfson 1981: 121)

constrained as to pattern productivity just as much as thanks or apologies. It should be remembered, however, that even if the patterns which can be established by quantitative methods are of interest, they have different properties from other routines.

At this point we need to make a distinction between different types of routine. According to Stenström, structures can be analysed both on the grammatical and pragmatic level (see Stenström's 1990: 172f multi-level analysis of so-called discourse markers). Coulmas (1979: 240), on the other hand, discusses the possibility of classifying routines into repetitive (recurrent) phrases and pragmatic idioms. 'Repetitive phrases' (such as *I really like NP*) do not have special syntactic characteristics, i.e. they are not restricted as to pattern productivity and they are not transformationally defective. 'Pragmatic idioms' are characterized by typical idiom features, such as a special meaning, fixed form and grammatical irregularities.

Finally, it should be noted that there is a fuzzy boundary between different types of phrase. As Lamb points out (1992, unpublished), there are a great many phrases which are only weakly or slightly idiomatized, i.e. they keep their literal meaning. Such transparent phrases are, for example, *the problem is ... , what I mean is ... , let me tell you something.*

1.8.2   *Prosodic fixedness*

Prosodically, conversational routines correspond to tone units. Tone unit boundaries and hesitation pauses within the tone unit therefore provide additional clues about the degree of fixedness of a conversational routine (see Altenberg and Eeg-Olofsson 1990: 18; Peters 1983: 10). There is a fixed set of tones to choose from. As Kuiper and Haggo point out, a fixed prosody makes 'storage and retrieval easier, as a filing system using cards of different colour in each section is easier to use than a single colour system' (1984: 228).

Keller (1981: 106f) regarded 'a drop in the intonational contour' as a more reliable criterion for 'gambits' (conversational routines with a discourse-organizing function) than syntactic independence or position in the utterance. Moreover, a characteristic intonation pattern can be chosen in stereotypic or standard situations illustrated by the tone on *sorry* when one bumps into someone (see Ladd 1978 – 'stylized intonation'). Finally, it should be stressed that although intonation is always to some extent fixed, a conversational routine may have several prosodic patterns each with complicated conditions of use. *Sorry* is, for example, used with a rise (fall-rise) tone if the speaker asks the hearer to repeat something, but with a fall tone to signal sincere regret.

A fixed prosody also means that the stress cannot be moved from its normal position to any other element of the phrase (see section 1.1). There are, however, degrees of prosodic fixedness, and changes in the prosodic pattern can be made for certain purposes (*thank you very mùch→ thank you vèry much*).

1.9   The processing of conversational routines

On a general level, the analysis of routines and idioms depends on whether language performance is regarded as governed by grammatical rules or as the 'putting-together' of ready-made or partly ready-made cognitive units stored in the long-term memory. In this connection it is fruitful to think of the 'language text' as being produced and interpreted according to two different principles.

According to the so-called 'open choice principle' discussed by Sinclair (1987: 319), the language text is the result of a number of 'slot-by-slot' choices made by the language user on different levels. A language text organized according to the 'idiom principle' imposes heavier constraints on what is said[13] since the principle presupposes that language users have at their disposal a number of lexicalized or semi-lexicalized phrases which are stored in the long-term memory (see Sinclair 1987: 320). Such phrases can be interpreted directly by the hearer without the need of semantic rules operating on the syntactic structure in a compositional fashion (see Morgan and Horn's notion 'short-circuited implicature'; see section 4.4). The idiom principle is compatible with a tendency to economy in language (see Leech 1983: 67) since the speaker can easily and rapidly get access to the lexicalized or idiomatized chunks which are stored in the long-term memory. Looking things up in the long-term memory is quick and provides the speaker with extra time to plan ahead.

Sinclair stresses the fact that the two models of language are incompatible with each other: 'There is no shading of one into another; the switching from one model to the other will be sharp' (1987: 324). On the other hand, the principles or processes for interpreting sentences do not represent an either/or choice in discourse interpretation, but operate in a parallel fashion:

> We should also recognize that the choice between understanding a combination on the basis of its components and understanding a lexicalized formation as a unit is not an either-or choice at all, since these two processes may both operate, in parallel. It is very likely that such parallel operation is usual for combinations that are as yet only slightly lexicalized.
> (Lamb 1992, unpublished, p. 1)

Parallel processing implies that the hearer has a choice between recognizing a combination of words as a lexicalized unit or analysing it on the basis of the grammar and the lexicon, and that switches from one principle to another can take place on-line. In Lamb's model there would be two possible processing routes (see Figure 1.3).[14]

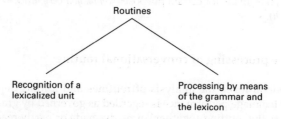

Figure 1.3 Parallel processing of conversational routines (strongly and weakly idiomatic phrases)

Even when a lexeme has been 'strongly' idiomatized, its components can still operate as such to provide connotations based on the meanings they have when occurring in isolation (cf. *frankly speaking, to tell you the truth*). If we take it that there are parallel ways of processing idioms, we can also explain that the semantic information associated with the component parts of the idiom can be recovered by means of 'recycling' (cf. Haggo and Kuiper 1983: 549 – 'semantic reanalysis'; Kjellmer 1991: 123 – 'manipulation'). An example is when *How do you do?* is responded to by *How do I do what?* for humorous effect (Makkai 1972: 175).

This view of language processing and interpretation means that many phenomena, which traditionally belong to grammar, may also be analysed as routines and patterns. Makkai advocates the view that much of grammar ought to be studied in an idiomatic perspective (1992, unpublished). Here are some examples:

- uses of words which are collocationally restricted
  (*now you come to mention it*)

- uses of words cooccurring with certain complements
  (*thank you for coming, sorry to trouble you*)
- words which are ordered in a special way
  (*perhaps you would like to come*)
- combinations of words which repeatedly occur together (indirect requests like *can you, would you,* etc)

There are many problems with studying utterances as routines or larger routinized patterns.[15] Even if one believes that the bulk of language is to some extent routinized, it is clear that speakers may differ with regard to what patterns they have stored and use. Moreover, it is difficult to formulate pragmatic rules or frames for indirect requests which are sufficiently constrained to explain how the extralinguistic situation is matched with lexical forms.

1.10   Routines and discourse

Minimally, a routine is a single word (e.g. *thanks, sorry*), but most routines consist of several words. It is clear that speakers can store quite long phrases in their long-term memories (e.g. the routine *can I keep you for a moment and tell you something* which can preface a message). A routine need not even be a syntactic constituent as is shown by routine phrases such as *the fact is* … , *can you* … . Some routines are discontinuous with a slot for lexical insertion: *as far as | … | is concerned*.

Routines do not only occur alone, but they can be repeated and juxtaposed. The structures which emerge are composed of single building-blocks, stored as units in the speaker's long-term memory, which appear in the order that they are generated. The combination of routines can be more or less fixed:

(1)   B   ^lòvely# .
           ^thank you !very 'much in:dèed#
(9.2. 568–9)

In general, the length and complexity of the gratitude phrase depend on the social situation and the amount of politeness it requires (see Chapter 2). Besides, we find sequences of routines. The smallest of the formulaic discourse structures can be described as an adjacency pair (Richards and Schmidt 1983a: 128; Schegloff and Sacks 1973). Adjacency pairs are sequences of utterances produced by two successive speakers such that the 'first pair part' constrains the other speaker to provide a response in the 'second pair part'. An exact copy of the first part is characteristic of pairs which are completely formulaic such as greetings (*Hello – Hello*). In discourse structures which are less tightly constrained, there is a choice between different strategies in the second part or the second part may be optional. Compare, for example, the following adjacency pairs consisting of a request and different second pair parts (from Richards and Schmidt 1983a: 129):

Request – Grant A: Can you mail these for me please?
               B: Sure.
– Put off   B: Sure, but I won't have time today.
– Challenge   B: Why do you always ask me to mail them *for* you?
– Refusal   B: Sorry, but I won't be near the Post Office.

Discourse patterns (which can be regarded as a special kind of adjacency pairs) may occasionally consist of three parts, all of which are routines.

> A: 'Would you pass the milk?'
> B: 'Here.'
> A: 'Thanks.'
> (after Goffman 1976: 69)

The first two moves of the conversational exchange are a request by A and the granting of the request by B. The third move (which is optional) acknowledges the response by B and closes the conversational exchange.[16]

Routines are frequent in certain discourse types which impose constraints on the speaker's short-term memory such as auctions (see Kuiper and Haggo 1984), sports commentaries (see Kuiper and Austin 1990), religious ceremonies (see Paul 1989). Another example is telephone calls where routines are found in the opening and the closing of the call (see Hopper 1989; Schegloff and Sacks 1973). This will be illustrated in the following chapters.

1.11 Conversational routines and grammatical analysis

To what extent can conversational routines be described grammatically? In the following sections I shall discuss if and what syntactic information must be specified for conversational routines.

1.11.1 Grammatical deficiency

According to Bahns et al. (1986: 695), formulas do not show any syntactic peculiarities. Many conversational routines can be analysed as sentences (*I am grateful for /your help/*, *I'm sorry, how do you do*), subordinate clauses (*as far as I know, if I may say so*), noun-verb structures (*I mean, you know*), non-finite clauses (*to tell you the truth, frankly speaking*), prepositional phrases (*in fact*), etc. There are also grammatically defective routines such as sentence fragments, independent subordinate clauses (*if you could help me*), irregular *wh*-questions (*how about coffee*), non-sentences (*next slide please*), and elliptical constructions of different kinds (*want a drink*).

Routinized sentence fragments can be of different kinds. The short phrases *sorry, beg your pardon* or *thank you* are analysed as sentence fragments because they lack the subject (or both subject and copula). Since the missing elements are known, the phrases must be analysed as the result of (situational) ellipsis (Quirk et al. 1985: 11.38).

Even if routines have a constituent structure, they are not necessarily generated by the grammar. To give an example, *you know* and *I mean* are a fixed combination of noun and verb which must be analysed as discourse markers (see Stenström 1990). Outside this group, however, noun-verb structures are an open-ended category. In comment clauses such as *he thought, he said*, etc, the verb can, for example, appear with an adverbial (*he said immediately*), and it can be exchanged for other synonymous verbs (*he reflected, he supposed, he mentioned*).

As pointed out above, conversational routines are usually multi-word units. One-word routines are difficult to describe in grammatical terms, and many of them would belong to Fillmore et al.'s class of 'extra-grammatical idioms' (Fillmore et al. 1988: 505). In *thanks*, for example, it is not clear what elements have been omitted as *thanks* could be expanded in more than one way. Both *I owe you my thanks* and *I give you thanks* are possible sources for *thanks* (Quirk et al. 1985: 12.34). Alternatively, we could argue that the syntactic properties of the phrase should be deduced from its syntactic sub-categorization. However, this is not very helpful since *thanks* can be sub-categorized in two different ways. The phrase must be a verb when it is followed by an intensifying adverb (e.g. *thanks very much*) but it can also be a noun which is premodified (*many thanks*). We conclude therefore that *thanks* is grammatically rather like *hello* which is not amenable to syntactic analysis.[17] Discourse-organizing routines such as *well, now* which function as 'openers' are also difficult to analyse grammatically. They can be analysed neither as elliptical structures nor as special parts of speech.

Moreover, whole sentences can be syntactically indeterminate, as illustrated by Haggo and Kuiper's (1983: 543f) example *there you are* (a formula used when giving somebody something). First, they say, this sentence is probably not a transformation of *you are there*. Secondly, we could hardly say that *you* is the subject of *are*. Thirdly, the status of *there* is difficult to determine.[18] Now if the phrase is not simply a transformational variant of the phrase *you are there*, this could be taken to mean that it should be analysed as a grammatical construction, i.e. 'a symbolic model that pairs syntactic conditions with semantic and pragmatic conditions' (Lakoff 1987: 471; cf. Fillmore et al. 1988). As a grammatical construction the phrase can have different syntactic, semantic and pragmatic properties from the corresponding simple sentences (see also the discussion of stems in section 1.11).

1.11.2 *Syntactic integration and position*

Conversational routines expressing thanks and apologies constitute independent conversational moves (see Stenström 1990: 147). On the other hand, routines with a discourse-organizing function (called discourse markers in Chapter 5) are partly integrated in another grammatical structure.

Following Andersson (1975) they can also be called speech-act adverbials because they have adverbial function and 'because they modify the speech act of saying something rather than what is said' (Andersson 1975: 27; my translation).[19] The adverbial constitutes a prosodic unit marked by a tone unit boundary. It has initial (or final) position in the utterance of which it is a part.

What is interesting about Andersson's analysis is that speech-act adverbials are characterized not only functionally and prosodically but also grammatically. In Figure 1.4, a distinction is made between speech-act adverbials, which have pragmatic function, and other elements (adverbs, clauses, etc), which are integrated in the proposition and have a propositional function.

The speech-act adverbial (= a) occupies a separate node in the tree diagram, indicating that its pragmatic scope extends over the whole structure although it is not part of the grammatical core. Elements which have a propositional function (= b) must be part of the propositional structure, which is interpreted compositionally by the semantic rules.

There are several arguments for distinguishing between two syntactic analyses. First, there is a contrast between speech-act adverbials and adverbs not referring to the speech act which is clear in pairs such as:

(a) Frankly (speaking), he behaved well
(b) He behaved frankly

Also, whole clauses as adverbials can have two interpretations reflected in different structural analyses. To give an example, *if I may say so* has pragmatic function and is not part of a conditional sentence. The clause contrasts with *if*-clauses which state the condition under which the main clause is true (*If it rains, I carry an umbrella.*).

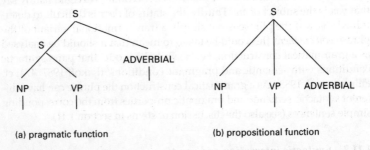

(a) pragmatic function   (b) propositional function

Figure 1.4 The constituent structure of (a) speech-act adverbials and (b) of other adverbials in final position (After Andersson 1975: 29)

Secondly, the analysis proposed in Figure 1.4 can explain the ambiguity of the following (constructed) example from Sinclair and Renouf (1988: 152):

> To be fair, Tom divided the sweets evenly.

In the pragmatic interpretation, the person who is fair is the person speaking or writing, and the phrase is a judgement on Tom. In this case, the phrase is attached pragmatically (as a speech-act adverbial or a disjunct) to the following utterance. In the other interpretation, *to* could be paraphrased as 'in order to', and the person who is fair is Tom. The infinitive is a purpose clause and belongs to the proposition.

In the well-known syntactic analysis of adverbials by Quirk et al. (1985: 8.121), adverbials which are only loosely integrated in the syntactic structure are called disjuncts. Their independent status is shown by various grammatical operations. For example, they are distinct from other syntactic classes of adverbials (adjuncts, subjuncts) because they cannot be made the focus of a cleft sentence (*it is frankly speaking that he did it*) or be the basis of alternative interrogation (*was it frankly speaking or strangely enough that he did it*).

1.12 A model for describing the structural flexibility of conversational routines

Can conversational routines be accounted for in generative grammar? As we have seen, conversational routines may be invariable and/or grammatically irregular; they can have idiomatic meanings and be bound to the situation. The majority, however, are partly productive and are not grammatically peculiar. Exactly how one describes conversational routines and other formulas seems to be a consequence of one's views on lexicalization and the boundary between the lexicon and grammar. Fillmore et al. describe the current grammatical scene as follows:

> Current formal models of grammar take a severe view of the distinction between knowing and figuring out: they assign as much work as possible to the computing or figuring out part of knowing how to use language, and they attempt to keep at a minimum those aspects of linguistic competence that have to be represented as stored or known.
>
> (Fillmore et al. 1988: 502)

In generative grammar a distinction is made between a grammatical rule component generating sentences and the lexicon representing those aspects of linguistic competence which are stored or known. It is possible, however, that generative grammar is, in a way, 'too perfect' to account for conversational routines. This leaves us with a number of possible models for describing conversational routines. In so-called Construction

Grammar (see Fillmore et al. 1988), conversational routines would presumably be grammatical constructions specifying syntactic, lexical, semantic and pragmatic information.

Recently, one has also seen different proposals for enriching the lexicon in order to account for structures which do not belong clearly either in the lexicon or in the grammar (see Jackendoff's 1975 discussion of full-entry theories using redundancy rules versus impoverished entries and Haggo and Kuiper 1983: 539f).

In the theoretical framework of the present study, which is based on Pawley and Syder (1983), the form of conversational routines is a fairly abstract sentence stem, consisting of a 'core' with possible extensions. The following lexemes are linked by family resemblance and related by a stem containing *sorry* as its core:

(2)　　I'm sorry to keep you waiting.
　　　　I'm so sorry to have kept you waiting.
　　　　Mr X is sorry to keep you waiting all this time.
　　　　(Pawley and Syder 1983: 210)

The stem is a collocational frame[20] with slots for grammatical categories.

　　　　NP be-TENSE sorry to keep-TENSE you waiting
　　　　(Pawley and Syder 1983: 210)

Clearly, the stem is different from a productive grammatical rule as it contains (lexical) elements which are not inserted by means of lexical rules. The capitalized elements represent slots into which, for example, a noun phrase or a tense morpheme may be inserted.

Lexicalized sentence stems are placed by Pawley in the 'ideal lexicographers' lexicon' (1986: 114). On a deeper level they are cognitive units which provide an economical way of storing linguistic variants which show some similarity, and they can be used ready-made in speech production. The availability and flexibility of the stem may explain why lexicalized sentence stems are so frequent in spoken language; the number of lexicalized sentence stems in English 'probably amounts, at least, to several hundreds of thousands' (Pawley and Syder 1983: 213; see also section 1.3).

From a formal grammatical point of view, a dictionary entry for a lexicalized sentence stem is a 'mini-grammar' (Pawley and Syder 1983: 216). The stem has the capacity to generate a number of 'possible routine phrases' and can be exploited by speakers for 'creative' departures (Fillmore 1984: 128). Variants are formed from the stem by substituting elements by 'inflection', modifying existing structures, combining elements into sets, embedding structures in larger discourse units and by deleting optional elements.

Grammatical constructions or lexicalized sentence stems can be compared with a finite state grammar without recursive properties (Kuiper and Haggo 1984: 221).[21] The grammar runs through a number of states with an initial and terminal state as endpoints, producing words at each transition, assigning to them a certain probability. Since the model represents the simplest type of generative grammar, it has little processing capacity (requiring only one slot in the short-term memory).

One can notice, finally, that although the lexicalized stems discussed by Pawley and Syder (1983) have the form of sentences, it is obvious that stems can also consist of clauses or phrases with fixed and variable parts and a specification of the elements which can fill an empty slot in the stem.

> ADVERB sorry to ...
> *very*
> *frightfully*
> *terribly*
> *awfully*
> *truly*, etc

Discourse-organizing routines (speech-act adverbials) consist of clausal or phrasal stems. For example:

> if I may be ADJECTIVE
> *frank*
> *honest*, etc

The adjective slot can be filled by *frank* or by a synonym.

What is fixed and what is variable can be seen by inspecting the stem. Consider *now you come to mention it*, which can be described by the following clausal stem:

> now you come to VERB PHRASE
> *mention it*
> *think of it*

The fixed part of the stem is *now you come to* since we cannot say *now that you come to ...* . There is a closed set of verb phrases which can fill the verb phrase slot.

Phrasal stems can be illustrated by *frankly speaking*, a routine phrase consisting of an adverb and the non-finite *speaking* in a fixed, stereotypic order:

> ADVERB speaking
> *frankly*
> *strictly*
> *broadly*, etc

The productivity of the stem is constrained by listing the forms which actually occur with their frequencies. Some forms are frequent, others are less frequent or non-occurring. In his corpus of apologies Owen (1983: 66) found that out of 24 possible combinations derivable from a syntactic frame (stem) with *sorry*, only twelve occurred, and of these only seven occurred more than once (see Figure 1.5).

$$\left(\left\{\begin{array}{l} \text{I'm} \\ \text{I am} \end{array}\right\}\right) \text{([intensifier]) sorry} \left(\left\{\begin{array}{l} \text{(that) S} \\ \text{to VP} \\ \text{if S} \\ \text{about that} \end{array}\right\}\right)$$

Figure 1.5   The syntactic frame used to describe apologies (after Owen 1983: 66)

1.13   The pragmatic function of conversational routines

1.13.1   *Conversational routines and illocutionary force*

Speakers must also know the function of conversational routines and the constraints on their conditions of use. It is important to discuss what is meant by function in this connection. It is generally assumed that speech acts are assigned illocutionary force by a special speech-act assignment mechanism (discussed in more detail in the following chapters) on the basis of certain formal 'cues' referred to as illocutionary force-indicating devices (IFIDs). (See Searle 1969: 30.) Obvious IFIDs are the performative verbs (*I apologize*); in thanks and apologies a noun or an adjective may play a similar role (as in *thanks, sorry*). At least for some speech acts, the methods by which illocutionary force is assigned to an utterance are less clear. Thus a compliment (such as *I really like your sweater*) is recognized as a compliment because of its formulaic composition only (cf. Haggo and Kuiper 1983: 535 for a brief mention of the problems involved). Moreover, special problems are created by devices which are ambiguous between a literal and a non-literal interpretation such as *can you*, which signals either a question or a request (see section 1.13.2).

Depending on what we mean by function, conversational routines can have many different functions. As Coulmas (1979: 254) points out, routinized forms also contribute to group membership, facilitate recognition and maintain 'orderliness' in the conversation by regulating certain emotional situations and providing the verbal means for communicating 'the right idea in the right place'. In addition, we must describe the situations in which conversational routines are used.

1.13.2   *Indirect speech acts*

The invention of new uses for things surrounding us is a familiar phenomenon in real life. As Weinreich writes:

> This phenomenon of superimposed meaning would be awkward and surprising if the doubling up of functions were not so familiar in other fields of human endeavor. I take a hammer and use it as a paperweight; its nail-driving functions are suspended while it functions to hold sheets of paper in a draft. A statue of a

goddess holds up the roof of a temple. A horn of a car, as it warns the pedestrians, sounds a melodic figure subject to aesthetic evaluation.
(Weinreich 1980: 259)

In a similar fashion, an utterance which is literally a question (*can you pass the salt?*) may function as a request. In linguistics, it is common to describe speech acts whose force results from the functional extension of the literal meaning of a sentence as 'indirect'. The indirect meaning can be inferred on the basis of utterance meaning, the preceding discourse, setting, etc and certain general principles of politeness and rationality. To give an example, the indirect meaning of *can you* (verb phrase) is motivated by the principle that it is polite to respect the hearer's autonomy and freedom not to comply with the request (see Chapter 4). By asking if the hearer is able to do something, the speaker gives the hearer the chance to refuse to comply because he is not able to.

Such principles are probably the closest we get to 'a grammar of functional extension' (Weinreich 1980: 259), and they have considerable explanatory power (see Chapter 4). Indirect speech acts may be analysed not only in a theory of indirect speech acts; when they are conventionalized, the pragmatic solution is less satisfactory.

1.13.3 *Conventionalization of indirect speech acts*

From the perspective adopted in this work, one can regard indirect requests as routine forms just as much as *thank you, sorry,* etc.[22] An indirect request is not generated by the grammar but the speaker uses a semi-lexicalized unit such as *can you*. What is special about (some) indirect requests is that they are pragmatically ambiguous. As a result, the routine *can you* can be either a request formula or a question formula (see section 1.3.2).

Moreover, indirect speech acts are more or less explicit. For example, when the speaker uses a performative formula, the illocutionary force is maximally explicit. When the speaker wants to be less specific, a less explicit or transparent marker is used, which is only indirectly associated with a certain function, although the link between form and function is conventionalized. It is in this sense that *I'm sorry* is an apology marker just as much as *I apologize*, although the phrase is less explicit.[23]

In this work, the rules for the use of indirect speech acts are closely linked with a particular language or culture. In other words, although the strategies are universal or at least very general, there may be cross-linguistic differences between indirect speech acts (see Blum-Kulka et al. 1989; Nattinger and DeCarrico 1989; Wierzbicka 1991). What makes some recent work in the area of indirect speech acts so interesting is that differences between speech acts have been found which are, to a large extent, motivated by different cultural norms and assumptions rather than by the strategy which is used (see Wierzbicka 1991).[24]

Indirect requests in the form of *can't you* are an example. Although the norm or the strategy which is used can be interpreted in terms of universal principles of rationality and politeness (what Leech 1983: 15f refers to as interpersonal rhetoric), the use of *can't you* is regulated by a complex web of language-specific social rules.

In Leech's analysis the sense of *can't you shut up* is spelled out semantically as follows: 'I have assumed that you cannot shut up. I now doubt whether this is true. I ask you to resolve my doubt' (1983: 123). What is interesting is that *can't you shut up* can be intended as an ironic reproach, in which case it is, of course, less polite than the corresponding affirmative question (Leech 1983: 122, 127).[25] In Swedish, *can't you* is less restricted and may also be used in polite requests. Thus, requests such as *kan du inte skicka saltet* ('can't you pass the salt') are frequent among friends or members of the same family. The point of the strategy is to make it easy for the hearer to refuse to comply. The presence of the negation therefore makes the request more polite.

Danish, not surprisingly, is like Swedish in that the use of interrogative form and negation can be associated with politeness in family discourse (Faerch and Kasper 1989: 227). In Japanese (Nattinger and DeCarrico 1989: 129), the conventions of use are again different: the negative question form is more polite than the affirmative question but it is associated with social distance and deference.

1.14 The pragmatics of conversational routines

All routines are to some extent constrained by the situation. They can be restricted with regard to the antecedent event, the setting, the participants in the conversation, etc. Only a few conversational routines, however, are completely frozen and restricted to a particular situation. An example is the phrase *YOU should talk* (Fillmore 1984: 129), which is formally invariable and tied to one particular situation or function (A scolds B 'for remarking on C's faults while ignoring B's own identical faults'), a single setting, etc. The majority of routines are more flexible, and the situations in which they are used more varied.

The pragmatic theory which is described in section 1.14.1 describes conversational routines in terms of the situational features which are needed by the hearer to match the form correctly with the extralinguistic situation, at least if the situation is stereotypic.

1.14.1 *Conversational routines and frames*

Conversational routines are difficult to describe because of their formal and functional variability. The problems, however, are multiplied when we want to describe the situation in which routine forms are used. The pragmatic information, or what Wolfson (1983) has called 'rules of speaking', for when and how a specific apology is used appropriately are not an unspecified list of contextual features but organized as frames. When an extralinguistic situation is perceived, it is matched with the 'frame' which the speaker selects from memory.[26]

The frame should be regarded as a hypothesis about speakers' stereotypic knowledge of a situation and how this knowledge is organized in the long-term memory. In artificial intelligence 'frame' is a 'memorized framework' which contains stereotypic knowledge about places, people, function, etc (Brown and Yule 1983: 238f). People have frames for 'rooms' or 'houses', as well as for linguistic facts like noun phrases, and there are probably also frames for thanking, apologizing, etc.

In order to understand why speakers' social and pragmatic knowledge is organized as frames it is necessary to say something about the emergence of routines and their gradual conventionalization (see Altenberg 1990a; Kennedy 1990; Coulmas 1981a: 3). It is clear that in the course of the communication many situations tend to recur. It is not surprising that when a situation is repeated the linguistic behaviour which has worked in the past is also repeated and becomes the established pattern for members of the speech community. In this way a linguistic form comes to be routinely associated with a greeting, thanks or apology and is used automatically when a type of situation recurs.

Since it represents the association between the social situation and a speech-act formula, the frame is a useful model when one compares routines in different cultures (Coulmas 1979: 242f; Fillmore 1984) and when one analyses functional and formal variants of a routine phrase.

1.14.2 Factors of speech-act frames

Exactly what situational factors are needed in a frame depends on what speech act is studied, but also on one's theory of what the factors of the communication situation are.[27] One can assume that in a speech-act frame, there will be slots for an antecedent event as well as for socio-linguistic information about the participants, the temporal and physical setting, the reason for the formula, sequentiality (e.g. information about whether the routine must be followed by a response), the communication channel, non-verbal behaviour accompanying the routine, etc.

Routines can be pragmatically restricted to a special medium (e.g. the telephone), an institutional context (e.g. the court, the classroom), to a special time of the day (e.g. greeting phrases) or to individuals of a certain age or sex. The following frame has been suggested by Coulmas (1979: 246f) for the routine phrase *Congratulations!* (see Figure 1.6).

The frame features suggested by Fillmore (1984: 135f) for formulas like *I'll tell you what* or *you should talk* also include 'prototype example' and ' "creative" departure', 'similar formulas', 'usage notes'.

I	Participants
	sex
	age
	social role
	hierarchy
	authority
	familiarity
II	Setting
	time
	place
III	The why and wherefore
	time
	reason
IV	Contextual restrictions
	sequentialization
	stylistic homogeneity
V	Concomitant activity
	gestures

After Coulmas (1979: 246f)

Figure 1.6   Factors constituting the frame for *Congratulations!*

A theory of frames presupposes a theory of communication. There must, for example, be a speaker and a hearer participating in the communicative event who share certain assumptions or general knowledge about the world organized as frames. A frame should also make it possible to explain that a pragmatic rule is broken if the recipient of a gift does not say *thank you* or if a person calls his employer by her first name without invitation or if one says *Congratulations!* when there is no reason for it (see Gleason and Weintraub 1976: 129).

Frames are compatible with several different cognitive theories of communication. In this book I shall explain what goes on in communication in terms of Sperber and Wilson's relevance theory (1986). According to Sperber and Wilson, what happens in communication is seen as a balance between the speaker's wish to be maximally relevant and the need for the hearer to be able to process the utterance with minimal effort. (These thoughts are developed in more detail in Chapter 5.)

1.15   Conversational routines and language teaching

It follows from the preceding discussion that conversational routines are pragmatic entities (speech acts, discourse markers or incomplete phraseological units) which can be taught and practised without any reference to grammar.

Lists of phrases which are functional synonyms have been compiled in course-books and communicative syllabuses (see Wilkins 1976; for more recent references, see Wolfson and Judd 1983). Phrases can also be combined into a conversation. The following example of a conversation with labelled 'lexical phrases' is taken from Nattinger and DeCarrico (1989: 130):[28]

A: Excuse me? (sustained intonation) (Summons: SI)
B: Yes? (response: SI)
A: the Saturday Market? (topic nomination: SI)
B: uh huh? (acknowledgment: SI)
A: Where is the Saturday Market (request: SI) (location: NT), please? (politeness: SI)
B: I'm not sure but I think (assertion: SI) (evaluator: DD) (fluency device: DD) it's three blocks to the right next to the Burnside Bridge. (location: NT)
A: O.K. (acknowledge: SI) So long. (parting: SI)

Classification code:
SI = social interaction
NT = necessary topic
DD = discourse device

In the conversation above, conversational routines make up a large part of the discourse. They provide necessary topics, they have social functions and contribute to the meaning or structure of the discourse.

There are several reasons why conversational routines should be taught. They are linked directly with function and can be taught as units without bringing in grammar. When Chomsky reviewed B.F. Skinner's *Verbal Behavior* in 1959 (Chomsky 1959), he argued against the idea that imitation and memorizing were techniques used in language acquisition. Much current research points in the direction that 'there is nothing wrong with memorizing some essential chunks, especially at the beginning stages of language learning' (Nattinger and DeCarrico 1989: 133). Routines may even be the basis for teaching verbal behaviour:

Perhaps we should base our teaching on the assumption that, for a great deal of the time anyway, language production consists of piecing together the ready-made units appropriate for a particular situation and that comprehension relies on knowing which of these patterns to predict in these situations. Our teaching therefore would center on these patterns and the ways they can be pieced together, along with the ways they vary and the situations in which they occur.
(Nattinger 1980: 341, quoted in Richards and Schmidt 1983: 190, Introduction to Chapter 7)

Teaching conversational routines is still something new. The reason is that pragmatic aspects of language have been regarded as being 'outside the language', although the need to add a pragmatic perspective in language has often been recognized (see Allwood 1987 (1976)). The importance of the social and cultural aspects of conversational routines has increasingly been stressed by sociolinguists and applied linguists with an interest in second language (L2) teaching (see Wolfson 1983: 85).

Conversational routines are difficult to teach because they are culture-bound and because their formal description and their situational frames are extremely complex (Yorio 1980). Learners of the language are usually not aware that there are rules governing these expressions but use phrases in a way which deviates from the native norm or which causes communicative misunderstandings. In tests with L2 learners it has, for example, been shown that they find it difficult to judge the politeness value of different apologies (Cohen and Olshtain 1981). Another experiment has indicated that there are considerable differences in native and non-native performance with regard to requests in response to written discourse-completion tests (Blum-Kulka and Levenston 1987; on cross-linguistic problems with complimenting, see, for example, Holmes and Brown 1980).

Any study of the use of language has to start with what Fillmore (1984: 134) calls 'small pragmatic facts' such as describing the forms and conditions of use of conversational routines. These facts can then be explained in the light of broad differences between nations and languages and in terms of politeness and cultural ethos. In the following chapters a start will be made to describe some small facts about speech acts and other conversational routines.

Notes

1 There is a diversity of terms in this area in which different aspects of formulas are emphasized: Bolinger (1976) – prefabrications (prefabs); Kennedy (1990) – collocations; Nattinger and DeCarrico (1989) – lexicalized phrases; Keller (1981) – gambits; Fillmore et al. (1988) – idioms with a pragmatic point. Especially in the psycholinguistic literature, it is common to distinguish between routines (or memorized sequences) and patterns (or stems) which are partly lexicalized. See, for example, Krashen and Scarcella (1978). The use of conversational routines in this work emphasizes the social as well as psychological aspects of different kinds of phrases which can be more or less lexicalized.

2 Among the detailed, pragmatically based classifications which have been proposed, one can mention Stenström (1990), Nattinger and DeCarrico (1989) and Edmondson and House (1981). 'Small talk' will not be further discussed here.

3 The original corpus which consists of 87 texts has later been supplemented with 13 texts which have not been included in the present study (Greenbaum and Svartvik 1990: 14f).

4 The symbols which have been used in the transcription of the examples in the text are explained in the Preface.

5 Cf. Makkai (1992, unpublished): 'Now it so happens that 75–80% of average North American English conversation consists of such

"prefabricated units" to quote Bolinger's term (1976)'. An even higher figure, although less well supported, is suggested by Pawley, 'My guess is that the bulk of laymen's lexemes in English – perhaps 90 percent of them – consists of phrases which are also literal expressions' (1986: 114).

6　See also the review of the role of formulas (routines and larger routinized patterns) in Krashen and Scarcella (1978) and of their neurolinguistic correlates in Hatch (1983: 212).

7　For an account of different positions regarding the status of formulas and frame structures in language acquisition, see Bohn (1986). Notice that in section 1.14 I use frame as a pragmatic rather than a syntactic notion.

8　The discourse structure rules operate as a file accessing system: 'Let us suppose that the discourse structure rules ... are actually a filing system for formulae and that the files appear in the order that the discourse structure rules would generate them' (Kuiper and Haggo 1984: 227).

9　For further discussion of conversational routines and function, see section 1.13.

10　Both accounts draw on the functional model proposed by Bühler (1965/1934). According to Bühler, each utterance has a symbol function (propositional function), a symptom function (expressive function) and a signal (textual) function.

11　The difference between the expressive and propositional functions, however, is far from clear with speech acts like thanking and apologizing. I agree with Holmes (1990: 158) that they have little referential meaning and are characterized, above all, by the expressive (affective) function.

12　Weakening of *how are you* (in American English) has resulted in *hi* which can be regarded as a new lexical item (see Ferguson 1981: 31f).

13　Cf. Blum-Kulka's discussion of 'the idiomatic process' (Blum-Kulka 1987: 142).

14　As pointed out by G. Lakoff (1987: 448), even 'strong idioms' may be pragmatically motivated: 'The relationship between A and B is *motivated* just in case there is an independently existing link, L, such that A-L-B "fit together". L *makes sense* of the relationship between A and B.' Clearly, not only 'semantic idioms' such as *spill the beans*, but also 'pragmatic' idioms such as *frankly speaking, as it were* or (conventionalized) indirect speech acts are motivated in the sense that there is a link between the literal and the idiomatic meaning.

15　Cf. also Sinclair (1987: 325): 'Areas of relevant study include the transitional probabilities of words, the prevalent notion of "chunking", the occurrence of hesitations etc and the placement of boundaries, and the behaviour of subjects trying to guess the next word in a mystery text.'

16 In Goffman's terminology, the 'offender' (the person who makes a request) is placed under some obligation to show appreciation after the ritual equilibrium has been restored by the granting of the request (Goffman 1976: 69).

17 See also Haggo and Kuiper (1983: 541) on the syntactic indeterminacy of single-word expletives like *damn* and *bother*. When the expletive *bother* has an object (*Bother the wind!*), it is treated as a different phrase.

18 There are also adverbial phrases which are syntactically indeterminate, e.g. *as it were, so to speak*.

19 Cf. Quirk et al.'s (1985: 8.123–26) category 'style disjunct'.

20 In *The BBI combinatory dictionary of English* a distinction is made between collocations ('words keeping company with each other') and free combinations, while, for example, Carter (1987: 63) recognizes degrees of collocational restriction. The sentence stem would be characterized as a semi-restricted collocation in Carter's terminology.

21 On finite state grammars, see Chomsky (1957: 20).

22 The point that (conventionalized) indirect speech acts should be regarded as 'bound utterances' is also made by Kiefer (1983: 746).

23 Carter (1987: 64), on the other hand, prefers to speak about a scale of transparency ranging from completely opaque to transparent phrases.

24 See also Horn (1989: 344): 'Since the short-circuiting of implicatures is a matter of convention, we expect to find differences between speakers and languages as to just which conventions of usage are operative. And indeed, as demonstrated by Searle (1975) and Green (1975), there is considerable cross-linguistic variation as to which questions can be used to convey which requests.' On short-circuited implicatures, see Chapter 4.

25 Wierzbicka (1991: 207) suggests that the meaning of *can't you do X* can be described by the following meaning components:
    • I see you are not doing something that you should be doing
    • I feel something bad because of this
    • I think you should know: this is bad
    • I say: I want you to say if you can't do this thing
    • I think you can do it and don't want to do it
    • I say this because I want to say what I think and what I feel.

26 Cognitive models, including frames, scripts, etc, are frequent, above all, as models for reasoning and categorization (see Lakoff 1987: 116f). Here frames explain discourse planning and processing.

27 For a discussion of possible features or parameters of the communication situation, see Biber (1988, Chapter 2).

28 Since Nattinger and DeCarrico (1992) was not available to me while writing this chapter, references have generally been to their earlier article.

CHAPTER TWO

Thanking

Middle-class children in our society are taught to preface every statement to an adult with a request of by-your-leave and to terminate every encounter, if not every interchange, with some version of thank you.
(Goffman 1976: 67)

2.1 Introduction

In the past, interest has primarily been devoted to 'general pragmatics' (e.g. principles of conversation, politeness), while the pragmatic description of particular expressions and speech-act forms has been ignored. Recently, however, the focus of interest has changed from general aspects of speech acts to how linguistic forms are linked to pragmatic and social rules.

From a cross-cultural perspective, speech acts may differ both with regard to strategies and the social and cultural rules for their use. The problems for foreign learners caused by speech acts are therefore considerable. In a study comparing native and non-native speakers, Eisenstein and Bodman (1986; see also Bodman and Eisenstein 1988) found, for example, that even advanced learners of English had problems with thanking due to the idiomatic nature of the phrases, and the sociopragmatic constraints on their use. When one compares English with other languages, there are differences in whom one says *thank you* to, when one says *thank you*, the settings in which thanking is expected, etc (on Marathi and Hindi, see Apte 1976; on Arabic, see Davies 1987; on Japanese, see Coulmas 1981b; on the differences between Swedish and English, see Aijmer and Olsson 1990).

This chapter deals with gratitude expressions with special regard to their functions and the forms and strategies which are used. Functionally, *thank you/thanks* is analysed on the speech-act level, as a politeness marker and as an element organizing the discourse. In addition, gratitude expressions are analysed pragmatically with regard to the factors of the social situation and text type constraints.

Thanking expressions can be reduced to a small number of lexicalized 'stems', which can be modified, expanded, etc. Pragmatically, they are associated with frames delimiting the range of application of the stem and the patterns derived from it. Several frames are needed to account for the fact that a minor favour provided by the telephone operator requires a different gesture of politeness than a generous offer from a friend, or that extra gratitude is expected when one thanks the host or hostess for the food on a social occasion.

As stressed in Chapter 1, a corpus is needed to pick out the phrases which are routinized and to provide a sociolinguistic and stylistic profile for the individual expressions. In collecting material, the emphasis has been on the examples which are found in the London-Lund Corpus. All the examples of routines for thanking in the corpus have been collected, and a description of the linguistic variants and their conditions of use has been undertaken. Additional examples come from the written part of the Survey of English Usage, the Birmingham Corpus of English Texts, from my own reading or have been provided by native speakers.

2.2 *Thank you/thanks* as an illocutionary force indicating device

Thanking and apologizing have much in common, which is the result of the fact that both are expressive speech acts, i.e. they express the speaker's psychological state towards a state of affairs or a person (see Searle 1976: 12). In addition, expressives subsume speech-act verbs such as condole, congratulate, greet, welcome, which will not be discussed here.

Since *thank* is expressive it has the following features:

- factivity, i.e. the truth of the state of affairs is presupposed by the speaker to be true
- a psychological state is expressed
- the propositional content expresses some property ascribed to the speaker or the hearer

The analysis of thanking by Searle (1969: 67) reflects the fact that the illocutionary point of the verbs in this class is to express an attitude and that they are factive. Searle considered *thank (for)* as an illocutionary force indicating device or IFID, which can be specified by a set of criteria or rules:

Thank (for)
Propositional content rule: Past act A done by H (the hearer).
Preparatory rule: A benefits S (the speaker) and S believes A benefits S.
Sincerity rule: S feels grateful or appreciative for A.
Essential rule: Counts as an expression of gratitude or appreciation.
(Searle 1969: 63)

According to these rules, the act for which the speaker expresses gratitude must be a past act done by the addressee, which benefits the speaker; the speaker feels grateful for the act (or behaves as if he does), and the utterance counts as an expression of gratitude.

As pointed out in recent sociolinguistic work (see Olshtain and Cohen 1983), speech acts can also be analysed in a larger perspective with regard to their responses, the set of strategies expressing the illocutionary function and aspects of the social situation. Moreover, the forms need to be described with regard to functional, grammatical and prosodic properties.

2.3 Thanking and politeness

In order to understand why some speech acts can be expressed in many ways, we must go beyond the illocutionary point of the particular speech act and consider its affective value or politeness. Holmes (1984: 346) distinguished between negatively affective speech acts such as criticism and reproach, which can be attenuated or mitigated, and positively affective speech acts, e.g. compliments or thanking, which can be modified by strategies 'boosting' illocutionary force. Leech (1983: 104) classifies speech acts into four different types of speech act depending on their social function: competitive, convivial, collaborative, conflictive. Competitive speech acts, such as ordering and asking, are essentially discourteous (Leech 1983: 105) and are often realized indirectly in order to minimize their inherent impoliteness (Leech 1983: 83). (Conflictive and collaborative speech acts are of less interest from the point of view of politeness.)

Thanking coincides with a convivial (intrinsically courteous or polite) function (Leech 1983: 104). When the illocutionary force is convivial, politeness consists in maximizing politeness (Leech 1983: 84 – 'positive politeness').[1] Positive politeness can be achieved by intensifying adverbs such as *very much, very much indeed*, etc (= lexical devices) and by prosodic devices highlighting the emotionality which can be associated with thanking. One of the most important strategies reinforcing politeness consists of the use of combinations and repetition.

Schematically, the different types of strategy for thanking someone can be represented as in Figure 2.1. However, it is difficult to draw a distinction between strategies of thanking (= neutral strategies; Haverkate 1984: 40) and reinforcing strategies (Haverkate 1984: 40) since thanking may itself be 'emotional' (see section 2.4).

2.4 Strategies of thanking

In this work the realizations of speech acts are regarded as strategies in the manner suggested by Haverkate:

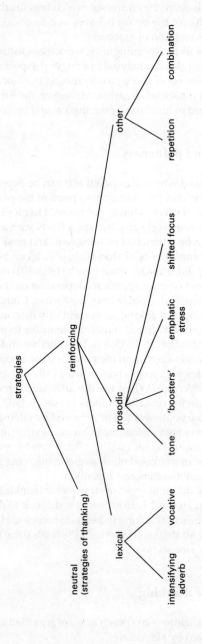

Figure 2.1 Neutral and reinforcing strategies

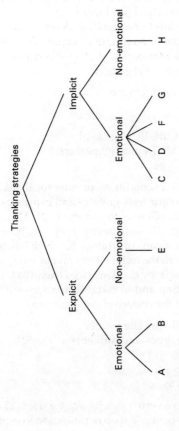

Code to strategies:

(A) thanking somebody explicitly
(B) expressing gratitude
(C) expressing appreciation of the addressee
(D) expressing appreciation of the act
(E) acknowledging a debt of gratitude
(F) stressing one's gratitude
(G) expressing emotion
(H) commenting on one's own role by
    suppressing one's own importance
    (self-denigration)

e.g. *thank you, thanks*
e.g. *I am grateful*
e.g. *that's kind of you, that's nice (of you)[2]*
e.g. *that's lovely, it's appreciated*
e.g. *I owe a debt of gratitude to …*
e.g. *I must thank you*
e.g. *oh (thank you)*
e.g. *I am an ingrate, I'm so careless*

Figure 2.2 Thanking strategies

> With respect to linguistic actions, (...) strategies are applied in all those cases where in the performance of the speech act the speaker is in a position to make a choice from a set of options concerning the concrete realization of that speech act. (Haverkate 1984: 40)

The relationship between the linguistic action and strategies is not clear-cut, however, as the speaker can obtain his goal in many different ways. There is an open-ended set of strategies or speech-act formulas, which can be classified with regard to directness/indirectness used and the degree of emotionality ('expressiveness') involved (see Figure 2.2).

Strategies A and B are the most direct ones. Strategy A was almost the only strategy which was used in the London-Lund Corpus, although it was sometimes combined with other strategies. Strategy B occurred only three times and was always realized by *I'm grateful*:

(1)   c   *((well it's)) . [i] . I'm* ^grateful to the
            'honourable :mèmber#
            es^pècially#
            as ^he is a !fellow of the same !{còllege as :{Ì
            was at#}} in !Càmbridge Mr 'Deputy {^Spèaker#}#
(11.5 53–5)

Strategies C and D refer to the felicity conditions or rules for thanking. The person who has received a favour feels grateful and expresses his appreciation either of the benefactor (C) or of the act itself (D). Although these strategies do not express gratitude directly, they can be used indirectly to express gratitude. By means of strategy E, which has been analysed as direct but non-emotional, the recipient of a favour recognizes the existence of a debt and 'pays for it' by thanking (see Owen 1983: 167). This strategy is restricted to writing and to certain situations such as thanking one's teacher or family in the preface of academic works:

> I owe a lasting debt of gratitude to my late teacher ...
> I am equally indebted to colleagues and students at the School of Oriental and African Studies ...
> A particular debt of gratitude goes to ...
> Very special acknowledgements to ...

Strategy F involves the performative verb (*I /hereby/ thank you for ...*) and can be reinforced by stressing the speaker's wish or obligation to express his gratitude (*I must thank you, I would like to thank you*). In less formal contexts, strategy A is used instead. Strategy G (literally an expression of surprise) is associated with a high degree of emotionality or 'gushing'. Strategy H was only found in writing, and always with other strategies.

Thanking is easy to recognize since the speaker nearly always uses an explicit strategy (usually strategy A). However, an explicit expression of thanking may be combined with more indirect strategies (see section 2.10.4).

2.5 Gratitude expressions

The expressions of gratitude consist of *thank you* and *thanks*, with or without intensifiers (Table 2.1):

Table 2.1: Relative frequencies of gratitude expressions in the LLC

	Realization	Number
(A) THANK YOU	*thank you*	134
	thank you very much	73
	thank you very much indeed	17
	thank you so much	2
Subtotal		226
(B) THANKS	*thanks*	33
	thanks very much	28
	thanks very much indeed	5
	thanks awfully	2
	thanks a lot	2
	many thanks	1
Subtotal		71
Total		297

Other patterns:	*I'm grateful (to NP) that ...*	
	ta ta love	–

Ta ta (informal) is a morphological variant of *thank you* (or *thanks*), which occurred twice in the corpus with the meaning 'goodbye':

(2) A +((2 sylls))+ ^I'll I'll ^give her enóugh#
      B ^yès#
      A ta ^tá love#
(7.2 461–3)

I am grateful was used in formal situations to express truly felt gratitude (see section 2.4).

2.6 Continuation patterns

It is clear that speech acts can have a fixed continuation, although this is not usually discussed in speech-act theory. The responses can also be characterized in terms of speaker strategies (see Table 2.2):

Table 2.2: Thanking 'responders'

	Type of strategy	Realization	Number
(A)	minimizing the favour	e.g. *that's okay*	1
(B)	expressing pleasure	e.g. *great pleasure*	2
(C)	expressing appreciation of the addressee[3]	e.g. *you're welcome*	–
Total			3

The motivation for strategy A (*that's okay*) is to restore the imbalance between the participants by minimizing the debt of gratitude incurred. Other realizations of the same strategy, not represented in the London-Lund Corpus, are *not at all, no problem, don't mention it, that's all right*. In strategy B, the focus is on the benefactor's pleasure in doing the favour. Strategy C, which is closely related to B, is frequent only in American English. Responders after an act of thanking had a fixed prosodic pattern with a rising (fall-plus-rise) tone:

(3)   B   ^wèll then#
           ^thànks for the cóffee#
       A   ^great pléasure#
           ^glad to !sèe you#
           ^bỳe#
       B   ^bỳe#
(3.2 736–41)

Responses to an act of thanking seem to be infrequent in English compared with many other languages (Swedish, Russian, German) and only a few strategies are represented.[4] In Swedish, four different strategies are used (see Table 2.3):

Table 2.3: Thanking 'responders' in Swedish

	Type of strategy	Realization
(A)	minimizing the favour	e.g. *för all del* 'by all means'
(B)	denying the cause for thanking	e.g. *ingen orsak* 'no cause'
(C)	leaving the hearer the option whether to accept the favour	e.g. *var så god* 'please'
(D)	thanking the hearer 'expressing appreciation of the hearer'	e.g. *tack (själv)* 'thanks yourself'

2.7 The grammatical analysis of gratitude expressions

In Quirk et al. (1985), expressions which are irregular or deficient are called formulas and are not analysed grammatically. However, it can be argued that this account is too simple. Many routines can be analysed as sentences, verb phrases, noun phrases, etc. But *thank you* and *thanks* are difficult to describe in grammar. As pointed out in Chapter 1, *thank you* is generally analysed as elliptic, although it is not certain what the subject is (*I*, *we*), but it may also be argued that it is a verb phrase. *Thanks* can be analysed as a noun phrase with exclamatory function (cf. *heavens, tops, my apologies*). Since the phrase can be modified by intensifying adverbs, it can also be analysed as a verb (see section 2.10).

There are also gratitude expressions which are fully grammatical (*I wish to thank you, may I take the opportunity to thank you*). Since these forms can be analysed in the grammar, no special grammatical properties need to be assumed when they are analysed as routines.

2.8 Prosody and fixedness

There has been comparatively little discussion of prosody and routinization. Couper-Kuhlen suggests that there are specific intonational patterns conveying attitudes:

> ... it appears that there are also specific intonational patterns in English associated with the expression of attitude. Which attitudes and what patterns, however, is still a subject of discussion.
> (Couper-Kuhlen 1986: 175)

In fact, thanking is one of the most stereotypic social speech acts, and the tone can be stereotypic as well. The so-called 'stylized' or stereotypic intonation sometimes associated with a calling contour is used only in situations such as to thank a waiter, a bus-driver, the telephone operator for favours of a routine character carried out as part of the speaker's professional duties (Ladd 1978: 523). A good example of a stereotypic tone from the London-Lund Corpus is the operator's *thank you* on the telephone:

```
(4)     A  ^òh#
           ^right óh#
           ^hold ón#
        B  ^thank y=ou# - - -
(8.1 1018–19)
```

The rise or fall-plus-rise tone sounds casual or non-committal and is compatible with the routinized situations illustrated in examples (5)–(7). It could not be used in situations which require 'serious' thanking, such as thanking for an expensive gift (see also Knowles 1987: 195). In example

(5), *thank you* is purely phatic in the answer to the enquiry about the Speaker A's welfare; the phrase acknowledges the reception of a letter in example (6) and marks the end of a telephone call in example (7).

(5) C ((are)) you ^wéll#
     A I'm ^vèry 'well thánk you#
(1.9 29–30)

(6) B ^I !got your lètter thánk you#
        ^and your nòte#
(9.1. 303–4)

(7) C ^will you hŏld#
     B [I'm] ^no I wòn't#
        ^I'll !call bàck thánk 'you#
(8.2 1028–30)

When the function of *thank you* is only ritual or polite, as in the examples above, the fall tone would be so emphatic as to sound impolite or brusque (Lindström 1978: 108; Quirk et al. 1985: 572).

The fall tone is more likely to signal real gratitude. It is also used in contexts where the favour is small, indicating that it is the speaker's perception of the extralinguistic situation that determines the amount of gratitude which is required:

(8) a [ə:] won't you sit *down
     B * ((2 to 3 sylls)) *
     A ^thànk you #
(3.1 10–12)

(9) A *good ^mórning#*
     a *good morning Miss*Detch how are you
     A ^fine ! thànk you #**
(3.1 1030–2)

In fact, the fall tone was more frequent than the casual rise tone and occurred in 64 per cent of the examples with either *thank you* or *thanks* (see Table 2.4).

2.9 Distribution of thanking over different texts

Thanking can also be constrained by text type or medium (speech/ writing). The distribution of the examples over different textual genres is indicated in Table 2.5. Even if thanking is relatively frequent in informal conversation, the majority of examples (37 examples per 10,000 words) occurred in telephone calls. The number of examples in discussions and debates is also noticeable. On the other hand, there were only isolated

Table 2.4: The distribution of nuclear tones in *thank you*[5] and *thanks*

Nuclear type	*thank you*	*thanks*
Fall	71	17
Rise	17	3
Level	4	1
Rise-fall	7	–
Fall-rise	15	–
No tone	2	2
Total	116	23

examples in unprepared public speech (speech addressed to an audience) and no examples in unprepared speech, e.g. sports commentary.

In written English, thanking is restricted to a few functions and situations. One thanks one's colleagues, old teachers, family, etc, for their help and support in the preface of an academic work, and one begins a letter by thanking the recipient for his letter, note, postcard, kind regards, help, etc. Also one may write a special thank-you letter thanking a relative for a present and accept an invitation by thanking for it. A variety of different expressions was used in the written part of SEU, including some which were not found in the spoken data (*very many thanks, many many thanks, I should like to thank you*).

(10)   Thank you for a lovely long letter.
(W 7–1)

Table 2.5: Distribution of *thank you/thanks* over different text types (the figures have been normalized to 10,000 words)

Text type	Number	Number per 10,000 words
FACE (surreptitious)	85	5
FACE (non-surreptitious)	14	2.3
TELEPHONE	186	37.2
DISCUSSION	10	1.7
PUBLIC	2	0.3
PREPARED	–	–
Total	297	46.5

(11)   Dear Mr Carter,
         Thank you for your letter of the 22nd. I had a reasonable holiday
         thank you and am now much involved in the usual turmoil.
(W 7–9)

(12)   Sir: I should like to thank you for a temperate reply to what may
         have seemed a somewhat intemperate letter. I am also grateful to
         Anthony Thwaite for revealing the source of the article in question.
(W 7–17)

(13)   Thanks again for your help.
         Yours faithfully, </Tony Stevens/>
(W 7–15)

(14)   Annwyl Judith, Many many thanks for your kind regards and letters.
(W 7–3)

(15)   Dear Michael. Very many thanks for your letter of the 23rd
         November.
(W 7–10)

(16)   Thanks for your invitation to tea tomorrow.
(W 7–31)

2.10 *Thank you/thanks* as stems

We also need to describe the variant types of thanking and discuss the
expressions which can be created by means of modification, expansion,
etc. Gratitude expressions range from short, fixed phrases such as *thank
you* or *thanks*, to elaborate patterns of considerable length expressing
intensification.

The model presented here to describe how new gratitude expressions
can be formed is based on the idea of sentential or phrasal 'stems' (see
Pawley and Syder 1983: 208f; Barkema 1992; see also Chapter 1). Stems
can undergo a number of grammatical operations (expansion, ellipsis,
embedding and combination with other units) resulting in new patterns
which have their own grammatical, functional and prosodic description.

It could be argued that the stem is sentential and that *thank you* is the
result of ellipsis (Ai). Alternatively, we could say that *thank you* is a verb
phrase inheriting certain properties from regular VP-constructions such
as cooccurrence with intensifiers and *for*-complements (Aii):

(A)   (i) $\left(\left\{ \begin{array}{c} I \\ we \end{array} \right\} \right)$ thank you (INT) (VOC) $\left(for \left\{ \begin{array}{c} NP \\ V\text{-ing} \end{array} \right\} \right)$

(A)   (ii) thank you (INT) (VOC) $\left(for \left\{ \begin{array}{c} NP \\ V\text{-ing} \end{array} \right\} \right)$

e.g. *I thank you very much Joe for your call, thank you very much indeed Joe, thank you Joe, thank you for ringing; we thank you,* etc

In a lexicalized stem such as (Ai) or (Aii), a grammatical element can be added or deleted in ways which are specified by the notation. Thus the elements within parentheses can be compared with optional grammatical rules of the rewrite type.

The stem in (Ai) consists of the verb *thank, you* (= the benefactor), *I* (= the person who benefits from the favour) as well as optional grammatical elements like INT ('intensifier'), VOC ('vocative') and *for NP* or V-*ing* (= the reason for the expression of gratitude).

Thanks can be expanded in the ways which are specified by the following stems:

(B)   (i) thanks (INT) (VOC) $\left(\text{for} \left\{ \begin{array}{l} \text{NP} \\ \text{V-ing} \end{array} \right\} \right)$

e.g. *thanks very much Joe for the book, thanks for the book, thanks Joe, thanks for ringing,* etc

(B)   (ii) (PREMODIFIER) thanks (VOC) $\left(\text{for} \left\{ \begin{array}{l} \text{NP} \\ \text{V-ing} \end{array} \right\} \right)$

e.g. *(very) many thanks for your help, thanks Joe, thanks for dropping in,* etc

The simple *thanks* in stem (Bi) can perhaps be regarded as a weakening of *thank you,* but would be analysed as a noun in (Bii).

2.10.1   Expanded forms of thanking

By means of expansion of the stem, the reason for gratitude can be made explicit. The type *thank you (INT) for NP* occurred in 15 examples and *thanks (INT) for NP* in 7 examples.[6] The speaker used the pattern to thank 'a benefactor' explicitly for the letter, the coffee, the sherry, for his time, etc:

(17)   C   ^thànk 'you# -
         for the ^shèrry# -
     a   *(laughs –)* a great pleasure Dai
     A   *(laughs –)*
(1.9 547–50)

(18)   B   ^[m̀]# -
         ^thanks for rínging#
     A   ^rìght# -
         ^bye#
     B   ^bye býe# .
(7.2 834–8)

(19)   A   ^thank you for dropping ín _Sam#
(1.1 1211)

(20)   A   ^thank you !vèry 'much for 'letting me knów#
(9.2 611)

The expanded phrase has a characteristic prosodic profile with a compound fall-rise tone. Alternatively, the onset falls on *thanks* and the nucleus comes at the end of the tone unit:

> thànk you for coming alóng (4 examples)
> ^thanks for rìnging (3 examples)

When *thank you* is followed by a name, part of the nuclear tone (or a stress) occurred on the name:

> thànk you Málcolm
> thànk you 'Sally

2.10.2   *Thanking and intensification*

Intensification is the most frequent device to create more polite gratitude expressions. *Thank you* occurred with an adverbial intensifier in 40.7 per cent of the examples and *thanks* in 53.5 per cent of the examples (see section 2.5). *Thanks* was also more 'creative' in terms of the types of intensifier it cooccurred with (*very much, very much indeed, awfully, a lot*).

The Birmingham Corpus (BIR) provides additional examples of intensifiers, as illustrated in Table 2.6. First names (*thank you* (Name) 9 examples; *thanks* (Name) 4 examples) or endearment forms (*love, dear*) signal politeness and can also be viewed as strategies maximizing positive politeness.

Table 2.6:   Intensified gratitude expressions

Thank you + intensifier	*Thanks* + intensifier
thank you very much	*thanks very much*
thank you very much indeed	*thanks very much indeed*
thank you so much	*thanks awfully*
thank you awfully (BIR)	*thanks a lot*
thank you ever so much (BIR)	*many thanks*
thank you a thousand times (BIR)	*thanks so much* (BIR)
	thanks ever so (BIR)
	thanks a million (BIR)

2.10.3 Prosody and intensification

Thank you very much occurred with a fall tone in 67 per cent of the examples (and in 70 per cent of the examples with *thanks very much*). A characteristic prosodic pattern is an onset on *thank,* a stress or a booster on *very* and a fall tone on *much* (82.4 per cent). On the other hand, *very* was normally unstressed in the phrase *thanks very much*, which occurred with a fall tone in 60 per cent of the examples.

Generally speaking, the nuclear tone must be compatible with the meaning of the gratitude expression. The rising tone was primarily used in situations requiring little gratitude such as the closing of a telephone call (9 examples).

In a number of examples, rising tone signalled a different interpretation from that indicated by the meaning of the gratitude phrase. For example, the effect of the rising (or fall-plus-rise) tone in *thank you very much* is that the speaker may sound sarcastic or amused:

(21) b ^ôoh#
        you can ^{lêave} :me ôut# .
        ^thank you very múch#
        *- ^wòmen's 'union's#
        a ^dead and a_live
    a *(- - - laughs)*
    (b hóle#
(6.2 652–6)

In example (22), *thank you very much* sounds dismissive:

(22) B ^I 'asked him *:straight ôut#*
        (A *:im!pŏrtable#* .
        ^yés you . ^yéah#
        and ^what [d] he sày#
    B ^he said !not on your :nèlly 'thank you 'very
        múch#
        he ^very much pre_fers !Cràwsville#
(8.4 1067–72)

Thank you/thanks very much indeed had an unmarked prosodic pattern (23 per cent of the examples), characterized by a fall tone on the last syllable, an onset on *thank*, and weak stress on *much*:

   ^thank you very 'much indèed

In addition, prosodic devices such as 'boosters' and stress may reinforce illocutionary force. In 29 per cent of the examples *very* received the booster (a step-up in pitch in relation to the preceding syllable), supporting Altenberg's findings that *very* has a high booster potential (Altenberg 1987: 136). The following example of *thank you very much indeed* contains several boosters (marked by!) as well as extra stress on the nucleus:

(23) b *look at your map ((and you must let me know
         about)) the telephone and things*
      A *oh ^thánk you very mùch#
         that's ^very nîce of you#* .
         ^[m̀]#
         ^thank you !very !much !!in"dèed# - -
(1.10 1031–5)

2.10.4 Patterns of compound thanks

As a result of the combination of several strategies, the number of forms available to the speaker to thank someone increases enormously. Of all the expressions of thanking 12.8 per cent (38/297) consisted of a combination of thanking strategies. The combinations found in the corpus are shown in Table 2.7.

Strategies C and D had a relatively fixed syntactic and lexical form:

> (that is) ADJ (e.g. *that is lovely, that is kind of you;*
> *lovely, very kind of you*)

Lovely appeared 21 times as a realization of strategy D, while other adjectives expressing a positive evaluation (*great, grand, good*) occurred only in isolated examples.[7] In the syntactic pattern containing strategy C, the only adjectives were *kind* (4 examples) and *nice* (2 examples).

Compound thanks are organized around an explicit expression of thanking. *Thank you/thanks* is reinforced by strategies, which either precede or follow the direct expression (see Faerch and Kasper 1989: 222 on external modification).

The explicit expression of thanks was present in (nearly) all the examples of compound thanks. In the two examples where it was missing, its absence can be explained as the result of ellipsis. Consequently, example (24) has been classified as (A)+D+D+D+D+C:

(24) C but . ^would you get . 'one of them to :bring you
         róund#
         and ^have a 'pint of béer with us 'just 'now#
         ((if you've)) ^tíme#
      A ^that would be lôvely# .
         *^that would be lòvely#
         ^yès# .
         ^rìght# .
         ^that would be !very* ((nice))
(1.9 520–7)

and (25) as a compound although the direct expression of thanking is missing:

Table 2.7: Combinations of gratitude strategies in the LLC

Combination	Number	Example
D+A	12	*lovely thank you very much indeed; that's lovely thank you*
G+A	6	*oh thanks*
D+D+A	3	*lovely lovely thanks*
(A)+C	3	*that's nice of you*
A+D	2	*thank you lovely; thank you very much lovely*
A+A	2	*thank you thank you (love)*
G+A+C+A	1	*oh thank you very much that's very nice of you (m) thank you very much indeed*
C+A	1	*that's nice of you thank you; that'd be very kind thank you*
(A)+D+D+D+C	1	(see example (26))
A+A+D	1	*thank you thanks lovely*
G+A+D	1	*oh thanks lovely*
G+A+D+D	1	*oh thanks lovely that's lovely*
G+A+C	1	*oh thank you that's nice of you; oh thank you that's very kind of you*
G+A+C+C	1	*oh thank you very much if you'd be so kind very kind of you*
G+A+G	1	*oh thank you very much oh*
G+D+A	1	*oh that's lovely thanks very much*
Total	38	

Abbreviations:

A = thanking (e.g. *thanks, thank you, thank you very much*, etc)
C = expressing appreciation of the addressee (e.g. *that's nice of you*)
D = expressing appreciation of the act (e.g. *that's lovely*)
G = expressing emotion (e.g. *oh, ah*)

(25) a **would you like to** take the . comfortable chair .
         ((2 sylls))
      A *that's* ^lóvely#
         (laughs .)
(3.1. 1033–5)

Oh can be analysed in two ways since it has a fairly independent status. In example (26) *oh* (= strategy G) is an 'external' modifier:

(26) A [ə:m] - - . ((I'll)) just ^put this 'back in the
         (('2 sylls)) . *:sùrvey#*

     B *((^I will)))* .
     A ^òh#
        "^thànk you 'very múch# .
        if ^you'd be so kínd#
        ^very kínd of 'you# .
(3.2 729–34) (= G+A+C+C)

Oh can also directly modify *thank you* as in (27):

(27)   A and the ^woman in thère 'said the ^chap's wìfe#. she ^sáid she
          was # - ^priced it at : ten_p
       B *oh ^thànk you Míke#
(1.7 832–4)

Patterns can be more or less frequent, and they can be more or less fixed
with regard to the number and order of strategies. To begin with, we
can notice that all the examples were combinations of only four different
strategies (A, C, D, G). Strategies B and E (see Figure 2.2) did not enter at
all into larger structures (in spoken language). Combinations of two
(explicit) strategies were most frequent (see Table 2.8).

One particular combination was more frequent than any of the others
(about one-third of the examples), namely D+A. For example:

(28)   B I'll ^write it 'on this :pròof#
          and ^go *and 'trans'fer it to*
       A *^one o^clock* :Sampa'nini's 'in - :Bàrrack
          'Street# .
       B ^yès#
       A ^lòvely#
          ^thanks 'very mùch# -
(9.1 681–6)

Table 2.8: Combinations of thanking strategies in the LLC (single
strategies have been included for comparison)

Type of strategy	Number
1 strategy	262 (88.2%)
2 strategies	23 (7.7%)
3 strategies	8 (2.7%)
4 strategies	3 (1%)
more than 4 strategies	1 (0.3%)
Total	297

As a result of repetition, the same strategy occurred twice (or even three times). However, the repeated strategies were normally not realized in the same way, and strategies of the same kind need not be adjacent:

(29)   b   and you must have a key of the house and you must
            *look at your map ((and you must let me know
            about)) the telephone and things*
       A   *oh ^thánk you very mùch#
            that's ^very nîce of you#* .
            ^[m̀]#
            ^thank you !very !much !!in"dèed# - -
(1.10 1031–5) (= G+A+C+A)

Although combinations of gratitude expressions are a characteristic feature of speech rather than of writing, they were not unusual in personal letters. Strategies A and D can be combined:

(30)   Thank you so much for this, it is appreciated.
(W 7.3. SEU)

One of the longest combinations in my material was found in a personal letter:

(31)   Dear Joan. I am a rat a swine an ingrate. I was terribly pleased to
       get your letter with Margaret's address, I really was – thank you.
(W 7.3. SEU)

The strategies of gratitude in example (31) involve self-denigration, the expression of pleasure (twice) and thanking (I+D+D+A).

In long, elaborate thanks it is difficult to sort out the effect on politeness of the individual strategies, and length itself is a factor contributing to the politeness of the speech act.

2.11   The functions of gratitude expressions

2.11.1   Thanking and ritualization

The function of gratitude expressions cannot be described only in terms of illocutionary force since *thank you* and *thanks* have functions which seem to violate the rules for the use of the illocutionary force indicating device. Eisenstein and Bodman (1986: 168) note, for example, that *thank you* can be used ironically and can have the illocutionary function of accepting or rejecting an offer and signalling the conclusion of the conversation.

There are several analyses of the functions of *thank you/thanks*, which go beyond speech-act theory or represent a different approach. From Goffman's sociological perspective (see Chapter 1, section 1.5), thanks are small supportive rituals associated with politeness and good behaviour in our society.

In Norrick (1978), it is argued that gratitude expressions have a number of social functions depending on what the speaker wants to achieve by means of thanking (Norrick 1978: 284f). Some of these functions could be analysed as perlocutionary,[8] but many of them go beyond the perlocutionary effects of the speech act and are conventionally associated with the utterance just as much as the illocutionary function of thanking.

The social effect of *thank you* is generally an acknowledgement[9] that one has benefited from an action by another person (Norrick 1978: 285), but *thank you* can also assure somebody in advance of one's gratitude for a service, offer, promise even though the truth of the propositional content cannot be presupposed (Norrick 1978: 285; Coulmas 1981b: 74). *Thank you* is also used to acknowledge small favours, e.g. when the bus conductor gives the passenger his ticket, the bank clerk hands the customer money over the counter or a waiter brings a guest a cup of coffee. Another function is illustrated when a person says *thank you* for being helped on with his coat and indicates that he can do the rest himself (Norrick 1978: 285), or when *thank you* is used to dismiss a person whose services are not needed ('the dismissive thanks').

Sometimes thanking has very little meaning. *Fine thanks* in the answer to the question *how are you* represents a 'phatic' use of thanking, i.e. thanking has no other function than to make the hearer feel good. In addition, *thank you* can accept a proposal to end the telephone conversation, in which case the phrase has a terminating or discourse-organizing function. Another interesting use is *thank you* with the illocutionary function of accepting an offer. However, when an offer is rejected, *thank you* is purely phatic (*no thanks*). Finally, there are derived uses of *thank you*, signalling irony, sarcasm, brusqeness, which are marked by a characteristic prosody (see section 2.10.3). A different type of example, where Searle's felicity conditions are violated, is *Thank you for not smoking*, where thanking for something which is undesirable and is still in the future is interpreted as a request not to do it. Some of the functions that *thank you / thanks* can have are summarized in Figure 2.3. In the Figure, I have made no attempt to distinguish between the illocutionary function of thanking, the social or perlocutionary functions and the discourse-organizing function of thanking.

An important task in this chapter is to describe the different functions that *thank you/thanks* can have. In addition, factors of the social situation, such as the type and size of favour, will be investigated.

2.12 Thanking as a discourse marker

Coulmas (1981b: 81) quotes Hymes as saying that 'while in American English, it (*thank you*) is still mainly a formula for the expression of gratitude, British "thank you" seems on its way to marking formally the segments of certain interactions, with only residual attachment to

	(i)	acknowledging a major favour
	(ii)	acknowledging a favour such as being handed something
	(iii)	assuring a person of one's future gratitude
	(iv)	dismissing a person or a person's services
	(v)	accepting a proposal that the conversation should end
thank you/thanks	(vi)	closing the conversation
	(vii)	accepting an offer
	(viii)	making the hearer feel good ('phatic' function) when an offer is rejected ('no thanks') or one answers an enquiry about one's health ('fine thanks')
	(ix)	irony, sarcasm, brusqueness
	(x)	negative request ('thank you for not ... ')

Figure 2.3   The functional domain of thanking

"thanking" in some cases' (Hymes 1971: 69). *Thank you* is, for example, used as a discourse marker with the function of signalling various stages in service encounters, when a ticket is sold on the train, or a person is handed something in a restaurant:

(Situation: the conductor hands over a ticket)
Conductor: 'Thank you.'
Passenger: 'Thank you.'
Conductor: 'Thank you.'
(From Coulmas 1981b: 91)[10]

The conductor says *thank you* on handing over the ticket, and the passenger accepts the ticket by thanking for it. The little interaction is terminated by the conductor's thanking.

Moreover, on the telephone people thank each other repeatedly, and *thank you* (or a variant form) can appear several times in succession:

(32)   B   and ^go *and 'trans'fer it to*
    A   *^one o ^clock* :Sampa'nini's 'in – :Bàrrack
       'Street# .
    B   ^yès#
    A   ^lòvely#
       ^thanks 'very mùch# -
    B   ^wèll#
       ^thank yòu very _much#
       +for ^being so !pàtient 'with it 'all#
       (– laughs)+
    A   +(laughs - -)+ ^thànk you# .
       ^rìght#
       ^rìght#
       ^see you thèn#
    B   "^yès#
    A   +^bye#+
    B   +^bye+ bye#
(9.1 682–97)

Thanking functions as a marker signalling that the conversational part-ners want to terminate the conversation. After thanking, the interlocutors exchange farewells.

What larger sequential patterns does thanking occur in, and what func-tions does it have in these patterns? It is clear that *thank you* is in many ways like utterances such as *OK* or *well*, whose function is due to their sequential (or syntagmatic) position in the discourse structure, although *thank you/thanks* does not entirely lose the function of thanking.

2.12.1 Thanking as a closing signal in adjacency triplets

In adjacency pairs such as compliment–thanking and well-wish–thanking, the gratitude phrase expresses evaluation and closes the minimal dialogue. When thanking occurs in larger units, consisting of three turns, it is less clear what function it has and under what conditions it is obligatory. Consider:

(33) A *is ^this a spare páper#*
      B (([ə] ^yèah#
         I actually ^got it for yóu#))
      A ^thank you very múch#
         ((1 syll)) *^thanks very much in:dèed#*
(1.1 36: 32–6)

According to Goffman (1976: 69), the interaction in example (33) is a remedial interchange consisting of an offence ('the request'), the relief ('the granting of the request') and an appreciation move, which has the function of restoring the social harmony between the participants.

However, in the following example, the function of *thank you* is diffi-cult to reconcile with Goffman's analysis of thanking as an appreciation move:

(34) 1 m I ^gìve it to you# - .
           ^will you sígn it# -
      2 b ^nò# .
      3 m ^*thànk you#* -
           ^((my)) . ^will you ^will you sígn it Mr *'Danby#
      4 d *^nò#* -
      5 m ^*thànk you#* .
           my ^question is ànswered# -
(5.6 86–93)

The excerpt comes from a debate about fox-hunting. It ends with the ques-tion whether Speaker b (and Speaker d) are willing to sign a petition for the abolition of fox-hunting. The function of *thank you* is not to express appreciation since the answer to Speaker m's request is 'no'. *Thank you* signals instead that a previous rejection is acknowledged (see Davidson

1984: 127 – thanking as a 'rejection finalizer'; cf. Tsui 1989: 556). On the level of discourse organization, the most important function of *thank you* is to convey that Speaker m is satisfied, that the issue is closed and that something else follows (see Tsui 1989: 560; Stenström 1984: 239f; Severinson-Eklundh and Linell 1983: 294f).

It is clear that the 'appreciation move' (the 'follow-up move' in an adjacency triplet) can have several functions, which may be present at the same time:

> ... we may say that at the level of organization of an exchange, the follow-up move has the general function of acknowledging the outcome of the interaction in an exchange. This general function can be realized specifically as evaluating the response; showing understanding, appreciation, or acceptance of the response; and showing a change of state of knowledge or information as a result of the response. At the level of organization of a sequence, the follow-up move has the function of signaling the end of the sequence.
> (Tsui 1989: 560)

Thank you/thanks as a closing signal can be followed by other elements such as *right, right oh, OK*, which also have a closing function.[11] Consider:

(35) 1 B [əm] could you ^give Pro'fessor :Worth's apòlogies#
             for ^[ði:] mathemàtical so_ciety _meeting# ^on !Friday the
             'seven:tèenth#
      2 C ^yèah# .
      3 B ^*thanks very mùch*# .
      4 C ^rĭght 'oh#
(8.1 710–13)

There is a close relation between follow-up moves and discourse type. An extra appreciation move is, for example, especially frequent in class-room discourse, debates and telephone calls (Tsui 1994). Sociolinguistic factors are also important. Stenström (1984: 243) found that the number of follow-up moves varied in individual conversations depending on how well the interlocutors knew each other, and Stubbs has suggested that the third move is obligatory when the participants in the conversation are strangers, but that it is optional if the conversation takes place between friends (Stubbs 1983: 145).

Examples where thanking closes a small encounter are relatively unproblematic. When we look at thanking as a closing signal in larger sequences than the adjacency triplet, the description is more difficult. As Tsui points out,

> ... (the function of a follow-up move) is not only to acknowledge the outcome, but to signal the end of the encounter as well. It is when the two functions are realized separately that problems of description are created.
> (Tsui 1994: 247)

2.12.2 *Thanking in proposal-acceptance sequences*

An offer or a request can, of course, be accepted immediately (Houtkoop-Steenstra 1987: 62). Thus offers of food or of small services have the form of adjacency pairs, i.e. the first part is followed by the second part without a gap. It is clear, however, that people interact with each other in complex ways, and that it would be a mistake to think of a request as always being complied with at once, information as accepted without questioning, promises (or offers) as immediately accepted by the other partner in the conversation. What we find is macro-speech acts or global speech acts of different length and complexity (see van Dijk 1977: 73).

Example (36) illustrates that thanking may have a fixed location in a sequence of speech acts made up of more than three turns:

```
(36)    1  A  ((that's)) . ^{Fèbruary} the :ninetèenth# .
        2  B  ^yès# -
        3  A  ^at ![twə] ^twelve thìrty#
        4  B  ^yès#
        5  B  at ^Long Màrket#
        6  A  ^[m̀hm]# .
        7  A  ^ÓK#
        8  B  ^rìght#
        9  B  ^thanks very múch#
       10  B  *^b̌ye#*
       11  A  *((^thǎnk you#))*
       12  A  ^b̌ye#
```
(8.2 1173–84)

Speaker B does not accept the arrangement in turns 1–3 immediately. *Yes* (with a fall tone) does no more than acknowledge the information ('weak' acceptance).[12] A request for confirmation and the confirmation itself (turns 7 and 8) is required before the proposal is finally accepted in turn 9. 'Strong' acceptance is expressed by *thanks*, which also has the function of indicating that Speaker B wants to close the conversation. As we can see from example (36) the sequence involves at least the following five steps:

1 making a proposal
2 weak acceptance
3 request-for-confirmation
4 confirmation
5 strong acceptance/sequence closing

(After Houtkoop-Steenstra 1987: 2)

Five-turn structures are used for making arrangements, proposals or offers referring to the future (Houtkoop-Steenstra 1987 – 'remote proposals'). The first part is a question, request, suggestion, offer, arrangement, etc, inviting the hearer's acceptance or compliance. The general category is referred to by Houtkoop-Steenstra as a proposal:

> ... I will speak of 'proposals' as a general category of conversational actions which all have in common that the recipient is asked to commit himself to the execution of an action: collaborating in bringing the present conversation to a close, passing on a piece of information to another person, calling somebody to the telephone, holding the line, accepting an offer, etc. All these actions have in common that they are initial or 'first' conversational actions to which the recipient is expected to respond.
> (Houtkoop-Steenstra 1987: 6)

Thank you signals acceptance of the proposal and brings the sequence to a close.

The pattern illustrated above has several variations. Proposals (requests, suggestions, offers) can be 'recycled', expanded or continued after a break, and the acceptance can be immediate or provisional, final or deferred. As a result, *thank you* can be found in different discourse patterns. In example (37), the proposal takes place in several steps and needs to be accepted 'in instalments' by thanking or by some other acceptance signal:

```
(37)  1  C   *and I'll ^let you 'know* how I 'go for . :bits and
              'pieces that are _going òn 'then âll *'right# .
              and ^I will -*
      2  B   *^rìght# .
              ^f=ine#
              ^thanks very 'much indèed#*
      3  (C  !go into your fi:nancial 'ramificàtions#
              ^âll right#
      4  B   ^ríght# .
              ^OḰ#
              ^I'll !have it . I'll ^have it 'down in dètail#
              ex^actly 'what we 'earn and :hòpe to 'earn#
              ^âll right#
      5  C   ^óh# .
              ^well I !don't 'worry a'bout thát#
              ^I ((was - I'll)) ^tǎlk to you#
              and ^I will !sort it 'out in a_bout ten mìnutes#
              *all ^ríght#*
      6  B   *^yès#* .
              ^fine#
              ^thanks very 'much in!dèed#
      7  C   ^bў̆e#
      8  B   ^bye bу́e#
(8.2 905–25)
```

In turn 2, *thanks very much indeed* accepts the first part of the proposal. Speaker C continues his turn, and the final acceptance of Speaker C's proposal does not come until turn 6. The sequence is characteristic of the closing of conversation, as seen from the fact that the interaction ends with farewells (turns 7 and 8).

A similar example is (38). *Thank you* occurred at several stages of the interaction signalling 'stepwise acceptance'. Final acceptance (at the end of the extract) is marked by more intensification:

(Situation: Speaker B is the interviewer and Speaker A the interviewee)
(38) A ^yès#
         I ^sěe ((what you can 'see as your 'point))# .
         *^*thànk you*#*
      B *^and [ə:]* !if you can ^if you can [ə: ? ə:]
         :wrĭte to us#
         and ^ăsk us for some 'help#
         we'd be "^věry 'glad#
         to ^gìve it to you#
      a [m]
      A ^all ríght# -
         ^*thànk you*#

(further down in the same interview)

      (B *and we'll* "^have to we'll ^have to 'let you
         knòw#
         ^whàt we# .
         de^cide a'bout your :applicàtion#
      A ^*thank you 'very mùch*#
         and ^now I 'have to 'see the [ə:] .
      B ^Tutor to 'Women Stúdents#
         and the ^sěcretary#
         will ^tell you 'how to fìnd her#
         . all ^ríght#
      A *^*thank you very much* indèed*# - .
(3.1 559–68; 1017–26)

The reason for such elaborate patterns may be that the proposal (e.g. a request or an offer) refers to an act in the remote future, that the proposal involves a major favour or that the relationship between the participants requires more politeness. Speakers are, for example, more likely to repeat thanks if the participants in the conversation are non-equal on the power scale.

2.12.3   *Thanking in telephone closings*

As always when the discourse extends over several turns, there may be several possible structural analyses, and *thank you* permeates discourse in ways which are not easy to analyse.

Openings and closings are structural units just as much as adjacency pairs and turn sequences. They are psychologically 'real', and they are typically marked by special boundary signals. Consider A's and B's use of thanking at the end of a telephone call in example (39):

(39) 1 B O^Ḱ# .
             ^wèll#
             I'll ^just 'drop you a nòte#
             ^àny'way#
             to con^firm _this mèeting# .
             ^which is the !twelfth at e'leven 'forty-five#
      2 A ^thànk you#
      3 B ^that's 'very !kìnd of you#
      4 A *^OḰ#*
      5 B *^thank you* 'very mùch# .
             +^bye býe#+
(8.3 1035–45)

The closing of the call takes time to achieve, and it involves ritual, repetition, etc. The analysis by Schegloff and Sacks (1973) of telephone closings helps us to understand what is going on. According to Schegloff and Sacks, the conversation is closed by the participants in two phases. In the first phase, an offer of assistance, a promise, an arrangement to meet, etc may be seen as an invitation to the other participant jointly to bring the conversation to an end.

In example (39), the confirmation of an arrangement in turn 1 (*I'll drop you a note to confirm the meeting*) is potentially a 'last topic' in the telephone call (a so-called closing-implicative topic; Levinson 1983: 317). It can therefore be analysed as a pre-closing device indicating that the speakers are willing to terminate the telephone call (Schegloff and Sacks 1973: 317). After pre-closing, the speakers proceed to leave-taking, a ritual which may also involve thanking each other.

Thanking before the closing of the telephone call can also be seen 'as a signature of a sort' (Schegloff and Sacks 1973: 318). *Thank you* at the end of the telephone call was found in eight of the nine business calls and only two of the personal calls in the London-Lund Corpus, which shows that it is almost mandatory in the former type. Example (40) represents a prototypal closing pattern consisting of double adjacency pairs. In the first adjacency pair the participants thank each other. This is followed by a pair in which the exchange of farewells takes place.

(40) C ^OǨ *then#
          ^fìne#*
      A *^rìght# .
          ^thank* you very 'much in+dèed#+
      C +^thank+ ýóu#

    A good ^býe#
    C ^bўe#
(9.2 317–23)

The 'echo response' in the second part of the pair (10 examples in the LLC) can be modified lexically and prosodically.[13] The position of the nucleus can be varied as well as the nuclear tone:

(41) B *^thanks very múch#*
      C *^thằnk you#;.*;
         ^look 'forward to sèeing you#
      B ^all rìght#
         ^bye býe#
(8.2 1244–8)

The rising tone of the second *thank you* can be compared with the falling tone in the first part of the adjacency pair:

(42) B +^yừp#+
         ^O!Ǩ 'then#
         ^rìght#
      A *((well))* ^thank you very mùch#
      B ^{thánk} yóu#
      A ^b=ye#
      B ^bye thère#
(9.2 249–53)

Thank you can also be followed by a simple *OK* or by *right* (*all right*) rather than by a 'responder' (*it's OK, great pleasure*).

(43) C ^well _Iəll [ə] !chèck thát#
         as I ^sáy#
         as "^soon as I get 'back to _my - [ə:mə]
         :UEDÉSN
         'papers# .
         ^and !give 'her a rìng a'bout it#
      A ^thank _you vèry much ((in'deed))#
      C ^all right thén# -
         [ə]
      A ^good *býe#*
      C ^good býe#

(44) A ^yèah# - .
         O^Ḱ#
      B ^[m̀]# -
         ^thanks for rínging#
      A ^rìght# -
         ^bўe#

B ^bye býe# .
   ^see you next wéek#
A ^sèe you#
B ((^sèe you sóon#))
(7.2 819–41)

The analysis of thanking at the end of telephone calls can also profit from a social perspective. Stubbs writes that some utterances have the function to 'take up an alignment, to make a commitment to a position, to claim fellowship or form alliances' (Stubbs 1983: 188). From this point of view, the closing of the telephone call can be analysed as a ritual displaying the speakers' alignments and commitments.

Thanking as a social ritual can be followed by apologizing before the exchange of farewells (see Chapter 3):

(45) B ^àll ríght#
         we'll ^dò that +_Judith#+
      A +that'd be+ ^very kìnd#
         ^thanks àwfully# .
         ^sòrry to 'bother you#
      B ^nò#
         ^not a !bìt# .
         look ^forward to !sèeing you a'gain 'one of these
         dáys#
(8.4 532–9)

Other examples of supportive rituals which are typical of social encounters are thanking for the coffee or for a meal or thanking the other person for ringing, for his patience, etc (see Severinson Eklundh 1986: 47):

(46) B ^wèll then#
         ^thànks for the cóffee#
      A ^great pléasure#
         ^glad to !sèe you#
         ^bỹe#
      B ^bỹe#
(3.2 736–41)

Here thanking and its response serve as an extra 'conversational loop' adding nothing to the topic development. The only function of the exchange is to make it possible for the conversationalists to claim social fellowship and confirm their desire to end the telephone call in a friendly way.

Phatic talk is another means of establishing convergence before the personal contact is interrupted by farewells:

(47) 1 B ^well ((we)) [? ə:] as !near two 'thirty as
            pòssible#

2 C ^yês#
3 B all ^ríght# - .
 ^that's fîne#
 ^thank you very mùch# .
 ^that'll en'sure that we'll get :some 'kind of
 :dày'light#
 (– laughs) ^even if *it's :ràining#*
4 C *^yès# .
 ^that* will 'be . ^that ((would)) be gòod#
 ^yê s#
5 B ^yès# .
 ^O'K fîne#
6 C ^fîne# .
 ((^êxcellent#));.;
7 B *^thanks very múch#*
8 C *^thànk you#;.*;
 ^look 'forward to sèeing you#
9 B ^all rìght#
 ^bye býe#
(8.2 1230–48)

In turn 1, an arrangement to meet is reconfirmed. The function of this turn is in the first place to invite the other person to close the conversation. The conversational move (turn 3) therefore serves as an agreement to close the conversation. The sequence is followed by social talk and ended by an exchange of farewells. Thanking is mainly of a phatic character although it also facilitates for the participants to close the conversation.

The patterns at the end of the telephone call can be varied depending on the type of call, the setting, the relationship between the participants, etc. Calls requiring efficiency and speed can end by thanking alone, especially if the caller and answerer do not know each other.

(48) B ^number's !Brì stol#
  ^five 'six :five 'six :èight#
  A ^five 'six :nine _six èight#
  B ^thank yòu#
  A ^thank yòu#
(8.2 1013–16)[14]

Example (48) has two possible analyses. Either *thank you* has the meaning of farewell, or the farewell exchange is implicit after the caller and the recipient have arrived at mutual agreement to close the conversation (see Clark and French 1981). Alternatively, the pre-closing and closing sections can be compressed into a single turn (Houtkoop-Steenstra 1987: 137).

(49) B [əm] – ((I)) ^think I'll :trỳ 'ringing a'gain in
  'quarter of an hóur then#

C ^rìght#
   ^OḰ##
B *'if he's* ^stĭll not a'round then# .
   ^yèah#
C ^rìght#
   +^bye býe##+
B +^thǎnk you##+ .
   ^bўe##

(8.1 941–3)

In example (50), thanking + *goodbye* comes immediately after the proposal in the first turn. As a result the whole closing ceremony occupies
only one turn:

(50) A I'll ^give you a 'ring back làter#
      B ^thanks very 'much indèed#
         ^thànk you# .
         ^bye býe#

(8.1 330–3)

A variant closing pattern consisting of two turns is illustrated in
example (51):

(51) C I'll look ^forward to sèeing you#
      B ^fîne# .
         ^thank you very *'much in:dèed Mr 'Parker#
         bye ^býe##*
      C *^thànk you#

(8.1 1303–7)

In example (52), Speaker C does not respond to Speaker B's thanking him but says farewell immediately. The whole closing takes three
turns:

(52) B I'll ^tèll him#
      C ^yès#
      B ^rìght#
      C ^y=es#
      C ^OḰ then#
      B ^thànks#
      C *(– giggles) ^bўe##*
      B *(– giggles) ^bўe##*

(9.1 1206–13)

Thanking as a closing signal has a special function in discussions and
debates. In example (53), thanking brings about the change to a new
speaker:

(Situation: Radio discussion)
(53) m we should .re^member those of our ancestors
         ((that)) we can find òut abóut#
         and ^take an ĭnterest in _them#
         because "^ŏut of _them#
         came ^everything that we âre#
      f ^thank you very múch#
         ^let's ask the psy:chòlogist#
(5.2 832–7)

The chairman (f) thanks person m for his participation in the debate and invites another speaker to take the floor.

In an (informal) discussion with many speakers, *thank you* is used by the two discussants as a 'floor-leaving device':

(54) b +^[m̀]#
         ^yèah#+ - - -
         ^yès#
      A *^[m̀]#* - - .
         ^wèll#
         ^gòod#
         that's grèat#
         ^thank you !very +mùch#+
      b +^gòod#+
         ^wèll#
         ^thank *yôu#*
         thank ^yòu#
(4.4 566–78)

Thank you is furthermore used alone or with other closing signals such as *end of message, that's all, goodbye* (12 examples) to mark the end of a message delivered on the automatic telephone answering machine. These examples are of special interest because *thank you* is used in a situation where no receiver of the message is present, and where the social function associated with *thank you* must be minimal.

(55) BB so per^haps you could 'telephone _me to ar'range
          an'other appóintment# .
          ^thănk 'you#
(9.3 676–7)

(56) AE thank ^yòu# .
          ^ènd of méssage#
(9.3 52–3)

(57) AZ [ə:] ^thàt's all 'thank you 'very ":múch#
(9.3 653)

A routinized intonation pattern (with a fall-plus-rise tone on *thank you* and a rise tone on *goodbye*) is illustrated in:

(58) AY [ə:m] . the ^other 'question((s)) I can dis'cuss
with him . 'when he rìngs# .
^thằnk yóu# .
good^býe#
(9.3 583–5)

2.12.4 *Thanking in different turn positions*

All larger discourse patterns cannot be analysed as sequential. Syntagmatic patterns containing *thank you / thanks* in different positions result from the merging of several conversational moves into a single turn:

(59) A *^my* !next 'shipment :ín of 'course#
will ^be con_siderably !dèarer#
B ^yès# .
^Ï see# -
^rìght# .
^OḰ#
^thank you 'very mùch#
A ^ríght#
B ^rìght#
good^býe#
A *((2 sylls))*
(8.1 611–21)

Speaker B's turn in example (59) is made up of a combination of moves (*yes + I see + right + OK + thank you very much*). Table 2.9 lists the distribution of *thank you*, *OK*, and farewells in the London-Lund Corpus. *Thank you + goodbye* (*bye, bye bye*, etc) was the most frequent combination (16 examples). The order of the elements was fairly fixed with thanking preceding *goodbye* in all but one example. One can also notice that weak acceptance (*yes, I see*, etc) generally preceded forms of strong acceptance (*thank you / thanks*). The most frequent individual patterns were *thank you# bye* (5 examples) and *thank you# bye bye* (4 examples) both of which had a fairly fixed intonation:

^thằnk you# ^bўe# (4 examples)
^thằnk you# ^bўe bye# (2 examples)

To sum up, thanking was frequent as a pre-closing or closing signal in telephone conversation. As shown in section 2.9 there were as many as 37 tokens per 10,000 words in telephone conversation to be compared with only five tokens in (impromptu) informal conversation. *Thank you/thanks* on the telephone does not, however, lose its meaning completely but can

Table 2.9: Combinations of *thank you* and other closing signals in the LLC

Type	Number
BYE+THANK	1
OK+THANK+THANK+OK+OK+BYE	1
THANK+OK+OK	1
THANK+THANK+APOLOGY	1
THANK+THANK+BYE	1
OK+OK+THANK	2
OK+THANK	2
THANK+OK	4
OK+OK+OK+THANK	5
OK+THANK+BYE	7
THANK+BYE	16
TOTAL	41

Abbreviations:
OK = *yes, I see, right, OK* (weak acceptance)
THANK = *thank you, thanks, thank you very much*, etc (strong acceptance)
BYE = *goodbye, bye bye*, etc
APOLOGY = *I'm sorry*, etc

also be analysed pragmatically as an act of thanking or as a signal of appreciation of the conversational partner.

2.13 The pragmatics of thanking

We need a description of the discourse situation associated with thanking which accounts both for the use of *thank you/thanks* and for the variants which can be created by means of intensification. The following discussion will focus on the object of gratitude and on the size of the favour.

2.13.1 *The constraints caused by the object of gratitude*

Parents spend considerable time teaching their children to say *thank you*, and *thank you* is among the first phrases that foreign learners are taught to say in English. There are rules for how, where and when such phrases are used; we are, for example, supposed to express our appreciation of the meal on social occasions, send a thank-you note to an aunt for a Christmas gift, say 'thank you' after a compliment, etc.

The classification of the situation I have undertaken is based on several different dimensions or factors. Following Coulmas, I regard the type of favour ('the object of gratitude' or benefaction) as the most important factor because it determines the degree of gratitude which is required (see Coulmas 1981b: 74). Other factors, such as the relationship between the participants and the size of the favour, are also important and will be commented on below. Whether one thanks a close friend or a stranger may, for example, have an effect on the form which is used. Moreover, there is a difference between small and large gifts, and between hospitality on social occasions (major favour) and small treats which are provided as a matter of course (minor favour). Another factor determining the type of thanks is whether the setting is the place of work or a person's home. In the former case, a small favour may be done routinely because it is the person's job to do it.

To begin with, thanks can be grouped into two main categories depending on whether the favour involves material things, like a gift or a service, or something immaterial such as a well-wish or a compliment. Favours classified as immaterial goods include offers, promises or suggestions which are only anticipated. Another distinction is between determinate and indeterminate favours:

(60)   C   I'll look ^forward to sèeing you#
       B   ^fine# .
           ^thank you very *'much in:dèed Mr 'Parker#
           bye ^býe#*
       C   *^thànk you#
(8.1 1303–7)

Several reasons for gratitude are possible in example (60): 'Thank you for ringing', 'thank you for talking to me', 'thank you for your attention', 'thank you for your time', 'thank you for your wishing to see me', etc. Table 2.10 summarizes some information from the London-Lund Corpus on different types of thanking ('benefactions').

A.   MATERIAL THINGS

Twenty-five per cent of the examples were thanks for material things such as a gift or a service. *Thank you* is used routinely when a person was handed a cup of coffee, a glass of wine, or a cigarette. The largest number of examples in this category occurred in connection with small services carried out by a person in his professional role. For example:

(Situation: Female research assistant and author (Speaker C) hands over a copy of her book to the secretary (Speaker A))
(61)   C   *yes ^hĕre we 'are# - - -
           ^you are :wĕlcome to have thìs# -

Table 2.10: Types of 'benefaction'

Type	Number
A. Material things	
letter	4
gift (small and large)	3
hospitality (food, drink)	42
services (major or minor)	11
visiting, phoning, letter, postcard	6
Subtotal	66
B. Immaterial things	
compliments, congratulations, well-wishes	3
carrying out a request (fulfilling a person's wishes)	14
interest in one's health	5
offer, promise, suggestion, invitation	28
information	18
a proposal to do something (e.g. to close the conversation)	131
Subtotal	199
Total	265[15]

```
        ((I ^xĕroxed you)) a !còpy#*
     A  ^thanks 'very mùch# - -
(2.14 167–70)
```

On the telephone, the caller acknowledges a favour by the operator by means of a simple *thank you* or *thanks*:

```
(Situation: Speaker A is the operator)
(62)   A  ^òh#
          ^right óh#
          ^hold ón#
       B  ^thank y=ou# - - -
(8.1 1018–19)

(63)   A  ^=anyway#
          I ^have !Barney "Bìmms#
          from ^Robert "!Nòrton on the 'line *_for you#*
       B  *^thank y=ou#*
       A  ^O_Ḱ#
       B  ^yĕs# - - -
(8.3 885–90)
```

(64)   C   hul^lo I'll !just 'put you 'through to :Mr 'Perll
           Jàmes#
       B   ^thànk you# .
(8.1 350–1)

Thanking is also required on social occasions. Guests are supposed to thank the host/hostess for the meal when leaving his or her house. It is also polite to praise the meal or compliment the host or hostess while one is eating. The amount of politeness may be increased by prosodic devices (stress, boosters) or by a combination of a compliment and thanking:

(65)   B   *it's a ^{very* 'nice} :sŭpper 'Jo#
           ^thank you +!very 'much in:dèed#+
(2.10 1258–9)

In example (66), the social occasion seems to demand a high degree of emotionality or 'gushing':

(Situation: Speaker B, a middle-aged male architect, has been offered a glass of liqueur)
(66)   B   ^Gòd#
           ^look at "!thàt#
           you're ^treating it as 'though it were !wìne# -
           ^blèss you 'dear#
           ^thank you vêry 'much# -
           ^lôvely# - -
           (. grunts)
(2.3 1–7)

Thanking a person for his hospitality may be the rule at the end of a visit before the exchange of farewells:

(67)   A   ^I'm going 'out !shòpping# .
       B   ^wèll then#
           ^thànks for the cóffee#
       A   ^great pléasure#
           ^glad to !sèe you#
           ^bỳe#
       B   ^bỳe#
(3.2. 735–41)

If some time has elapsed after the social event, gratitude is shown in writing rather than in speech (a thank-you letter or a thank-you note).

English-speaking people express thanks both for small services and for big favours, causing trouble or inconvenience for the benefactor:[16]

... (they) verbalize their gratitude for all sorts of big and small favors, for gifts and compliments; they use gratitude expressions in situations involving exchange of goods and services for monetary payments; they use them in a

variety of other informal and formal situations, for example, cocktail parties, gatherings of relatives and/or friends for special occasions, press conferences, entertainment shows, etc. ... The use of these gratitude expressions ... is so pervasive that it becomes almost mechanical.
(Apte 1976: 84f)

Even small favours may result in profuse gratitude depending on the speaker's perception of the extralinguistic situation:

(Situation: One of the guests at a party has asked for cherries)
(68)   c   ^could I !hǎve one#
       a   ^yèah# –
           ^here's one for :yòu 'Fanny# -
       B   ^òh#
           ^thánk you 'very mùch#
           ^òh# - - -
(4.6 525–30)

In example (69) a spouse is thanked for getting up early to make breakfast:

(69)   b   ^thànk you very 'much for 'getting up this 'morning and
           'making bréakfast#
(4.1 624)

Thanking an interlocutor for coming along, for ringing, for being patient, etc, may have the additional purpose to signal that the conversation is coming to an end (see section 2.12.3):

(70)   A   ^thank you for dropping ín _Sam#
(1.1 1211)

People are expected to express their gratitude when they receive a letter in speech or in writing or on the answering machine:

(Situation: Message left on the answering machine)
(71)   BL   [ə:] . ^thank you Jàmes#
            ^very !m=uch# .
            for your ^lètter todáy# .
(9.3 770)

B. IMMATERIAL THINGS

The majority of examples (75 per cent) referred to favours which can be classified as immaterial objects. One is, for example, supposed to say *thank you* to acknowledge a compliment, a congratulation, a well-wish or an invitation. A compliment is any utterance which is flattering, complimentary or just polite:

(72)   A   ^I'll take you 'out for a :drĭnk in a 'minute
           {^Jóel#}#

```
      *(laughs - - )*
   a  *that's the spirit Nick*
   A  ^thànks# - - -
(2.9 680–3)
```

(73)　A　oh ^Dàniel#
　　　　I [ə] I ^hope I 'see you wèll#
　　　D　you ^dò#
　　　　　^thànk you#
　　　　　+. ^yès#+
(4.4 798–802)

A well-wish is illustrated in example (74) and a congratulation in example (75):

(74)　A　en^jǒy your'self#
　　　　^have *a 'nice tíme#*
　　　B　*^thǎnk you#* ^bўe#
　　　A　^bўe#
(7.2 62–6)

(75)　a　hello Ann it's Joan
　　　B　hel^lò {Jòan#}#
　　　a　(sings Happy Birthday)
　　　B　(…) ^thànk you#
(7.11 1157–8)

The proper way to accept an invitation is to thank for it:

(76)　A　^thànks for your 'invitátion you ((['həu]
　　　　　^throwing a *!pàrty#))*
(1.4 12)

Thanking is needed to acknowledge that the speaker's request has been complied with:

(77)　A　*is ^this a spare páper#*
　　　B　(([ə] ^yèah#
　　　　I actually ^got it for yóu#))
　　　A　^thank you very múch#
　　　　((1 syll)) *^thanks very much in:dèed#*
(1.1 32–6)

Generally speaking, gratitude should be expressed for all types of information (names, telephone numbers, the way to the station, etc). For example:

(78)　B　do you ^want the !tĕlephone 'number#
　　　A　[ə:m] . ^might as well háve it I *sup'pose#*
　　　B　*^yèah#* .

[əu] ^óne# -
  A ^yés# .
  B ^one "two óne# .
  A ^yés#
  B ^five 'one 'seven èight# -
  A ^thanks very múch#
(8.1 655–63)

There are a few situations in which thanking is required for politeness only. An example is *thank you* after *fine, well,* etc in the response to a routine enquiry about a person's well-being:

(79) A *good ^mórning#*
     a *good morning Miss* Detch˙how are you
     A **^fine !thànk you#**
(3.1 1030–2)

In this use, *thank you / thanks* was often attached to the preceding tone unit as a nuclear 'tail' (examples (80) and (81)). In other examples, the gratitude expression had a rising or falling tone:

(80) B well ^how are you Tímothy# -
     A ^áll 'right 'thanks#
(1.7 511–12)

(81) A * ^how are yòu#*
     B *[ə:m]* . I ^I'm very wéll 'thank you#
        and ^yóu#
(8.1 6–8)

(82) C ((are)) you ^wéll#
     A I'm ^vèry 'well thánk you#
        ^yès#
(1.9 29–31)

Potential favours followed by thanking are offers, arrangements, suggestions, etc (see Coulmas 1981: 74):

(83) B I'll ^ring you _bàck#
     A ^thank you 'very múch#
     B ^bўe#
     A ^bўe#
(8.1 1000–3)

A generous offer may require effusive gratitude:

(84) B I'd be ^most gràteful#
        if you could ^pass that òn#
     C ^OḰ#
        I'll ^do my bést#

```
        ( . giggles)
    B   ^thank you :sŏ 'much#
    C   ^OḰ# .
        *^g=ood#*
    B   *^good*býe#
    C   ((good))^bўe#
(9.1 65–72)
```

Thanking in response to an offer is closely linked with polite behaviour and etiquette. Such routine uses may be what Robin Lakoff (1975) had in mind when she wrote that women are supposed to be particularly careful to say *please* and *thank you* and to uphold the other social conventions. Thanking is used both to accept and reject an offer.

```
(85)    B   +((d'you ^wánt some 'coffee#))+
        A   +((oh)) ^thànk you#+
(2.4 1320–21 )
```

```
(86)    a   *[ə:] won't you sit* down
        B   *((2 to 3 sylls))*
        A   ^thànk you# - -
(3.1 10–12)
```

Depending on the occasion, the size of the favour, etc, gratitude can be expressed more or less profusely:

```
(87)    c   ((^Máisie will you 'have an'other one#))
        B   ^oh yĕs#
            ^thànk you#
            ((how)) ^lòvely# .
(4.3 925–9)
```

```
(88)    B   you can ^ĕasily 'have one#
        A   *^lòvely#* -
            ^lòvely#
            ^thànks#
(2.5 845–8)
```

When the situation is formal, thanking can be expressed indirectly:

```
(89)    a   ^would you 'like to 'take some lùnch . **'young
            Páuline#**
        b   **^[m̀]# .
            ((that would))** be ^very !nìce pléase# -
(6.2. 1038–40)
```

Thanking (for food) can be replaced by other acceptance forms, e.g. by *yes please* (with rising tone):

(90) B would you ^like one of !thŏse# .
      A ^yes pléase#
(2.11 316–17)

Thanking is also needed to soften the rejection of an offer of food, drink or a small service:

(91) c and wanted to go there *. do* you want a drink
         darling
      D *^yêah#*
      c I've got some thanks
      a oh good
(1.12 133–6)

A routine rejection of an offer is associated with a polite rise (or fall-rise) tone:

(92) b *((let's)) give you some more*
      (C 'something at :lŭnch-'time# - .
      C ^and was !just _going to go 'off and :have a _cup
         of !tèa# .
         ^nò thánks# .
(2.7 783- 5)

(93) A ^what a_bout a cigarètte# .
      A *((4 sylls))*
      B *I ^wòn't have one thánks#* - - -
(1.8 148–9)

(94) a ^if you 'wish to 'wash hànds etcétera# -
         a^long the cŏrridor#
         on the ex^treme 'right-*hand sìde#*
      b *[ə:m]* . I ^dòn't thánk you# -
(6.2 1045–8)

On social occasions, the rejection of an offer is regarded as a face-threatening act, which requires politeness and conscious attention. In example (95), the speaker expresses gratitude profusely (with 'gush'; Edmondson and House 1981) and adds a compliment:

(95) C ^you !can *_have a you can ^have a* **'spoonful
         of** :crèam with 'these if you líke#
      B I ^really 'won't 'thanks áwfully# -
         ^they're !!tèrribly#
         ^gŏod#
(2.10 1377–89)

2.14 Frames for thanking

Speech acts and other pragmatic phenomena have often been described in an informal way by sociolinguists. The importance of formulating pragmatic rules in a more careful way has been stressed by Haggo and Kuiper:

> We believe … that it is essential for the rules of pragmatics to be as carefully formulated as those of a generative syntax. If they were, then we might know how speakers match their lexical output of formulae with their perceptions of the situation in which they are speaking and (to quote Chomsky again) 'succeed in acting appropriately and creatively in linguistic performance'.
> (Haggo and Kuiper 1983: 550)

As pointed out in Chapter 1, it is clear that pragmatic 'frames' or some similar notion (see Olshtain and Cohen 1983 – 'speech act set') are needed to describe the social knowledge associated with routine phrases. In artificial intelligence, frames are knowledge representations of communication situations, such as going to a restaurant, and play an important role in utterance interpretation by facilitating and speeding up the matching of the extralinguistic situation with the information of the situation in the speakers' mental lexicon. Since routines play an important role in speech production and discourse interpretation, they also need to be organized as frames. The frames for gratitude expressions represent the language users' knowledge of the social rules of thanking (i.e. rules due to the constraints imposed by the setting, who the participants are, their relationship to each other, etc.). (However, in the figures below, frames are stated as lists of situational features and not as rules.)

Frames are not easy to define even for highly routinized speech acts since the numerous variables present in natural contexts make the pragmatic analysis of the situation difficult (see Eisenstein and Bodman 1986: 169). The distinction between standard and non-standard situations may be useful to understand the notion speech-act frame.

In standard situations certain situational parameters (setting, the relationship between the participants, the type of favour) are set beforehand. Hoppe-Graff et al. describe 'standard' and 'non-standard' situations as follows:

> In standard situations, such as often-recurring routine situations, the actual input is interpreted and dealt with as if 'following a script.' The perception of situational characteristics leads to the activation of knowledge (scripts, schemata) specific to that class of situations and to the insertion of schema variables. The result is that the recognition of the situation and the consequent information processing depends almost exclusively on the activation and specification of what is already known. In uncommon or rarely occuring [sic] situations – non-standard situations – the interpretation and mastery of the situation depends on the use of more general declarative and procedural

knowledge (plan, heuristics, etc) and on extensive application of information drawn from the context.
(Hoppe-Graff et al. 1985: 90)

Below I suggest some situational parameters and their values when the speaker says *thank you* or *thanks*. The speech-act frame of thanking must, for example, take into account the 'object of gratitude' and the speaker's perception of the size of the favour. Moreover, I have no doubt that sociolinguistic factors such as age and sex of the participants are needed to explain the use of thanking. In a study of children's acquisition of politeness, Greif and Gleason (1980: 164) found, for example, that mothers used more polite *thank you*s than the fathers did.

FRAMES FOR THANKING

A   The simple *thanks/thank you*

Formal features	**Situational features**
Function phatic, closing signal, acceptance, politeness, etc	*Setting* at work, at a person's house
Intonation rising tone stereotypic tone	*Participants* Social roles: operator-caller; host-guest; secretary-employer; chairman-participants in a debate Personal relations: friend-friend
Continuation patterns that's okay you're welcome *Discourse-specific features* occurs mainly in telephone closings	*Types of thanking* ('minor favours') acknowledging the receipt of a small favour or treat, closing a telephone call or a debate, returning greetings, responding to a congratulation or well-wish, accepting or refusing an offer

According to Eisenstein and Bodman (1986: 168), the most frequent use of thanking is a quick, almost automatic, thanks which is typically used in service encounters, when one receives a ticket from the bus conductor, when someone holds open the door, when one is served food at the restaurant, etc. In the London-Lund Corpus, the simple *thank you / thanks* was typically a response to minor services or duties, which rarely expressed real gratitude. The short *thank you/thanks* was further found in polite greeetings, to accept or reject an offer in a polite way and routinely when a person was handed some food or drink. Other uses of *thank you/thanks* are institutionalized, such as thanking in response to the operator's *hold on* on the telephone. In addition, *thank you / thanks* was frequent at the end of a telephone call as a pre-closing or a closing signal and in debates when the chairman thanked a participant for his contribution. Notice that thanking may appear in the form of paired routines consisting of thanking followed by a response (*thank you / that's OK*), and that it has a special prosody.

2.14.1 Variation in standard situations

There are also situations where thanks must be intensified for greater politeness. From a psycholinguistic point of view, one can assume that intensifiers are used with little conscious attention and that intensified expressions are associated with frames. The following frame indicates what the situational variables are when *thank you/thanks* is intensifed:

FRAMES FOR THANKING

B   The intensified *thank you/thanks* (*thanks very much indeed*, *lovely thanks*, etc)

Formal features	Situational features
Function expressing sincere gratitude	*Setting* at a person's house, social occasions
Intonation fall tone	*Participants* friends, members of the same family; strangers (unequals)
Continuation *that's okay*, etc	*Types of thanking* ('major favours', 'potential favours') invitation, social hospitality, major
Discourse-specific features none	service, generous offer, gifts

Reinforcing strategies such as intensification were used to express gratitude for major services as well as for unexpected or generous offers. The use of intensification was also due to other social variables such as power and social distance between the participants (Holmes 1990: 185f).

Even long and elaborate structures (such as example (96); identical with example (66)) can be described by a frame.

(96)   B   ^Gòd#
              ^look at "!thàt#
              you're ^treating it as 'though it were !wìne# -
              ^blèss you 'dear#
              ^thank you vêry 'much# -
              ^lôvely# - -
              (.grunts)
(2.3 1–7)

What is routinized here is the direct expression of thanking. It can be reinforced by strategies and be adapted to situations which have some similarity to the standard situations associated with thanking.

2.15 Conclusion

Thanking is probably one of the most stereotypic speech acts since speakers nearly always use some form of *thank you/thanks*, even when they express their gratitude for a major favour. *Thank you* and *thanks* are routines which need to be described in terms of a fixed number of functions, prosodic patterns, distribution in different text types, etc. Grammatically, they are stems or grammatical constructions which can be intensified, expanded and reinforced by strategies which come into play when extra politeness is required. Pragmatically, gratitude phrases are associated with frames which are activated when a certain extralinguistic situation recurs. It may be suggested that the features of the frame are not so specific as has been suggested in the discussion above, since the frame can also be activated in situations which are similar to the recurrent or standard situation.

Notes

1   By politeness is meant absolute politeness rather than politeness which is relative to the situation. Only in the absolute sense is, for example, *thank you very much indeed* more polite than the simple *thank you* (see Leech 1983: 83).

2   Notice that both *that's nice of you* and *that's nice* have been subsumed under strategy C.

3   No example was found in the London-Lund Corpus.

4   But notice the high frequency of *you're welcome* in American English.

5   In a few examples, the nucleus falls on *you* rather than on the verb. Expanded forms of *thank you/thanks* have not been counted.

6   According to Searle (1976: 18), all the expressives are characteristically followed by *for* + *ing* rather than by *to* + infinitive or a *that*-clause. In my account, this follows from the fact that they are stems.

7   *Great, grand* and *good*, together with thanking, were restricted to the closing of the conversation (telephone call).

8   On the distinction between illocutionary and perlocutionary function (acts), see Searle (1969: 25).

9   According to Bach and Harnish, thanks and apologies are classified as 'acknowledgements' rather than as expressives. Acknowledgements are often 'issued not so much to express a genuine feeling as to satisfy the social expectation that such a feeling be expressed' (Bach and Harnish 1979: 51).

10 This pattern is described by Coulmas as Australian English but occurs in British English as well.

11 No other signals were found in the London-Lund Corpus after *thank you / thanks*. According to Goffman (1976: 70), *you're welcome, that's all right, think nothing of it, it's okay* can, however, occur in this position.

12 See Stubbs's category 'acknowledge' (Stubbs 1983: 189f).

13 Cf. Ferguson (1981: 27): 'This kind of full echo response is so common in formula exchanges that one is tempted to claim its universality or at least the high probability that every speech community has at least some politeness formulas which have this kind of response.'

14 As shown by the transcription, A got the number wrong when repeating it.

15 A number of examples were difficult to classify with regard to situation.

16 The fact that the reference is to speakers of American English only can probably be disregarded.

CHAPTER THREE

Apologies

'I beg your pardon?' 'It is not respectable to beg', said the King. 'I only meant that I didn't understand', said Alice.
(Lewis Carroll, *Through the looking glass*, 1962: 280)

3.1 Introduction

In every society there are polite rituals, such as apologizing when one bumps into another person in the street.

One pedestrian trips over another, says 'Sorry', as he passes, is answered with 'Okay', and each goes on his way.
Goffman (1976: 67)

The example illustrates the use of routine phrases such as *sorry* and *okay* to apologize when a small offence has been committed. According to Goffman, the ritual work of apologizing 'allows the participants to go on their way, if not with satisfaction that matters are closed, then at least with the right to act as if they feel that ritual equilibrium has been restored' (Goffman 1976: 68).

Although a large number of studies of apologizing have been carried out (e.g. Edmondson 1981; Fraser 1981; Holmes 1990; Blum-Kulka et al. 1989; Olshtain and Cohen 1983; Owen 1983; Trosborg 1987), the authors have not generally focused on forms or utterances that are routinely employed as apologies. In the majority of cases, however, the speaker apologizes in a relatively fixed way. When this is the case, we can account for the association of form with the extralinguistic situation by means of pragmatic frames, i.e. combinations of forms and a situational type.

In the first part of the chapter, apologies are defined and described as strategies or forms with regard to wording, function, grammatical irregularity, prosody and distribution in different text types. In the second part, the pragmatic and sociolinguistic aspects of apologies are described. As in the previous chapter, the examples come mainly from the London-Lund Corpus.

3.2   Defining apologies

Semantically, apologies are strategies (also called semantic formulas) which people use as a means to obtain their communicative goals. There are, however, a number of problems. How does one recognize a strategy? How many strategies are there? What does a taxonomy of apology strategies look like? Edmondson (1981: 279) asks, for example, whether we should accept utterances such as the following as apologies:

- I've gone and broken your record-player
- I wish I hadn't been so careless with your record-player
- It was really bad of me to break it

(Data fabricated)

Ultimately, it is how one chooses to define an apology that determines whether a particular utterance counts as an apology strategy. The analysis of speech acts by Searle (1969) is of great interest in this connection because explicit criteria for the function of speech acts are proposed. In speech-act theory, apologies like thanks are associated with IFIDs (illocutionary force indicating devices) such as the performative *I apologize*, which can be described by a set of felicity conditions (Searle 1969: Chapter 3; see also Chapter 2). Even though the rules for apologizing have not been discussed in detail by Searle, it is easy to mention a few conditions which must be fulfilled by the illocutionary force indicating device (see also Bach and Harnish 1979: 51f). What seems to be necessary is that the 'apologizer' has done something which is annoying or damaging to the person to whom the apology is addressed. The apologizer now regrets having done the act and takes responsibility for it by uttering an apology. Some 'minimal' conditions on apologizing following from a speech-act analysis of apologizing are summarized by Holmes (1990: 161) as:

(a) an act has occurred;
(b) A believes the act has offended B; and
(c) A takes some responsibility for the act.

Apologies can also be treated in a sociolinguistic model with more attention to strategies and the range of expressions realizing the speech act (see Olshtain and Cohen 1983).

In a sociolinguistic approach to apologizing, the social function of the speech act is basic. Holmes describes an apology as a social act aimed at the hearer's face-needs:

> An apology is a speech act addressed to B's face-needs and intended to remedy an offense for which A takes responsibility, and thus to restore the equilibrium between A and B (where A is the apologizer, and B is the person offended).
> Holmes (1990: 159)

81

Apologies have several social functions. By apologizing, the speaker may aim at maximizing the hearer's well-being. According to Gu (1990: 241), apologies are, for example, 'face-caring', while Edmondson and House (1981: 47f) suggest that they are consistent with the hearer-supportive maxim ('Support your hearer's costs and benefits and suppress your own!').[1]

Stripped of intensifiers (*I am*) *sorry* is a neutral apology. Intensifiers have the effect of emphasizing the speaker's feelings, empathy and concern for the hearer (Vollmer and Olshtain 1989: 213) and are associated with what Leech (1983: 84) calls positive politeness (see Edmondson and House 1981: 95 – 'gushing'). An example is (1):

(1)　b　and ^may I** now +^don't
　　　m　**[':m] - - ac^cording to**
　　　(b　interrúpt#
　　　　　we ^didn't ***interrúpt ((you#))+***
　　　m　+^yès# .
　　　　　I'm *^sò sorry# .
　　　　　^I'm sò+ sorry# .
　　　　　^yès#*
(5.6 477–83)

3.3　Apologizing strategies

The range of possible apology strategies can be expected to be enormous. Thus, even if one restricts oneself to certain basic strategies, it is difficult to arrive at a taxonomy of speech acts. Fraser (1981: 263) establishes a taxonomy of apologies based on nine strategies. Olshtain and Cohen (1983), on the other hand, distinguished only four basic categories but recognize a large number of subcategories. I have found it convenient to distinguish 13 different apologizing strategies (see Figure 3.1), even if all of them were not found in my material.

Although it may be impossible to enumerate a finite number of apology strategies, one can specify the strategies people seem to prefer. These have a fixed form, and they tend to recur. Thus, in 83.7 per cent of the examples in my material, people used an explicit form like *sorry* alone or together with other strategies (see section 3.4). In data based on elicitation from role-plays, the ratio of direct apologies is lower. In Trosborg's investigation (1987: 164), the direct apology strategies corresponding to simple explicit apologies amounted only to 7.2 per cent of the total number of strategies used by native speakers (see also Holmes 1990: 170).

Apologizing strategies can be subclassified into explicit and implicit strategies and into strategies which are emotional or not. The most direct strategy is to apologize (A) or to present, give or offer one's apologies (B).

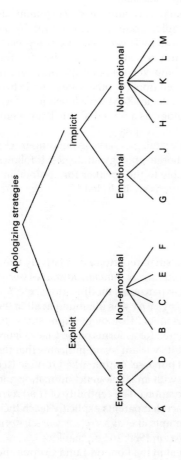

Code to strategies:

(A) explicitly apologizing
(B) offering (giving, presenting) one's apologies
(C) acknowledging a debt of apology
(D) expressing regret
(E) demanding forgiveness
(F) explicitly requesting the hearer's forgiveness
(G) giving an explanation or account
(H) self-denigration or self-reproach
(I) minimizing responsibility
(J) expressing emotion
(K) acknowledging responsibility for the offending act
(L) promising forbearance from a similar offending act
(M) offering redress

e.g. *I apologize (for)*
e.g. *I present my apologies*
e.g. *I owe you an apology*
e.g. *I'm sorry, I'm afraid that*
e.g. *pardon me, excuse me*
e.g. *I beg your pardon*
e.g. *(I'm sorry) it's so unusual*
e.g. *how stupid of me, how awful, I ought to know this*
e.g. *I didn't mean to ..., I thought this was ..., I was thinking it was ...*
e.g. *oh (I'm so sorry)*
e.g. *that was my fault* (Fraser 1981: 263)
e.g. *I promise you that that will never happen again* (Fraser 1981: 263)
e.g. *please let me pay for the damage I've done* (Fraser 1981: 263)

Figure 3.1   Apologizing strategies

A strong form of a direct apology is to say that one is indebted to another person (strategy C).

Strategies A and D are emotional as well as explicit, i.e. they express the speaker's attitude towards a state of affairs which is presupposed to be true.[2] The emotionality can be strengthened with more politeness as the result (see section 3.9.2). Strategies E and F, which ask the offended person for forgiveness, are direct but non-emotional.

Implicit apologies consist of 'softeners', accounts, excuses, minimizations of responsibility, etc. For example, strategy G is not literally an apology but an excuse or account.[3] Strategy H expresses a self-reproach by the speaker, and strategy I minimizes the responsibility for the damage. Strategies G, H and I may, however, serve as apologies in the appropriate context. Strategy J is different from the other categories in that it cannot occur alone as an apology. Strategies K–M have functions which follow from the definition of an apology as a remedial act. They were, however, not found in the London-Lund Corpus.

As Holmes (1990: 167) points out, the strategies serve as building-blocks for constructing longer and more elaborate apology strategies. It follows that the number of strategies available to the speaker for apologizing increases dramatically when combinations are included.[4]

3.4   The form of apologizing

Apologies are generally made up of a small repertoire of relatively fixed expressions representing verbs (*apologize, excuse, pardon*), adjectives (*sorry, afraid*) and nouns (*pardon*) and their expansions, modifications, etc. *I'm sorry* is used rather than *I regret*, and *forgive me* was not found at all in the London-Lund Corpus (see Table 3.1). Out of 215 apology expressions, the majority (83.7 per cent)[5] can be accounted for as forms of *sorry* (see Figure 3.2). The frequency of *I'm sorry* (and its variant *sorry*) indicates that the phrase has developed into a 'general purpose' or unmarked routine (see Ferguson 1981: 27). It is pronounced with an 'apologetic' intonation and is more or less automatic in many situations. The centrality of (*I'm*) *sorry* as an apology is also shown by the fact that parents explicitly teach their children to apologize by means of prompts like *say sorry, can you say sorry, what do you say*, etc (see Greif and Gleason 1980: 163 on thanking).

Other expressions were less frequent in the London-Lund Corpus and had restricted conditions of use. The strategy of using a performative verb as in *I apologize* was, for example, limited to formal contexts. *Pardon* only occurred in situations where a person had not heard what was said. *Excuse me* was used to apologize for minor offences involving social etiquette rather than for genuine apologies (see Frame C on p. 121). *I'm afraid* was used only in a few examples. The phrase has the function to apologize just as much as *I'm sorry*, as indicated by the following quotation:

Table 3.1: Relative frequencies of (direct) apology expressions in the LLC

		Realization	Number
		sorry	107
		I'm sorry (I am sorry),	
		we're sorry	57
(A)	(I AM) (WE'RE) SORRY	*I'm terribly sorry*	4
		I'm very sorry	4
		I'm awfully sorry[6]	1
		I'm so sorry	7
Subtotal			180
		I beg your pardon	8
(B)	(I BEG YOUR) PARDON	*beg your pardon*	1
		pardon	8
Subtotal			17
(C)	EXCUSE (ME)	*excuse me*	10
Subtotal			10
		I apologize	2
		I owe (you) an apology	2
(D)	APOLOGIZE (APOLOGIES)	*give one's apologies*	2
		present one's apologies	1
		pass on one's apologies	1
Subtotal			8
Total			215

Other patterns:	*I am afraid*
	unfortunately
	regrettably

I'm afraid I haven't got one. 'Don't make excuses', said the guard.
(Lewis Carroll, *Through the looking-glass*, 1962: 267)

It can be argued that *I'm afraid* does not presuppose the truth of the state of affairs expressed in the complement clause like other apology phrases, and that it serves the same function as an adverb such as *regrettably*, *unfortunately*, namely, to express the speaker's 'apologetic' attitude towards a proposition which is asserted or announced. *I'm afraid* is, for example, used to apologize for unwelcome information produced in response to a question (see Owen 1983: 90):

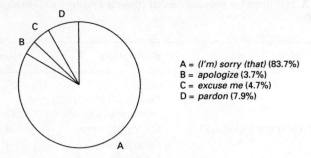

Figure 3.2 The distribution of apology expressions in the London-Lund Corpus

(2)   B   ^could you 'tell me what [ði:] :starting
           :sǎlary#
           ^of a - a ^teacher 'coming . a ^qualified 'teacher
           from a 'college of 'edu!càtion [?] ís# .
      A   [ə:m] I'm a^fraid I càn't#
           the ^person you 'want to :spèak to#
           is at ^lunch at the :mǒment# .
(8.3 1146–50)

In example (3), the apologetic *I'm afraid* is parenthetical:

(3)   A   you ^can't "{ùse the 'thing} :ǒther'wise#
      B   ^yès#
      A   yes ^none of us !thòught of it I'm afráid#
      B   (. *.* laughs)
(8.4 40–3)

I'm afraid is an apology only in those examples where the speaker intends to remedy an offence or atone for some personal insufficiency. In example (4), on the other hand, *I'm afraid* expresses the speaker's reservation:

(4)   A   *(- - laughs)* ^òh 'dear# .
           ^I'm ^I'm a!fraid I 'spoke to Pro:fessor 'Sharp
           èarlier#
           ^do a"pǒlogize 'to him#
           ^if it ^if it was ^if it's :nĕcessary#
(8.3 766–71)

In these cases, *I'm afraid* is primarily a 'disarming apology', i.e. the speaker uses the phrase to apologize before an intrusion or an offence.

3.5 Continuation patterns

Apologies can be introduced by various remarks and be followed by supportive conversational moves. They may even constitute a whole interaction, although this was not illustrated in my material. Another property that they have is that they may occur with a fixed continuation pattern. This does not mean, however, that they always have a continuation, or that the absence of a response to the apology is necessarily noticeable. The speaker uses a restricted set of 'responders':

(Situation: Speaker B has been cut off by the telephone operator (Speaker A))
(5)   B   (- - - long pause) she's ^just cut me !òff# - - -
        A   ^sorry I 'cut I ^cut you òff#
        B   it's ^all rìght#
(8.1 839–41)

When the apology is acknowledged verbally, the responder plays down the need to apologize or denies it altogether. Only a few forms were found, most frequently *that's (it's) all right*, often in combination with *well*, *no* and *oh*. Less frequent realizations of the same strategy are *don't worry*, *never mind*, *not a bit*. Consider:

(Situation: Speaker B apologizes for a time offence)
(6)   A   ^thanks for phòning# .
        B   ^sorry it 'wasn't _last nìght#
        A   ^oh 'that's all ríght#
            (untranscribable murmur)
(7.2 1096–9)

The prosodic pattern in the responding phrase is relatively fixed. Besides a fall-rise tone, the simple rise was used:

(7)   a   ^just 'one sècond# - - -
            (speaks on telephone - - -) - .
            [ə] – ^sòrry
            about thís 'Ralph#
            *I .
        B   *^don't wórry# .
            ((^don't !wòrry#))*
(5.11 15–19)

(Situation: Speaker A apologizes for inconveniencing Speaker B)
(8)   B   we'll ^dò that +_Judith#+
        A   +that'd be+ ^very kìnd#
            ^thanks àwfully# .
            ^sòrry to 'bother you#
        B   ^nò#

    ^not a !bìt# .

    look ^forward to !sèeing you a'gain 'one of these
    dâys#

(8.4 533–9)

The responses can be long and elaborate as a result of extra components:

(9)   B I'm ^sòrry I've 'been so *lóng#*
        A *no* ^nò#
           it's ^it's [':] I ^wasn't I ^wasn't "certain you
           'felt you'd 'have to 'look thròugh them 'all#

(2.6 1254–6)

In most cases, the apology occurred without a 'responder', in particular when the object of regret is not specified. Especially if the offence is trivial, there is no need for a minimizing response. It is also noteworthy that all but one example were found in telephone conversation. It is possible therefore that a non-verbal response is used instead in face-to-face conversation.

3.6   The grammatical analysis of apology expressions

Like other elements which have a fixed form, apologies may be grammatically irregular. *Sorry* or *pardon* can be analysed as 'radically elliptical' or fragmentary since they can be related to fuller forms such as *I am sorry* or *I beg your pardon* (Norrick 1985: 85; see also Quirk et al. (1985: 838).[7] Alternatively, they can be regarded as syntactically indeterminate one-word sentences. However, the majority of apology phrases, including the full form *I am sorry*, are perfectly grammatical and only weakly lexicalized.

3.7   Apologies and prosody

An interesting question is whether apologies can have 'stylized' intonation, signalling an element of stereotype in the message (Ladd 1978). Stylized intonation may be accompanied by 'chant' or by a special calling contour. A stylized apology intonation is appropriate in the interaction between shop clerk and customer or between strangers if no serious apology is intended. As Ladd points out (1978: 324), we can squeeze past people in a crowd using a casual tone, but it would not do to use the same tone when bumping into people in the supermarket, causing them to drop the eggs all over the floor.

    In my material a fall-rise or a rising tone was most common in casual apologies. Fall-rise tone has been regarded as the unmarked apologizing

Table 3.2: The distribution of nuclear tone on *sorry* in the LLC

Nuclear tone	Number
fall	29
fall-rise	29
rise	23[8]
rise-fall	–
level	–
Total	81

tone associated with casual apologies, but a rising tone was almost as frequent in the London-Lund Corpus (see Lindström 1978: 39, 116; Owen 1983: 99) (Table 3.2). The two prosodic extremes are represented by a low fall and a high rise tone on the apology:

> With a low fall the apology tends to sound more genuine and regretful. At the other extreme we find RH [high rise, KA], which tends to sound perfunctory. This tune may also retain its usual meaning of contradiction: the speaker refuses to admit responsibility.
> (Lindström 1978: 177)

Prosody can also signal if the apology is disarming (anticipatory) or remedial (retrospective), and the degree of politeness or emotionality associated with the apology.

3.8 Distribution of apologies over different texts

Table 3.3 demonstrates how *sorry* was distributed over different varieties or genres in the London-Lund Corpus. The largest number of examples with *sorry* was found in the predominantly interactive categories of conversation and telephone calls. On the other hand, *sorry* was missing altogether from prepared commentary, and the expression was infrequent in public speech.

Excuse me, pardon, apologize were restricted to a small number of discourse types (see section 3.4). *Apologize* (and the noun *apologies*) did not occur at all in conversation, but the few examples in the corpus were found in (formal) telephone calls (11), messages on the answering machine (10) and in public speech (12):

(10)　　AF　I a^pòlogize# .
　　　　　　^for the de'lay . in ac:knòwledging#
　　　　　　[ə:] your ^kĭndness# - .
(9.3 85–7)

Table 3.3: Distribution of *sorry* and its variants in the LLC (the figures have been normalized to 10,000 words)

Text in LLC	Number	Number per 10,000 words
FACE (surreptitious)	69	4.1
FACE (non-surreptitious)	21	3.5
TELEPHONE	69	13.8
DISCUSSION	18	3
PUBLIC	3	0.5
PREPARED	–	–
Total	180	24.9

(11) B ^=and# .
      ^I . !just pre!sĕnt my a'pologies#
      for ^not being 'able to at!tènd 'the#
      [?] ex^ecutive com'mittee :meeting . at 'ten
      thírty# - -
(9.1 54–7)

(12) d she said ^I – I ^owe you an apòlogy# -
      I said you ^owe me !mŏre than 'that#
      you ^owe me :nearly a !hundred and *'twenty-'five
      quìd#
(11.3 629–31)

In written language, apologies were found mainly in letters. People apologize, for example, when they cancel an appointment, for not having written earlier or for their handwriting:[9]

(13) I was extremely sorry that I was unable to get to your father's funeral owing to an attack of gastric flu on Thursday evening.
(W 7–2)

(14) Thank you for a nice letter. I'm sorry I haven't had time to answer it.
(W 7–2)

(15) I apologize for this writing – it is my last viable biro.
(W 7–2)

(16) Sorry about the paper – but I am in a dash.
(W 7–31)

3.9 Collocational fixedness and flexibility

There are degrees of fixedness. On the one hand, there are phrases which have a fixed form and function (*excuse me*). On the other hand, there are phrases such as (*I'm*) *sorry*, which are more flexible. This restricted flexibility is accounted for by analysing the utterance as a sentence stem (see Figure 3.3).

$$
\begin{bmatrix} I & am \\ We & are \end{bmatrix} \text{(INTENSIFIER) SORRY} \begin{bmatrix} \text{(that)} & S \\ \text{to} & VP \\ \text{about} & \begin{Bmatrix} NP \\ V\text{-ing} \end{Bmatrix} \\ \text{if} & S \\ \text{but} & S \end{bmatrix}
$$

Code: Parenthetical elements are optional. Elements in brackets represent discrete choices.

Figure 3.3   Sentence stem containing *I am (we are) sorry* as the nucleus

The stem can be embedded in a matrix (*let me tell you how sorry I am*); forms can be expanded ((*I am*) *sorry to be late*) or shortened (*sorry*),[10] and more polite apologies can be created by intensification (*I'm so sorry*). A measure of the flexibility of the stem is the number of grammatical modifications which can take place. In the London-Lund Corpus 19.6 per cent of the examples were, for example, expanded (cf. Holmes (1990) 20.7 per cent; Owen (1983) 37.7 per cent). A comparison with Owen's and Holmes's data is given in Table 3.4. A tendency towards shortening is also evidenced in *pardon* and *beg your pardon*, which are variants of the stem (*I*) (*BEG YOUR*) *PARDON*. On the other hand, *excuse me* cannot be shortened although the expression can be phonologically weakened (*excuse me* →*'scuse me*).

Table 3.4:   A comparison between apology phrases containing *sorry* in the LLC, Owen (1983) and Holmes (1990) (cf. Holmes 1990: 172)

Type of apology phrase	LLC	Owen	Holmes
(Intensifier) *sorry*	107 (49.7%)	20 (24.1%)	66 (37.9%)
I'm/I am (intensifier) sorry	31 (14.4%)	21 (25.3%)	36 (20.7%)
(*I'm*) *sorrry (that) S/ to VP if S/for VP*	30 (14%)	22 (26.5%)	24 (13.8%)
(*I'm*) (*intensifier*) *sorry about that (this)*	12 (5.6%)	9 (10.8%)	12 (6.9%)
Total	215	83	174

Note: Totals include other patterns with apology phrases.

3.9.1 *Fully expanded apology expressions*

Each pattern 'generated' by the stem can be characterized formally, prosodically, functionally and situationally.

A. *I'M SORRY ABOUT THAT*

The apology (*I am*) *sorry about that*, *sorry about this* (12 examples in all) typically conveys that the speaker refuses to take responsibility for the offence and that the offence is now in the past (see Owen 1983: 86). When *this* and *that* point backwards to an offence, *that* suggests greater remoteness or less responsibility for the offence than *this*. *This* can also point forwards cataphorically to the reason for the apology (example (19)). Example (17) illustrates how the phrase is used:

(17)   a   ^just 'one sècond# - - -
           (speaks on telephone - - -) - . [ə] - ^sòrry
           about thís 'Ralph#
           *I .
      B *^don't wórry# .
          ((^don't !wòrry#))*
(5.11 15–19)

The apology pattern *sorry about that* (with a characteristic fall-rise tone) reflects the fact that the speaker apologizes for an inconvenience which is beyond his control.

   In example (18), the apology conveys ironic distance to a situation:

(18)   A cos . because ^some 'stupid "twít#
          didn't ^fìnish it in 'time# .
      B oooh oooh ^whimper :whìmper# - -
          I'm ^sòrry about thát# .
          ^can't you 'do it this afternŏon#
(7.3 1109–12)

In (19), the apology precedes a piece of unwelcome news for which the speaker does not wish to take responsibility:

(19)   A [ə:] if ^{wè were to 'tell him} "làter#
          ^well we're !sŏrry a'bout this#
          but ^you're not !èligible#
(2.6 3–5)

B.   *I'M SORRY THAT S, I'M SORRY TO VP*

*(I am) sorry + that/*zero clause (18 examples) was used in situations where
the speaker had committed a small time offence such as being late for an
appointment. Various subtypes can be distinguished:

(a) the offence is in the past

(20)   B   ^or 'like +[əm]+ for exàmple# .
           a ^Rŭssian# .
           ^will _s=ay# - -
           I'm ^sorry I was láte# .
           ^my !train . 'didn't arrìve# -
(2.11 531–5)

(b) the offence is ongoing

(21)   C   hel^lo !Líz# .
           ^sorry 'I'm láte#
(2.7 9–11)

   I'm sorry to VP (12 examples) was used for what Owen (1983: 78) refers
to as 'continuing offences' (cf. category b). In the London-Lund Corpus,
this type of apology was almost entirely restricted to telephone calls:

(22)   B   I'm ^very 'sorry to :tròuble 'you# .
       A   ((it))'s all ^rʏ̆ght#
       B   I'm ^very gràteful 'to you#
           ((3 to 4 sylls))
       A   ^ŎK#
       B   ((good))^bỳe#
       A   ^goodbỳe#
(9.2 222–8)

3.9.2   Apologizing and intensification

Sorry occurred with intensifiers in 8.9 per cent of the examples (see section 3.4). Although the potential number of intensifiers is very large, only
four intensifiers appeared in the London-Lund Corpus (*so, very, terribly,
awfully*),[11] which are identical to those found in an earlier study by Owen
(1983: 73). In the written material (personal letters from SEU), however,
intensification was also expressed by other intensifiers (e.g. *extremely*). In
addition, *sorry* was frequently reinforced by *oh* with the variants *ah, oh
gosh, oh dear* and by address forms or endearments:

(23)   f   ^Honor Bàlfour# -
           ^oh I'm sòrry#
       (c   [ə:] . *I ^want -* - ^I'm !sòrry# .
           ^àll I was _going to {^sày _was#}# .

93

       I ^don't know :how much [ði: ə: ?] the !cost is
       in!vólved#
       in ^putting the thing :úpright# -
       or . what^ever what^ever the :question !wás#
(5.4 222–7)

(24)   A ^sòrry 'love# - - -
       you ^got a 'special cŭp# - - .
       ^sòrry Béssie#
       I'll ^move òver# -
(8.4 395–8)

3.9.3 *Prosodic devices emphasizing the politeness expressed by the apology*

Prosodic reinforcing devices include the transfer of the nucleus from its normal, unmarked position to a different (usually a preceding) item in the tone unit (Altenberg 1987: 160 – 'marked focus') and the use of boosters and emphatic stress strengthening the nuclear tone.

    Generally speaking, such devices contribute to 'gushing' or emotionality. Several different prosodic features (booster, movement of the nuclear tone) are illustrated in example (25):

(25)   A e^leven 'twelve :thirteen 'fourteen
       B ^darling I !àm sorry a'bout that
          cham+págne#+
       A +^fĭf+teen# - .
       A oh "^that's a póint#
(2.10 1153–6)

3.9.4 *Compound apologies*

Apologies, like thanks, can be made up of a combination of strategies. In a compound apology, an extra element or conversational move has been added to an explicit apology. The apology expression functions as a core or the stable part of a sentence stem to which other strategies are added. Following Faerch and Kasper (1989: 237), the extra conversational move will be referred to as an 'external modifier'.[12]

    Table 3.5 shows the possible combinations of strategies occurring in LLC. Five generic apology strategies (A–E) have been distinguished:

A = explicit apologizing (*sorry, I beg your pardon*)
B = an explanation or account (*sorry it's so unusual*, etc)
C = self-denigration or self-reproach (*how stupid of me, how awful, I ought to know this*)

Table 3.5: Combinations of apology strategies (with *sorry*) in the LLC

Type	Number
A+B	6
A+D	7
A+C	4
C+A	1
A+C+B	1
C+A+B	1
E+A+B	1
E+A+D	1
E+A+C	1
Other combinations (see example (26))	1
Total	24

D = minimizing the responsibility (*I didn't mean to ..., I thought this was ..., I was thinking it was ...*)

E = reinforcing or gushing (*oh, oh God*)

Excuses, accounts, and acts of self-reproach modifying the apology are the result of a polite maxim that the speaker should be modest by conveying a bad impression of himself (see Leech's 1983: 132 – 'Modesty Maxim'). Strategy E, on the other hand, is associated with emotionality and gush and can be compared with intensifying adverbs. Certain strategies are especially frequent in a compound apology. These are an account (= strategy B) and the strategy minimizing the responsibility for the offence (= strategy D). The combination of strategies A and B is illustrated in:

(26) A now ^what wàs it# - - -
       ^sǒrry# -
       my ^memory's a !{lìttle 'bit} . [ə:] :hither and
       yòn sómetimes# -
(1.14 582–4)

Each of the nine patterns in Table 3.5 can be analysed as consisting of a necessary component or core (= A) and one or more modifiers. The patterns are characterized by a fairly fixed order with strategy A normally in the first position. The combinations A+B, A+C and A+D accounted for almost three-fourths of the examples. On the other hand, there are certain gaps in the material such as C+D.

In Holmes's (1990: 170) investigation, about half of the exchanges containing an apology involved more than one strategy. This is a much higher figure than in the LLC where only about 13 per cent of the examples contained more than one strategy (see Table 3.6).

The use of several strategies is illustrated in:

(27)　B　^I'm !sòrry about the - méss#
　　　　　^how !stùpid 'of me#
　　　　　((oh ^thère's - ^1 sỳll 1 syll#
　　　　　I'm ^sùre I put a [prókmi] *on#
　　　　　it's))*
(1.11 283–7)

The speaker apologizes for the damage he has caused (= A). The apology is followed by a self-reproach (= C) and an additional excuse (= B).

The apology in example (28) is made up of seven different moves, not all of which are easy to characterize:

(Situation: Speaker A apologizes for some inconvenience or annoyance to the hearer)
(28)　A　*^whère#
　　　　　^whère#
　　　　　^whère# .
　　　　　^oh I !bèg your párdon# .
　　　　　I ^běg your 'pardon#
　　　　　I'm ^sórry#
　　　　　I I'm* ^tòtally un+:{òriented#}# .
(3.4 433–9)

The apology section is very long and includes a question which is difficult to classify as an apology strategy. The apology is repeated and is followed by a conversational move which I have analysed as a self-reproach (*I'm totally unoriented*). When *I beg your pardon* is repeated, a change in the position of the nucleus takes place simultaneously.

Table 3.6: The number of apologizing strategies in the LLC

Number of strategies	LLC (%)
1 strategy	86.7
2 strategies	10
3 strategies	2.8
more than 3 strategies	0.6
Total	100

3.10 Apologies and function

Many linguists have noted the ritual character of apologies (see Knowles 1987: 193f). Most of the time, an apology is simply a polite gesture which does not express the speaker's true emotions. Ritual apologies tend to occur in stereotypic situations where speakers apologize for something trivial; the apologies have a characteristic intonation, and they have a fixed form. They contrast with more serious apologies in which the speaker expresses stronger regret (see Figure 3.4).

According to Bach and Harnish (1979: 51), a casual apology involves 'weak acknowledgement' and is issued not so much to express a genuine feeling as to satisfy the social expectation that such a feeling be expressed. Casual apologies are recognized intuitively by speakers. As Vollmer and Olshtain point out,

> In each language the speakers intuitively recognize the IFID variants [= the illocutionary force indicating devices], which carry only acknowledgement features since they are usually highly recurrent and routinized as opposed to the stronger and more *sincere/genuine* performative verbs and their respective modal extensions.
> (Vollmer and Olshtain 1989: 198)

The social function of routines is best described in terms of social and pragmatic factors. A ritual apology is not only appropriate for trivial offences, but also serves as a disarmer or softener, as an attention-getter, and as a phatic act establishing a harmonious relationship with the hearer. The illocutionary point of the apology is social, as emphasized by Norrick:

> The illocutionary point of apologizing is to express regret, the intended perlocutionary effect is to get the addressee to believe that one is contrite, but the social function may be to evince good manners, to assuage the addressee's wrath, or simply to get off the hook and be on one's way.
> (Norrick 1978: 280; cf. Holmes 1990: 164)

Bach and Harnish (1979: 51f) argue that apologies should be given different felicity conditions depending on whether the speaker's acknowledgement is strong or weak. However, on a deeper level, the difference between casual and serious apologies must be accounted for in terms of the constraints of the social situation rather than illocutionary force.

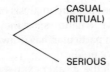

Figure 3.4 Two types of apology

The relationship between routines and function is, however, notoriously difficult to describe since the fact that a certain speech act is linked to a particular function and situation does not necessarily mean that this association is completely fixed. This is also emphasized by Edmondson:

> That a particular 'fixed expression' has an associated recognizable 'function' in discourse does not mean that the communicative or other act realizing that function has a predictable distribution, nor that *any* realization of that communicative 'function' will necessarily involve the use of the 'fixed expression,' as opposed to the use of some other linguistic (or para-linguistic) token. There are grounds for confusion here as there is an observable tendency for what we may loosely call fixed expressions to be used in predictable ways and in predictable circumstances: this is precisely why such expressions have become standardized.
> (Edmondson 1981: 275)

In other words, the fact that *pardon* was only found when a speaker did not hear does not mean that the speaker is always obliged to use this expression in the same situation.

What complicates the functional description of the function of apology routines is that apologies may also focus on 'upcoming' text and soften a following action which is thought to threaten the hearer's negative face. A typical case is when a person apologizes before pushing his way through a crowd or interrupting another speaker. The examples in the London-Lund Corpus are of a different kind. For example, *sorry* points forwards when the speaker asks the hearer to repeat the information.

3.11   Retrospective and anticipatory apologies

The 'time' factor is important for the analysis of many expressive speech acts such as thanking, congratulating, apologizing. In Coulmas's pragmatic analysis of congratulations (Coulmas 1979: 246), the event to which the congratulation referred was, for example, specified as 'non-future'. In apologies, however, the relationship between time and the offence is more complicated.

In order to get a clearer picture of the functions of apologies in discourse, I have found it helpful to classify them into two major groups, depending on whether they are responses to an offence or they anticipate an offence. According to the standard analysis of apologies in speech-act theory, they are retrospective in nature since they are semantically factive (see section 3.2). Norrick, in particular, has drawn attention to the factive presupposition of expressive predicates such as *sorry* or *apologize*, i.e. that the state of affairs for which the speaker expresses regret is presupposed to be true (Norrick 1978: 277). Similarly, Holmes (1990: 161) picks out 'factivity' as one of the properties defining apologies.

On the other hand, Edmondson has claimed that the speaker apologizes not only for a fact but also for an intention (Edmondson 1981: 282), or for the need to perform a particular speech act (Edmondson 1981: 283).

It is probably impossible to subclassify all the examples of apologies into one of these two categories. However, a rough estimation indicates that a little more than half of the examples referred to an intended, predicted, expected or simultaneous offence.[13]

While the function of the anticipatory apology is 'disarming' or 'softening', the retrospective apology is remedial, supportive (face-saving) and self-demeaning (see Owen 1983). The retrospective *sorry* can stand alone as a response signal or be followed by a *that*-clause specifying the offence. In example (29), *sorry* serves as response to a preceding event since Speaker B apologizes for having been unclear:

(29) B ^yès#
    ^yès the ^Hìgh 'Street# .
    it was *((the)) ^Hìgh 'Street#*
    C *^Hĭgh 'Street#*
    B ^yes it :wàs#
    ^sòrry#
(8.1 1143–7)

In example (30), the speaker apologizes 'on-line' for a mistaken assumption:

(30) A ^Greece the 'week befóre was it# .
    ^yès#
    a [ə] oh no no *.* it was days and days before that
    A *^òh#*
    ^yès#
    +^sŏrry#+
(1.9 285–90)

Whenever a *that*-clause is present, the apology is retrospective:

(31) C *hel^ló#* .
    ^sorry I'm láte#
    a +(. laughs) that's all right+ are you -
(2.7 2–4)

The focus of the apology is on remedying a past offence. *I'm sorry about* … also implies that the offence is in the past:

(32) A e^leven 'twelve :thirteen 'fourteen
    B ^darling I !àm sorry a'bout that cham+págne#+
    A +^fĭf+teen# - .
    A oh "^that's a póint#
(2.10 1153–4)

A retrospective apology can be recognized by the presence of extra moves justifying the apology or expiating the offence:

(33) c you ^see+ I was !on your !sîde#
      B **^sŏrry#;-**;
        it's ^so unûsual#
(4.3 316–18)

Finally, the retrospective apology can be followed by a 'responder' in which the apology is recognized, minimized or denied (see section 3.5):

(34) C O^Ḱ#
        ^thanks 'very múch#
        ^sorry to . 'give you all this "bóther#
        . "^bye#
      A *^that's all ríght#*
        ^bye b=ye#
(8.3 824–9)

When *sorry* has anticipatory function, it can be analysed as a polite preface or discourse marker with a softening or disarming function. Disarming apologies are found before speech acts which are in some way non-cooperative, unwelcome to the hearer or disruptive (Edmondson 1981: 282).

The disarming apology is needed when the speaker asks the hearer to repeat or clarify something, and it is used to soften a face-threatening action, for example when the speaker needs to convey bad news. The disarming function accounts for two additional uses of *sorry*: as a request for repetition and as a device for saying 'no' to a request, offer, invitation, etc. In the following sections, the disarming apology will be discussed in more detail.

3.11.1 Disarming apologies

Apologies belong predominantly to the expressive or interpersonal component of language. Thus when the speaker apologizes before an unwelcome or face-threatening action, the reason is that he wants to maintain the social harmony between the participants. Cancelling an appointment or saying that one will be late for a meeting requires a softening apology since these actions may be received in a negative way by the hearer:

(35) BF ^yĕsterday#
        I ^made an ap!pointment :with Pro!fessor 'Cobley
        at "!ten fif'teen this mòrning# -
        I'm ^sŏrry#
        but I'm un^able to !kèep this appóintment# .
(9.3 710–13)

(36) A so I ^ràng ((up saying)) I'm 'terribly sórry#
         but I ^shan't be !with you until !five past
         !tèn# .
(1.5 180–1)

An intrusion upon another person's privacy or 'physical space' should
be prefaced by an apology. A request involving an effort for the hearer is
an example:

(37) B ex^cùse 'me sír#
         ^would you !{clàrify a} !point in your !lècture#
         ^which _I !couldn't under!stànd# -
(1.6 1123–5)

(38) BO ^this is Léssin 'speaking# -
          [ə:m] . I'm ^sorry to impose . 'yet [ə] a :further
          [ə:m] 'task on Ma:lĭnda# -
          ^in the 'way of [ə:] "!bòok scróunging# .
          ^but I would be ex!tremely grăteful# .
(9.3 820–3)

Any unpleasant or unwelcome message may need a 'disarmer' in order
to soften its effects on the hearer. In example (39), the speaker apologizes
for not knowing something (cf. the discussion of preference in section
3.11.1.3):

(39) A *I ^didn't 'know 'many* :children !hàd this
         a'bility#
         I'm **^sorry to 'have to sáy ((yes))#**

In the preceding examples, the event apologized for has been in the
future. The speaker can also apologize for an offence which is simultaneous with the apologizing. The offence is expressed in a non-finite
infinitival clause:

(40) B I'm ^very 'sorry to :tròuble 'you# .
      A ((it))'s all ^rĭght#
      B I'm ^very grăteful 'to you#
         ((3 to 4 sylls))
      A ^ŎK#
(9.2 222–6)

(41) A ^sorry 'to [ə:] :put 'so 'many ":awkward
         quéstions#
         ^on yóu#
         [?] ^all at ònce# - .
(9.3 558–60)

3.11.1.1 DISARMERS AND CORRECTIONS

One of the most frequent uses of the disarming apology is before a correction. The apology is uttered after a 'trouble spot' and signals that a preceding word or phrase in the same turn will be replaced by a more appropriate word or phrase (*excuse me, I'm sorry*):

(42) B and ^so they !should know :sŏmething about it#
            or do they ^only 'know a'bout [ði:] .
            :pràctical# .
            ex^cuse me ex'peri:mĕntal 'aspects#
            of ^rèading# -
(2.4 735–8)

(43) B no ^not "sèventy-'eight#
            yes "^èighty-'eight#
            ^no I'm sórry#
            ^sìxteen 'years#
            yes "^èighty-'eight#
(1.13 238–42)

(44) AY ^there are !two !quèstions . oh "^sòrry#
            ^one quèstion#
            which I'd ^like to :àsk 'him# .
(9.3 573–5)

Notice the collocation of *sorry* with *no* (in the first example) and with *oh* (in the second example).

3.11.1.2 DISARMERS AS REQUESTS FOR REPETITION

The disarming *sorry* can also be followed by a request for repetition (*sorry what was that/this, sorry you were saying, sorry how much*, etc), or by an announcement that the speaker has not understood or misheard something (*I beg your pardon I misheard you, sorry I couldn't quite catch that, sorry I didn't get that, sorry I didn't catch that*).

(45) B [ə:] ^that 'thing that came :up a'bout the [s]
            :sessional ex!àms the 'other 'day#
        a ^sŏrry#
            *^[wo] ^what was thìs#
        B *the ^point is that [ə:]*
        a ^can you* 'ink ^ink me !ĭn +on this#+
(5.11 113–17)

(46) B [ə:m . ə] it ^stărts#
            with a ^bloke s=aying#
            I ^made an !awful [si:] :song and dànce#
            a^bout [ə:m]

A ^sórry#
^I ![kəu] 'couldn't _quite cătch 'that#
B ^sòrry#
^he ![sad - ə] . :said . it's a ^dìalogue#
(8.4 863–70)

In example (46), *sorry* was used by both parties in the conversational exchange. The second *sorry* (pronounced with a fall tone) is retrospective since Speaker B apologizes for not expressing himself clearly.

The apology can also stand alone with the function of a request to the interlocutor to repeat or clarify some information. In example (47), *sorry* (with a rising tone) is, for instance, directly followed by a clarification:

(47)   B   but I ^don't know if ^whether you could !get
            anybody :ĕlse to 'do it# - - -
       A   ^sórry# .
       B   "^lĭterally go through Èlstead#
            to ^get to Farnham thát way# .
(1.11 712–14)

3.11.1.3   DISARMERS IN DISPREFERRED RESPONSES

A disarmer may also be a device making it easier to turn down a request, refuse an invitation or an offer and to avoid answering a question. In the ethnomethodological theory of preference (see Levinson 1983; Pomerantz 1984; Davidson 1984), responses are either preferred or dispreferred. Dispreferred responses are illustrated by rejections, denials and disagreements. Preference refers both to the structural organization of the utterance in terms of markedness and to the special form ('turn shape') of the preferred or dispreferred component. *Sorry* is said to preface dispreferred second parts in an adjacency pair. For example, when an invitation is given, the expected or preferred response is presumably acceptance. A refusal is marked by components such as pauses, the particle *well* or an apology (*sorry*) to indicate that the response is dispreferred:

(48)   (c [ə] Prudence says she can't come sorry but
            Mo [ə]
            might come
(7.1 627)

There is obviously some functional overlap between *sorry* in dispreferred responses and the use of *sorry* as a softener of speech acts which are unfavourable or threaten the hearer's face. However, the occurrence of *sorry* in responses is explained in structural rather than functional terms.[14]

Disarming apologies are expected before refusals of offers or requests, denials, disagreements, etc. In example (49), *I'm terribly sorry* softens the effect of the cancellation of an appointment:

(Situation: Speaker A tells the interlocutor how she refused an invitation)
(49)   A   so I ^said !well I'm !tĕrribly 'sorry but# .
                ^yŏu know#
                ^that's how it's 'going to bé#
                cos I'm ^going to be awáy#
                for ^ten dáys# .
(2.12 948–52)

Questions have alternative answers, which can be distinguished in terms of preference. The preferred response to a question corresponds to the expected answer. In dispreferred responses to a question, the recipient does not know the answer or refuses to answer because he or she is not interested in the problem or is unable to answer, etc.

When *sorry* introduces a dispreferred answer to a question, it is frequently combined with an account of why the question cannot be answered:

(50)   B   so ^I said but - :what !dìfference does it 'make#
                and he said ((oh)) I'm ^sòrry# .
                ((he said)) it's the di^réctor's rùling# -
                it's ^school pòlicy#
                or ^something équally dènse# -
(2.4 623–7)

In example (51), *sorry* introduces a non-cooperative or insufficient answer since the answerer is not sure that he can give the information which is requested:

(51)   B   and ^what sort of rates do you !pày for 'this sort
                of 'thing# .
             A   [ə:m] - ^wéll# .
                [ə:] - - - I'm ^sòrry# .
                I ^ought to knòw this#
                I ^think it's a'bout one 'fifty an :hòur#
                or ^something of thàt kind# -
(3.2 240–3)

Another dispreferred answer is illustrated in example (52):

(52)   B   ^what is that 'poem a:bòut ((do you
                'think))# - - -
                I'm ^s=orry#
             A   I don't ^knów it#
(3.1 1342–4)

In addition, a disarmer can be expected if the speaker disagrees with the previous speaker; if he or she does not fully understand what has just been said or is not in the position of knowing the answer to the question:

(53)   D   ^I . '[ju:zd] :brèak# -
           is the ac^cepted 'usage of this 'tense in
           !Mònkland# .
           ^yours sin!cèrely#
       A   I'm ^sòrry#
           I [hae] I ^don't 'under'stand *the* !sèntence#
(9.2 1029–33)

(54)   A   he ^said I'm "!nòt interested in 'crime
           órdinary#
           ^[?]I'm !only 'interested in 'crime po:lìtical#
       b   oh –
       A   ^so !my re_tòrt wás#
           I'm ^sŏrry# .
           ^{Ì'm not 'interested in} . [ə] crime
           po:lĭtical#
           I'm ^only 'interested in 'crime òrdinary# .
(1.14 457–63)

If a request cannot be complied with, the refusal is dispreferred and can be preceded by an apology. All my examples are from telephone calls where the person the caller wants to speak to is not available:

(55)   A   ^hellŏ#
       C   *((1 to 2 sylls))* - - - ^hel!lŏ#
           I'm ^sòrry#
           ^Doctor :Mărshall isn't ìn at the móment#
           ^can I 'take a méssage 'please#
       A   ^{yès} plèase#
(9.2 272–6)

(56)   A   hel^lŏ#
       B   hel^lŏ# .
       A   ^sŏrry#
           ^he's !just playing !squàsh at the 'moment
           appárently#
       B   ^oh !rèally#
       A   but ^they're ex!pecting him bàck#
           be^cause _he's (. giggles) !got to collèct his
           _stuff#
(8.4 344–50)

In addition, *sorry* can stand alone as a denial that something is the case or as a 'turndown' of a request. Even if no example was found in my corpus, it seems clear that examples like (57) are quite natural:

(57)   Can you lend me ten pounds
       Sorry John
(From Edmondson 1981: 283)

3.12 The structural function of apologies

An apology can also be described as an element of larger conversational patterns. While greetings and farewells are almost obligatory rituals in a social encounter, apologies are generally optional. Apologies, like thanks, had functions which were specific to the opening and closing of the telephone call.

3.12.1 Apologies in telephone openings

Apologies are placed after greetings and have special functions such as apologizing for disturbing the answerer or for not getting in touch earlier. On a deeper level 'telephone apologies' can be analysed in terms of social and cultural norms:

(58) B   I'm ^sorry to 'get you to the :phŏne#*
      (A   I'm ^not even - ^I've _[drib] ^dragged myself 'up
           :nòw#
(7.2 18–19)

(59) B   *((hel^ló 'Arthur#)) .
          ^yès#
          good ^mòrning#* -
      B   hel^lò#
      a   [ə] sorry I've been so long in getting in touch
          with you I rang ((a)) couple of times yesterday and
          you weren't in
      B   ^no I was in !còllege 'yesterday#
(7.1 1385–90)

3.12.2 Apologies in telephone closings

Thanking and apologizing often occur together at the end of the telephone call with a ritual function. Leech (1983: 125) uses a mercantile metaphor to describe the social function of apologies and thanks (see section 3.2). An apology implies a transaction in that it is a 'bid to change the balance-sheet of the relation between s (speaker) and h (the hearer)'. Thus we speak of owing a person an apology, which suggests that apologizing (and thanking) may be regarded as an acknowledgement of an imbalance in the relation between the speaker and the hearer, and to some extent, as an attempt to restore equilibrium (Leech 1983: 125).[15] In this perspective we can explain apologizing at the end of telephone calls as a strategy re-establishing ritual equilibrium between the speakers before leave-taking. The ritual 'supportive' function of apologizing is illustrated in the following example:

(60)   A   ^just and ^I shall just 'tell them _that [əm]
            you're 'going to chìvvy# - -
            ((3 to 4 sylls))
        C   ^yèah# .
            O^Ḱ#
            ^thanks 'very múch#
            ^sorry to . 'give you all this 'bóther#
            . "^bў̆e#
        A   *^that's all ríght#*
            ^bye b=ye#
(8.3 821–9)

Example (60) illustrates several techniques for bringing the telephone call
to an end. One device used by Speaker A is to refer to an earlier arrangement (Turn 1). This can be understood as the last topic in the telephone
conversation and as the first move of the closing section. In the second
turn, Speaker C responds to the proposal, thus confirming that he is willing to close the call (*yeah OK*). Apologizing and the response have the
ritual function to confirm social alignments. According to Schegloff and
Sacks (1973), apologizing is also a pre-closing device since the action provides the caller with an additional opportunity to show that he wants to
close the call.

The fixed order between thanking and apologizing in the discourse
should also be noticed. Only in one example did apologizing precede
thanking:

(61)   B   I'm ^very 'sorry to :tròuble 'you# .
        A   ((it))'s all ^rǐght#
        B   I'm ^very gràteful 'to you#
            ((3 to 4 sylls))
        A   ^ŎK#
        B   ((good))^bỳe#
        A   ^goodbỳe#
(9.2 222–8)

Sometimes apologies are recycled with the result that the little farewell
ceremony may be quite long:

(62)   A   ^thank you !very mùch Bérto#
            ^sorry to bòther you# .
            ((that))
        B   ^y=es# .
            ^all wéll#
        A   ^{yȇs} fîne# -
            ^chugging awáy#
            ^very "hòt#
            (- giggles)

B ^yès#
^yès#
((^most [ig'zo:] exhàusting#)) -
^O'K wéll#
^sorry to have 'been so slów#
^I .
A ^no nò it's *all ríght#*
(B *!just* 'got 'caught 'up in òther 'things +all the
_time#;.+;
A +^côurse#;-+;
^OḰ#
^bye býe#
(8.4 453–71)

Speaker B apologizes three times. The third time the apology has the form of an account ('just got caught up in other things all the time'). The response to the apology is a simple (*of*) *course*.

Summing up, apologizing was frequently used in telephone conversation to mark the approaching closing of the call. In addition, it could be a part of the telephone opening. These uses may explain why *sorry* was more than twice as frequent on the telephone as in face-to-face conversation in LLC (see section 3.8) although the difference in frequency between the two text types was not as large as it was for thanking. Apologizing needs also to be analysed pragmatically, above all with regard to the type of offence.

3.13 The type of offence

The type of offence (see Coulmas 1981: 75 – 'the object of regret')[16] associated with an apology is important because it determines the variation between different forms. Different types of offence can be recognized. By taking over the categories used by Holmes (1990: 177) to classify the types of offence, it is possible to compare the apologies found in the respective corpora. The distribution of different categories of offence is shown in Table 3.7. The most frequent category of offence was a violation of conversational rules. Speakers apologized for interrupting, making digressions, changing topics, not having heard, not speaking clearly, making a pause or hesitating, etc. The apologies found in the London-Lund Corpus also reflect the importance of keeping agreements and appointments. As in Holmes's analysis, 'inconvenience' was a large category in the London-Lund Corpus (41.6 per cent), although it was not as large as 'talk offences' (45.4 per cent). On the other hand, the category 'possession' was absent in my material, and there were only a few examples where the offence could be analysed as 'social gaffe' (see Table 3.8). The categories will be discussed in more detail in the following sections.

Table 3.7: Types of offence calling for an apology

Category of offence

A Talk
   interruption
   not having heard or understood what sb says
   'slip of the tongue'
   digression
   correction
   not having made oneself clear
B Time
   being late
   wasting another person's time
   causing delay
   keeping another person waiting
   not keeping in touch
   cancelling an appointment
C Space
   disturbing or bothering another person
   intruding on sb's privacy
D Social gaffe
   clearing one's throat
   hiccuping
   coughing, etc
E Inconvenience or impoliteness to another person
   mistaking sb's identity
   leaving the room before the conversation is finished
   interrupting the conversation in order to answer the telephone, etc
   non-compliance with a request, invitation, proposal, etc
F Possession
   damaging a person's possessions

3.13.1 Talk offences

In the London-Lund Corpus, *sorry* was typically a device for solving communication problems. Any kind of disturbance in the flow of conversation can be looked upon as an offence which needs to be remedied by an explicit apology. The speaker apologizes for 'slips of the tongue', for intended or non-intended interruptions, for not speaking clearly, for pausing or hesitating, for having to hunt for the correct word, for corrections and modifications of the message, etc.

Not making oneself clear is an example of an offence which requires remedial action:

Table 3.8: Type of offence (in the LLC and Holmes 1990: 178)

Type of offence	LLC	Holmes
Inconvenience/impoliteness	90 (41.6%)	72 (39.3%)
Space	5 (2.3%)	30 (16.4%)
Talk	98 (45.4%)	30 (16.4%)
Time	21 (9.7%)	26 (14.2%)
Possession including money	–	20 (10.9%)
Social gaffe	2 (0.9%)	5 (2.7%)
Total	216	183

(Situation: Speaker A has failed to make it clear what he has in mind)
(63) A to make ^that kind of :"{lìmit} "!clèar#
         ^wóuldn't it#
      B ^in the ad!vèrtisement#
      A ^yèah#
         ^in the advèrtisement#
         I'm ^sòrry#
(2.6 62–7)

Sorry is part of the speaker's on-line editing of the message and is followed by a correction:

(64) A i^dèally we néed#
         a "^multiple type :bùilding# .
      ? ^sùre#
      ? *^yès#*
      C *^[m̀]#*
      A *[ə:]* ^{sòrry} a 'building with !mùltiple 'type
         'rooms#
(3.4 157–62)

An apology is appropriate whenever the speaker anticipates that the listener will have difficulty in following what is said. In example (65), it comes after a minor 'slip of the tongue':

(65) B I be^lieve it's '[bi:] . ex^cùse me#
         been ^sold to 'somebody 'who's a ooh :big nob in
         :bùsiness of _some sort#
(4.3 458–9)

Both speakers may end up apologizing (cf. Edmondson and House 1981: 156):

(66) b ^this méans#
         that at ^one and the 'same :tìme# - -
         we ^pay the !salaries of the stŭdents# - -
         the ^gránts#
         of [ði:] – ^*sòrry*#
      a ^salary of the stàff#
         ^*sòrry*#
      b ^this 'means that at '!one and the 'same
         ":tı̆me# -
         we ^pay the !salaries of the stáff# .
         the ^grants of the stúdents# -
(6.1 943–52)

Speaker b apologizes for interrupting the conversation to search for the
right word. Speaker a apologizes for his intervention.

Sorry can be used alone after some trouble in the conversation to invite
the hearer to repeat or clarify something in the immediately preceding
turn. For example:

(67) C *^Pirandéllo#* .
      B ^sórry# .
      C ^Pirandéllo# - -
      B (sighs -) ^yès# .
(3.6 925–8)

In telephone calls, names, addresses and numbers are difficult to hear
and need to be checked by means of *sorry* or some other apology phrase:

(Situation: Speaker B has difficulties in hearing a name)
(68) A ^Léa# .
         ^L 'E À# -
      B ^I'm !sórry#
      A ^Lèa# .
         ^L E À# .
      B ^Lĕa#
      A ^yéah# .
      B ^yèah#
(8.2 980–6)

(Situation: Speaker A has difficulties in hearing a number)
(69) B (- - - long pause) ^helló#
      A ^yés# .
      B ^Banque Natio'nale de Libán# - - -
      A ^yés#
      B ^nine to 'thirtéen# .
      A ^sórry#
      B ^nine . 'to . :thirtéen#

A ^yéah# .
(8.1 636–43)

Several apology phrases can function as requests for repetition or clarification. The tone was always rising (see Table 3.9). *I beg your pardon* was used both as an apology with remedial function (2 examples) and with the function of a 'repeat-request' (3 examples), while the elliptical *pardon* was used only as a request for repetition. The short phrase *sorry* was preferred to the complete utterance *I am (I'm) sorry.*

Table 3.9: Types of apology with the function of asking for repetition

Apology phrase	Number
sorry	16
I am sorry	4
pardon	7
I beg your pardon	5
Total	32

Interruptions and overlapping speech were typical talk offences (32 examples). In example (70), the speaker apologizes for taking the floor before the previous speaker has finished his turn:

(70) B I think ^lectures 'should be 'more pre:cìse# .
         than per^haps . they 'were when . when :Ì was an
         under*graduate#*
      E *^you like* +'concentràtion# .
         ^sòrry#+
(3.6 282–5)

The speaker may apologize both before and after an interruption. An apology before an interruption may serve as an attention-getter:

(Situation: Debate on the cruelty of fox-hunting)
(71) m ^if you 'think *you 'know :better than thèy do#*
      d *ex^cúse me# ^I 'am* "!nót# –
         ^I am re!ferring to the re'port of the com!mittee of
         the 'cruelty of :wild ànimals# **((^nineteen))**
(5.6 423–7)

In example (72), the apology is accompanied by a reason for the interruption:

(72) b ^sórry#
         ^just a sécond#

I'll have to - ^hold that ùp *a 'bit#* -
^rìght#
a *^oh yès#*
(6.1 186-90)

Both the 'interrupter' and the person who has been interrupted apologize before the conversation continues:

(From a telephone call)
(73)   B   **but ^I have !come into** - - ^sǒrry#
       A   ^sórry#
            ^go ón#
       B   I ^say I've !come into 'college and a :colleague
            has :kindly 'offered to 'baby-_sit
(7.2 956-9)

In example (74), Speaker m apologizes as a response to the other person's wish to 'go back a bit' in the conversation:

(74)   j   ^*one sécond#*
            ^can we 'go báck a bit#
       m   ^sǒrry# .[b]
       (j   be^cause he's !Gèoffrey todáy#
       m   ^yès#
            (laughs)
       j   ^so *it's !interesting*
       m   ^sórry#
            +^yés#+
(6.5 679-87)

Moreover, a digression may be followed by an apology:

(75)   A   àrmies#
            had ^really sort of - - - ^anyway I'm :sòrry#
            I was di^grèssing# .
            but ^what I 'mean ìs# - -
            the ^German 'General Stàff#
(2.3 364-8)

But *sorry* also marks an abrupt change to a new topic:

(76)   c   [m] - -
       B   I ^bèg your párdon#
       A   (- - *-* laughs)
       d   *it's not* been +you know+ - -
       c   +sorry+ - [m] have any books been written about
            this Frank .
(2.4 177-81)

113

For talk offences such as interruptions, overlaps, not hearing something, being unclear, etc, a simple *sorry* is often enough. A more profuse apology after a talk offence is illustrated in example (77):

(77) b and ^may I** now +^don't
      m **[ə:m] - - ac^cording to**
      (b interrúpt#
          we ^didn't ***interrúpt ((you#))+***
      m +^yès# .
          I'm *^sò sorry# .
          ^I'm sò+ sorry# .
          ^yès#*
          ++((^nò))++
      d *** *^no ^no*** ((we ^d=id 2 sylls#))*
(5.6 477–85)

I beg your pardon in example (78) is hardly a serious apology:

(78) n the ^flogging has got thìs to _do with it# -
          and I ^don't like your con:tinuous use of the word
          !flògging# -
      w ju^dicial bèating# .
          I ^beg your pàrdon#
      n ju^dicial beating's a !rather different [ə:] - a
(5.3 696–9)

Speaker n has said something which Speaker w finds offensive. The use of *I beg your pardon* after the correction should be taken as ironic or sarcastic and as a way of discouraging the previous speaker (cf. Edmondson and House 1981: 157).

3.13.2 Time offences

Arriving late, keeping somebody waiting, holding up a person's time, not keeping an appointment, disturbing a person who is busy, and being slow are typical time offences for which an apology is expected. When the addressee has been kept waiting, an explanation may also be appropriate:

(Situation: The telephone operator apologizes for a delay)
(79) B ^sorry to keep you wáiting#
          I ^can't !fìnd Mrs Cúmmings *at the 'moment#*
(8.3 536–7)

A common pattern is a form of *sorry* followed by a *that*-clause or an infinitive clause. The apology is followed by a response in which the apology is minimized:

(80) C ^sorry I'm láte#
  a +(. laughs) that's all right+ are you -
  b +(- laughs murmur)+
  C ^yès# .
(2.7 3–6)

The apology may be accompanied by long excuses:

(81) A *((I'm ^awfully))* _sorry a'bout _your :lĕtter# -
    but ^I [ə] ^I've been !so "bùsy ((at the
    móment))#
    ((that)) I've ^not ^just 'not had tíme#
    to ^send them !òff to you# -
  B ^I !sèe#
(8.3 440–4)

3.13.3 Space offences

A typical space offence is bumping into other persons or occupying someone else's seat. No examples of this kind were found in the London-Lund
Corpus, but I have included in this category examples in which the
addressee is bothered or disturbed by the speaker:

(82) A ^àngel#
    ^thank you !very mùch Bérto#
    ^sorry to bòther you# .
    ((that))
  B ^y=es# .
(8.4 452–6)

(83) a and she ^said [ə] . (. coughs) I'm !sorry to
    'burst :ìn 'like thís# -
    but I ^saw the 'light was still 'on at this
    :hŏur#
(11.3 66–7)

3.13.4 Offences involving social behaviour

Apologies are the rule after a breach of social etiquette: clearing one's
throat, coughing, hiccuping, sneezing, belching, sticking one's tongue out,
etc. A variety of expressions can be used such as *sorry, excuse me, pardon,*
I beg your pardon:

(84) b she ^said she didn't . 'think we were upstàirs# - /
    (clears throat) '^scùse me# .
    (clears throat)
(4.1 70–2)

A strong apology in the form of an exclamation followed by *I'm sorry* was chosen when the speaker apologized for licking his plate at table:

(85) A ^that is +"!vĕry "nàsty+ 'Gordon# - .
      B +((^good)) Lôrd#+
      C I'm ^sòrry#
         ((that's)) ^what !wè used to 'do as kíds# - -
(2.10 1347–50)

3.13.5 Offences involving inconvenience

The apology may be caused by an offence the speaker thinks will annoy or inconvenience the hearer. To this category belong apologies for errors committed, for mistaken assumptions and for other personal inadequacies. The speaker cannot answer a question or comply with a request, or has forgotten to do something which he or she has promised to do. The speaker may apologize for not being able to give the expected answer to a question:

(86) B and ^what sort of rates do you !pày for 'this sort
         of 'thing# .
      A [ə:m] - ^wéll# .
         [ə:] - - - I'm ^sòrry# .
         I ^ought to knòw this#
         I ^think it's a'bout one 'fifty an :hòur#
         or ^something of thàt kind# -
(3.2 240–5)

In example (87), Speaker A apologizes for the absence of an ash-tray. The apology is followed by the speaker's promise to redress the offence:

(87) B *^Jo we're !slightly* 'stuck for :àsh-'trays#
      A ^oh !I've gót 'one#
         ^I'm **so sórry#**
      d **here's another** one - -
      B ^lòvely# .
(2.10 628–32)

More serious 'errors', because they involve personal shortcomings, are not remembering a story or not recognizing a place where one has been several times. 'Gushing' and excuses are needed to remedy the offence:

(88) A [ə:m] - - - I ^think it's a :slightly fùnnier
         'story#
         (- - - pause about 15 secs)
      b [m]
      A ^no I'm sórry#
         it's ^not ((2 to 4 sylls)) - ^nò# - .
         ^funny !thìng#

```
        the ^bráin#
        ^ìsn't it# .
(1.14 591-8)
```

Oh sorry may be used 'on-line' when the speaker discovers that he has been misinformed or made a mistake:

```
(89)   m  *but you ^àre#
           a ^member* of the 'blood 'sports socíety#
           ^are you nót#
       b  ^nó# .
           I'm ^nót# -
           ((I)) ^never *!hèard of the 'thing#*
       m  *I ^thought* you wêre#
       b  ^nô#
           **^nò#
           ^nò#**
       m  **oh I'm ^so sòrry#**
(5.6 1120-30)
```

Heritage (1984) has characterized *oh* as a change-of-state token. Examples (88) and (89) show that *sorry* may also have this effect.

In example (90) the speaker apologizes for being a bore, which requires a denial as a response:

```
(90)   B  ^sòrry to be a bóre#
       C  ^you're !not a 'bore a bít#
           ^we'll !miss you :very mùch#
       B  ^àah#
           *- O^Ḱ#*
(7.2 1372-6)
```

Excuse me is preferred to *sorry* when the speaker has to leave the room or interrupts the conversation to answer a telephone call. Although other classifications of these examples are no doubt possible, the offences have been classifed as inconveniences.

```
(91)   b  *I'm ^((sùre)) you
       m  *I'm ^sùre you 'have#*
       (b  'want to* 'be constrúctive# .
           [m] ex^cŭse me a *_moment#*
(5.6 689-91)

(92)   A  [ə:] . ^n=ow#
           ^just you ex'cuse me !twŏ 'minutes#
           while I ^try and find :out this [ə:] :figure#
           (exit) - - - (enters) it ^ìs 'one fífty#
(3.2 418-20)
```

117

(93)   A (answers telephone) ex^cùse me#
           (speaks for some time on telephone) "^stupid
           ":bàstard#
(3.2 123–4)

3.14   Apologies and pragmatic frames

In Brown and Levinson's (1978) model of politeness, the factors determining the form and prosody of an apology which is needed in a certain
situation are the social distance between the participants (D), the asym-
metric relation of power (P) and the cultural ranking of the offence (R).
Together, these factors make up the weightiness of the act (see Holmes
1990).

In this work I have argued that communication is facilitated if hearers
look up things in the mental lexicon rather than figure out the intended
meaning by means of inference. The link between a form, its function and
prosody on the one hand, and the recurrent extralinguistic situation on
the other, can be represented as a speech-act 'frame'. The emphasis in my
description of the situation is on the type of offence and the legitimacy of
the apology, i.e. the rights and obligations of the participants to apologize.[17]

The sociolinguistic factors of the frame are, however, difficult to
describe. Some contextual factors are more important than others since
they determine the variation between different forms, e.g. between *sorry*
and *I'm terribly sorry* or between a simple strategy and a combination of
apology strategies. Other factors are the participants and their communicative goals, the severity and type of offence, the setting (time and
room), the channel (oral or written) and style (formal or informal). The
frame also specifies how an apologizing move is continued, and how
apologies are used in the opening and closing of the conversation.

However, there are several problems about frames and their use which
need to be stressed. In what situations do people use routine phrases and
frames to interpret what is said rather than infer what is meant on the
basis of computing the external factors of the communication situation?
How many frames are there? When do we have one situation rather than
several situational types? It may, for example, be suggested that speakers
use different apology frames when they speak to a stranger and when
they speak to an intimate friend; when they put their shoes on the table
and when they keep a person waiting.

The attitude adopted in this work is that the flexibility and referential
indeterminacy of conversational routines present no problem for the
hearer. Even if the fit between the world and the situation represented by
the cognitive frame is imperfect, the hearer may make sense of what is
said because the extralinguistic situation is sufficiently like the frame

concept. What such examples demonstrate is that interpreting what is said by means of frames is an active creative process where also 'new' uses of an utterance can be interpreted by analogy with, or on the basis of, the existing frames.

In the following sections I shall deal with the situational frames associated with apologies. The difference between (*I'm*) *sorry, excuse me, pardon,* etc, which have partly different but intersecting frames, will be discussed. Secondly, since the forms are not only of the simple type we associate with the simple *sorry,* the frames corresponding to the related 'expanded stems' will be discussed.

3.14.1 Frames for standard situations

It is clear that speakers have a repertoire of apology expressions to choose from which are appropriate in different standard situations. The following examples illustrate the difference between two types of apology:

(94) A has ^made me 'think of an:òther 'one# - .
         now ^what wàs it# - - -
         ^sŏrry# -
         my ^memory's a !{lìttle 'bit} . [ə:] :hither and
         yòn sómetimes# -
(1.14 581–4)

(95) A oo ^díd I#
         I'm ^so sórry#
         you see I was ^so ex!cĭt*ed#
         at ^seeing*
(1.9 22–5)

In (95), a long, elaborate apology is used after the offence. In the first example, the simple *sorry* was enough. The difference between the two situations must be accounted for.

As Coulmas claims, the idea that for each routine formula a distinct frame can be construed 'is much too simple' (1979: 250). Routines are flexible units which can be extended to new situations. It follows that it is economical for speakers to store as much information as possible about a form, and the situations in which it is used, in the same cognitive frame (see Bahns et al. 1986: 722; Coulmas 1979: 250). Moreover, frames are not completely distinct, but they may be similar to other frames or overlap with them.

Below, I give some examples of frames for apology utterances. I have analysed the situational frame for the simple *sorry* as well as for the intensified *I'm (very) sorry.*

FRAMES FOR APOLOGY UTTERANCES

A The frame for the simple *sorry*

Formal features	Situational features
Function mainly disarming	*Setting* at home, at work
Intonation rising tone stereotypic tone	*Time* (mainly) anticipatory
Continuation it's okay, that's all right	*Participants* friends, family, strangers operator/caller, caller-answerer
Discourse-specific features occurrence in the opening and closing of telephone calls	*Types of offence* most frequently talk offences

The simple automatic *sorry* was frequent in institutionalized contexts such as the telephone, although it was slightly more frequent in ordinary conversation. As expected, the most typical type of offence when the simple *sorry* was chosen was talk offences. *Sorry* was used both among friends and in institutionalized contexts where people have special roles. Finally, it was noteworthy that the simple *sorry* was nearly always disarming and anticipatory and contrasted in this respect with *I am (very) sorry*.

Just as modfied apologies (e.g. *I am very sorry*) have their own form and prosody, they need to be described situationally. This is represented in frame B as a variant of the frame (in A). When *sorry* was intensified it occurred less frequently in telephone calls, but the large number of examples in discussion is noteworthy.

B The frame for *I am (intensifier) sorry*

Formal features	Situational features
Function remedial	*Setting* at home, at work
Intonation falling tone	*Time* past events
Continuation pattern it's okay, etc	*Types of offence* inconvenience, talk, time
Discourse-specific features face-to-face conversation, discussion, telephone calls	*Participants* friends, family, strangers

Excuse me was linked to talk and inconvenience offences. No examples involved time offences. Unlike other apologies it was not found in telephone calls, but occurred primarily in face-to-face conversation and discussion (see C below).

C   The frame for *excuse me* (only a selection of features has been given)

Formal features	Situational features
Function e.g. asking someone to repeat something	*Setting* at home, at work
Discourse-specific features face-to-face conversation, discussion (not telephone calls)	*Time* anticipatory
	Types of offence space, inconvenience, talk, social behaviour

The majority of examples of *I beg your pardon* involved talk offences and was used primarily in face-to-face conversation. It is noteworthy that the simple *pardon* has been conventionalised as a request for repetition and clarification.

D   The frame for (*I beg your*) *pardon* (only a selection of features has been given)

Formal features	Situational features
Function e.g. asking someone to repeat something	*Setting* at home, at work
Discourse-specific features (mainly) face-to-face conversation	*Time* anticipatory
	Types of offence talk

3.15   Conclusion

Philosophers have argued about how many uses of language there are. Searle's position is clear:

... there are not as Wittgenstein and many others have claimed an infinite or indefinite number of language games or use of languages. ... If we adopt illocutionary point as the basic notion on which to classify uses of language, then there are a rather limited number of basic things we do with language.
(Searle 1979: 29)

From a linguistic point of view, it is natural to try to link form and strategies with function and with the social situation, even if there are examples which are difficult to classify. In this chapter I have argued that there is a distinct set of apology strategies which are associated with a relatively fixed wording. Links have developed between grammatical form and situation or function, as well as between intonation and situational features. Speakers not only know what form an apology has, but also what types of offence it is used with and whether it has a disarming or remedial function. The speaker's knowledge can be represented as frames consisting of semi-restricted collocations with constrained conditions of use which speakers match with the extralinguistic situation they perceive.

Notes

1 See Leech's Tact Maxim (Leech 1983: 107f).
2 Unlike Fraser (1981: 263) I have classified strategy D (expressing regret) as direct (explicit).
3 Following Goffman's (1976) well-known analysis of remedial interchanges, a distinction here is made between account (an explanation or justification) and apology. According to Goffman (1976: 68), apologies, accounts and requests are remedial moves functioning in a remedial dialogue.
4 Holmes, in fact, found more than 183 apology strategies, including combinations (Holmes 1990: 167).
5 In Holmes's New Zealand data, the corresponding figure was 79 per cent (1990: 175).
6 'I'm awfully' was, however, marked as 'unclear' in the corpus.
7 Cf. Norrick: 'It makes sense to speak of a . . . form as elliptical so long as its surface structure represents a proper subset of the constituents in a plausible syntactically complete paraphrase of it' (1985: 838).
8 One reason why the rising tone is so frequent may be that this is the normal tone when *sorry* has the function to ask the hearer to repeat the request.
9 The examples are taken from the written part of the SEU Corpus.
10 Shortening or ellipsis to a one-word utterance is illustrated by *sorry* via the following steps suggested by Norrick (1978: 675):

$$\text{I am sorry about} \begin{Bmatrix} \text{NP} \\ \text{V-}ing \end{Bmatrix} \rightarrow \text{sorry about} \begin{Bmatrix} \text{NP} \\ \text{V-}ing \end{Bmatrix} \rightarrow \text{sorry}$$

As pointed out in section 1.11.1, it is, however, far from clear how one-word utterances should be described grammatically.

11 It is noteworthy that no examples of intensifiers were found before a single *sorry* (see Owen 1983: 66).

12 Faerch and Kasper discuss request modification only but there is no reason to believe that their distinction between internal and external modifers could not refer to apologies (or to thanks). See Chapter 2.

13 See Edmondson, 'Apologies occur more frequently in the corpus used as disarming moves in discourse' (1981: 281). See also Edmondson's footnote 12, 'Though the corpus is small, I would hazard the opinion that the relative frequencies obtained here might well be reflected in a larger sample of conversation' (1981: 288).

14 In relevance theory, the disarming uses of *sorry* would have in common that they signal that the context created by the utterance is not the optimally relevant one for the interpretation of the utterance (Sperber and Wilson 1986; cf. also Jucker 1993: 450).

15 See also Edmondson's (1981: 284) discussion of 'ritual firming exchanges' at the end of business negotiation.

16 In Edmondson, the object of regret is referred to as 'complain'. The relationship between the two speech acts is described as follows: 'We note that in the case of the APOLOGY and the COMPLAIN, the same event P might be involved such that what from one conversationalist's viewpoint constitutes a ground for a COMPLAIN constitutes a ground for an APOLOGY for his interlocutor' (1981: 278).

17 On standard and non-standard situations, see, for example, House (1989: 107).

CHAPTER FOUR

Requests and offers

We could imagine a language in which all statements had the form and tone of rhetorical questions; or every command the form of the question 'Would you like to ... ?'. Perhaps it will then be said: 'What he says has the form of a question but is really a command'. – that is, has the function of a command in the technique of using the language. Similarly one says 'You will do this' not as a prophecy but as a command. What makes it the one or the other?

(Wittgenstein, *Philosophical investigations*, 'remark' 21, 1967)

4.1 Introduction

In many studies of requests, the emphasis has been on direct and indirect requests and the derivation of indirect speech acts from direct ones. In this chapter, the focus will instead be on the forms and patterns encoding requests and their situational and pragmatic constraints.

My starting-point is the observation that there are linguistic forms such as *can you, will you*, which can be viewed as 'routines' or fixed patterns and be analysed with regard to grammatical and semantic structure, prosody, function, sequentiality, text type, style and situation.

In the first part of the chapter I shall be concerned with the formal and functional description of request expressions. In the second part, situational and discourse aspects of requests are discussed. *Can you* and other conventionalized requestive expressions can be associated with a situational frame made up of a number of recurrent features (setting, the relations between the participants, type of requestive goal, etc). Imperatives and offers are dealt with separately.

4.2 The speech-act assignment mechanism and indirect speech acts

To begin with, I shall discuss some problems with the traditional view of how utterances are assigned illocutionary function. In speech-act analysis, as we have seen in previous chapters, the relationship between form and function is accounted for by saying that each utterance is associated with a certain illocutionary force indicating device or illocutionary act potential (Searle 1969). However, the 'IFID' does not on its own determine the illocutionary function of the utterance, but the interpretation also depends on inference and general conversational rules and maxims such as the cooperative principle suggested by Grice and the maxims which can be derived from it (Grice 1975).

In the following example from Searle (1979), quoted by Nattinger and DeCarrico (1989: 125), there is nothing in the form of Speaker B's answer which indicates what pragmatic force it has.

(1)   A Let's go to the movies tonight.
       B I have to study for an exam.

Speaker A infers what Speaker B means by forming hypotheses on the basis of the literal sense of the utterance, the extralinguistic context, and the assumption that certain conversational principles are adhered to: 'B has to study for an exam. Therefore he has no time to go to the movies.'

One of the problems is that it is far from clear what cues speakers use to assign illocutionary force to the utterance. Van Dijk (1981: 218) proposed that all of the following (linguistic and extralinguistic) factors have to be considered in determining the illocutionary force of an utterance: properties of the structure of the utterance and paralinguistic properties, perception of the present situation, knowledge of the speaker, knowledge of the superstructure or form of the episode, the relevant propositions and presuppositions, rules and norms and other knowledge of the world. As McLaughlin points out, if all of these factors are brought to bear on the interpretation, the search for a specific speech-act assignment mechanism relating an utterance to its pragmatic function would probably be futile (McLaughlin 1984: 67).

Another issue has to do with whether all utterances can be assigned a specific illocutionary force. Speech-act theory has been criticised for ignoring the fact that the majority of utterances are functionally indeterminate (Levinson 1983; Leech and Thomas 1990; Allwood 1987/1976). Levinson claims, for example, that it is sometimes impossible to assign a single force to an utterance since 'responses to utterances can attend to both the literal force ... and the alleged idiomatic force ...'(Levinson 1983: 269). Consider:

(2)   A Can you please lift the suitcase down for me?
       B Sure I can; here you are.
(Levinson 1983: 269)

According to Levinson, the utterance introduced by *can you* has to be interpreted both as a question and as a request in order to explain that the first move in Speaker B's response seems to answer the question, and the second component signals compliance with the request. *Sure I can* is, however, not necessarily a response to a question 'as there is no necessary relation between grammatical form and communicative function' (Tsui 1994: 46).[1]

Moreover, it is clear that most of the time we know what people mean because of what they say. The reason that we do this is that there are links between linguistic forms and function (see Fillmore et al. 1988; Nølke 1991: 203; Stubbs 1983; Wierzbicka 1991). Stubbs writes, for example:

> Any discourse analysis must integrate an account of what is said, into an account of what is done: first, because otherwise we have no realization rules or recognition criteria for underlying categories; second, because speakers themselves are condemned to stand by what they say, not by what they mean or intend.
> (Stubbs 1983: 177f)

4.3 Indirect speech acts and pragmatic principles

A number of analyses have been suggested for indirect requests which will be reviewed in this and the following section. According to Leech (1983: 16), communicative behaviour is constrained by 'interpersonal rhetoric', e.g. by the cooperative principle and the politeness principle. These principles can explain the difference in force between *will you shut up* (order) and *will you sit down* (offer) which have different propositional content. Sarcasm, exaggerated politeness, irony and other perlocutionary effects may also be derived from the literal meaning by means of inference and special principles. An example is *can't you*, where the negation must be interpreted ironically (Leech 1983: 123; cf. Chapter 1). As illustrated by example (3), a potentially formal or over-polite way of offering something can be understood as amusing if the context requires a less formal variant:

```
(3)     B   *^so he s=aid#*
            ^òh#
            ^wéll [ə:m]# -
            ^yŏu know# .
            ^may I 'be per'mitted 'to [ə:m] - 'offer 'you
            [ə:m]
            a 'small "gàteau#
            ^compliments 'of [ði:] . rèstaurant#
(7.3 1059–64)
```

Leech 'goes the whole pragmatic hog' (Leech 1983: 117f) and has attempted an explanation of indirect speech acts in terms of general pragmatic principles. Verbal behaviour, however, is not only the output of such principles, but is also determined by social and cultural norms. As a result, we must take into account both the insights provided by the theory

of speech acts and how principles of 'cultural rhetoric' constrain the interpretation of messages (see Wierzbicka's 1991 discussion of differences in
cultural logic).

4.4   Indirect speech acts and implicature

A speaker may utter the sentence *I want you to do it* and mean it as a
request. In order to account for the fact that sentence meaning and the
speaker's utterance meaning may 'come apart', Searle (1979: 34) postulates a number of inferential steps bridging the gap between the two types
of meaning. The 'apparatus necessary to explain the indirect part of
indirect speech acts' includes Gricean conversational principles and
shared background knowledge (Searle 1979: 32).

There has been much discussion about 'the theory of indirect speech
acts' and the conversational principles which are necessary to explain the
derivation of indirect speech acts. To begin with, all problems cannot be
solved within this theory:

> Why is it that some syntactical forms work better than others? Why can I ask
> you to do something by saying 'Can you hand me that book on the top shelf?'
> but not, or not very easily, by saying 'Is it the case that you at present have the
> ability to hand me that book on the top shelf?'
> (Searle 1979:48)

Searle's answer (1979: 49) is that certain forms tend to acquire conventional uses and that there are conventions of usage besides meaning conventions. However, Searle has no explanation why certain forms become
conventionalized and not others.

Secondly, the characterization of indirect speech acts as a series of
inferential steps is counter-intuitive for conventionalized indirect speech
acts (see Tsui 1994: 110). According to Horn (1989: 343), the derivation of
can you and similar forms[2] involves 'short-circuited implicature' (see also
Morgan 1978). Such implicatures are in principle 'calculable ... but are not
in fact calculated by speakers operating with the relevant usage conventions' (Horn 1989: 343). A more general issue has to do with what we
mean by implicature and by conventions of usage. Compare Horn:

> That a given pragmatic inferencing mechanism may operate with varying
> degrees of directness (or unconsciousness) is by now clear; this question is allied
> to the broader issue of the 'conventional' vs. 'natural' status of implicature in
> particular and pragmatic rules in general ... .
> (Horn 1989: 252)

Horn proposes that conventional implicature is distinguished from
'natural' or conversational implicature since it is not calculable by the
hearer (see Horn 1989: 144 for a discussion of other criteria such as the
non-cancellability of conventional implicature).

Other theories of indirect requests do not refer to the notion of implicature or inference. According to Blum-Kulka, *can you, will you*, etc, are linked to the illocutionary function as requests by means of one or more 'pragmalinguistic conventions' (1989: 40). Alternatively, linguistic forms may be analysed as linguistic cues to the indirect interpretation. For example, Sperber and Wilson (1986)[3] outline a discourse model (not unlike Horn's) in which linguistic and prosodic cues play an important short-cutting role in the interpretation process:

> What undeniably exists is not a well-defined range of syntactic sentence types but a variety of overt linguistic devices – e.g. indicative, imperative or subjunctive mood, rising or falling intonation, inverted or uninverted word order, the presence or absence of Wh-words, or of markers such as 'let's' or 'please' – which can guide the interpretation process in various ways.
> (Sperber and Wilson 1986: 247)

It is clear, then, that conventionalized indirect requests can be accounted for by means of short-circuited implicature or as psycholinguistic cues guiding the interpretation process. From a different perspective, indirect requests may be regarded as 'markers of a specific syntactic construction' or as 'fixed expressions', just like *thank you* or *sorry* (Wierzbicka 1991: 245f), since they have a fairly fixed form and function.

In this work I explore a 'pragmalinguistic' approach and try to establish conventional links between form and function on the one hand, and between form and situation on the other. *Can you, would you*, etc will be regarded as routines or fixed expressions although they are not complete utterances.

4.5 Pragmatic ambiguity

Even if there is a close linking between illocutionary force and utterances, this does not mean that the illocution of indirect speech acts is always straightforward. A problem which needs some discussion is the pragmatic or functional ambiguity of indirect requests. According to the so-called ambiguity thesis (see Bach and Harnish 1979: 174), *can you pass the salt* is ambiguous between the direct use as a question and the indirect function as a request. As a result, a sentence introduced by *can you* has potentially at least two different meanings or forces, one of which (or both) may be most appropriate in the context ('pragmatic ambiguity'; Blum-Kulka 1989: 45). The type of ambiguity needs to be further discussed.

Ambiguity is, of course, a common phenomenon in language. However, the ambiguity of indirect requests seems to be of a special type. It would be strange to say that *can you VP* is ambiguous in the same way as *the shooting of the hunters was horrible* (see Clark and Lucy 1975: 69), which can be given two different structural analyses. The type of ambiguity which is illustrated by *can you* implies that the hearer has to decide when the utterance is used directly or indirectly. As with all types of ambiguity, the context is an important guide to the intended interpretation. Thus, the most plausible interpretation of the following sentence is as a question:

(4)   Can you lift the table?

and example (5) is most likely a request:

(5)   Can you pass the salt?

The ambiguity of *can you* is more like lexical ambiguity where one meaning may dominate (because it is more frequent, is found in more contexts, etc). Some evidence that the indirect function represents the unmarked or preferred choice comes from the fact that the ambiguity of indirect requests may result in 'garden path phenomena'. The garden path theory of ambiguity implies that speakers compute only one reading for an ambiguous construction. If the unmarked interpretation is intended, the hearer is forced to revert and choose the other interpretation (see Clark and Clark 1977: 80). According to Blum-Kulka, this is the result of the fact that hearers tend to 'focus on' the indirect interpretations:

> Given an appropriate context, and given a conventional request of the 'salt passing' variety, hearers will tend to focus on the requestive interpretation. If the requestive interpretation is found not to match the pragmatic context, or if the hearer or speaker deliberately choose to opt out, then either or both can revert to a second literal interpretation.
> (Blum-Kulka 1987: 142)

In this work I go one step further and say that *can you* is directly linked with the requestive interpretation.

4.6   Defining requests

Requests have been described by Searle (1969) in terms of felicity conditions and by Bach and Harnish (1979: 48) as a speech act expressing the speaker's desire that the hearer do something with the additional proviso that the hearer take this expressed desire as the reason to act. According to Searle (1969: 66), whom I shall follow here, the performative verb *request* is associated with the following rules:[4]

Preparatory[5]	1. *H* is able to do *A*. *S* believes that *H* is able to do *A*.
	2. It is not obvious to both *S* and *H* that *H* will do *A* in the normal course of events of his own accord.
Sincerity	*S* wants *H* to do *A*.
Essential	Counts as an attempt to get *H* to do *A*.

In Searle's classification of speech-act types, requests are directives, i.e. their illocutionary point 'consists in the fact that they are attempts … by the speaker to get the hearer to do something' (1976: 11). The verbs in this class include *order, request, demand, beg, advise, offer,* etc (Searle 1976: 11).

Felicity conditions are not the only way of explaining the meaning of requests. The most radical break with speech-act theory is Wierzbicka's (1991) proposal to describe (conventionalized) indirect speech acts in a semantic metalanguage rather than in terms of illocutionary function. This would, however, result in a proliferation of phrases with a similar description. Tsui (1994: 92), on the other hand, suggests 'prospected response' as a criterion for defining requests and describing subclasses. This definition results in a distinction between 'requestives', which give the addressee the option whether to comply or not, and directives, which do not. In this work, request is used as an umbrella term similar to Searle's term 'directives', including a number of subfunctions which will be defined. Orders or commands, however, have not been included unless they are used as strategies to make polite requests or offers.

On a deeper level, a request can be analysed as a ritual which achieves a 'balance between two conflicting tendencies in our natures as human beings. On the one hand, we have a need for contact with our fellow-men, which leads to a desire for cooperation, sharing and mutual responsibility; on the other hand, we have a need for privacy, which leads to a desire for possessions, private territory, a need to keep other people at bay' (Edmondson and House 1981: 99).

The complexity of the speech act of requesting cannot be overrated. Much has been written about the depth of indirection when the speaker does not want to 'go on record' as having asked a request (see Stubbs 1983: 163). In standardized situations, however, it is appropriate to use a conventional strategy and a special routine phrase to ask for something.

4.7   Requestive strategies

The conventions associated with indirect requests are made up of strategies ('conventions of means') and 'conventions of form' (Clark 1979: 442; cf. Blum-Kulka 1989: 41). In speech-act theory, the emphasis has been on the conventional nature of the so-called performative verb. Other types of formal conventions are prosody, a certain word-order, etc. It is much more difficult to pick out the strategies which are conventionally used to make requests since there are so many ways in which a request can be carried out and it is difficult to define what we mean by request. The speaker may make a request by asking a question, making an order, suggesting something, etc. The strategies found in the London-Lund Corpus are illustrated in Table 4.1.

As indicated by Table 4.1, I have grouped requests into 18 different strategies. There is, however, little agreement about how many strategies there are and which they are. Fraser found, for example, as many as 20 different strategies (including hints and imperatives) for requesting (reported by Walters 1981). On the other hand, Blum-Kulka et al. (1989: 18) classified requests on 'a nine-point scale of mutually exclusive categories'.

Notice that it is, in principle, impossible to say how many strategies there are linked to a certain function. From one perspective (see Holmes 1990), the number of strategies available to express a request is indeterminate since the speaker can always think of new ways of getting the hearer to do something. What we focus on here is the set of strategies which have turned out to be functionally most appropriate and therefore been codified linguistically (cf. the notion 'speech-act set' proposed by Olshtain and Cohen 1983). Even from this perspective we have to deal with the question 'why these strategies and not others?'.

Just as in the previous chapters certain strategies can be regarded as more explicit than others. Strategies A and C are, for example, associated with the preconditions for a request and can be regarded as the most explicit ones. Other strategies make a more indirect reference to the preconditions of the request. The distinction between explicit and implicit indirect strategies will be discussed in more detail in the following section.

4.8 A taxonomy of requests

The functional definition of requests in speech-act theory is not detailed enough to characterize requests or to explain what strategies are used to make a request. In addition, we need to distinguish functional subclasses. For example, the morphosyntactic pattern with *perhaps you could* has a different function from *could you*. *What about* presupposes that the verbal action which is referred to is beneficial and has the function of a suggestion. Thus a variety of different functions can be expected.

Several authors (Leech 1983; Markkanen 1985; Bahns et al. 1986: 699), however, have expressed a pessimistic attitude with regard to the possibility of establishing criteria for different types of request. Leech and Thomas write:

> For the majority of illocutionary acts it no longer seems plausible to argue that any *formal* linguistic criteria can be established to distinguish, say, 'order' from 'request' (although an understanding of social role relationships, together with other contextual and paralinguistic features, certainly helps to narrow the range of possible interpretations).
> (Leech and Thomas 1990: 196)

And Markkanen, who carried out a cross-linguistic study of requests, writes that 'no division of the directive speech act into subcategories is felt

Table 4.1: Types of requestive strategies in the LLC

Strategy	Number
A Asking about the hearer's ability to do something [ABILITY] e.g. *can you* ...	132

B Asking about the possibility of the desired act happening [CONSULTATION]
 e.g. *is it possible* ...
  you haven't got ...
  would you mind ...
  have you ...
	9

C Asking whether the hearer is willing to do something or has any objection to doing something [WILLINGNESS] e.g. *will you* ... *would you (like)* ...	37
D Expressing a wish that the agent should do something [WANT][6] e.g. *I would like you to* ...	80
E Expressing a need or desire for (non-verbal) goods [NEED] e.g. *I want* ... *I need* ...	5
F Stating that the hearer is under the obligation to do the desired action [OBLIGATION] e.g. *you must* ... *you have to* ...	17
G Stating that it is appropriate that the hearer performs the desired action [APPROPRIACY] e.g. *you should* ...	3

H Asking an idiomatic wh- question [WH-QUESTION]
 e.g. *what about* ...
  why not ...
  how about ...
  why don't you ...
	9

Table 4.1: *Continued*

Strategy	Number
I Referring to a hypothetical action [HYPOTHESIS] e.g. *if you would …* *perhaps you would …*	18
J Expressing that one would appreciate, be pleased, feel gratitude if a hypothetical desired action were realized (cf. Strategy I) [APPRECIATION] e.g. *I would be grateful if you would …* *I would be glad if …*	6
K Asking for permission to do something [PERMISSION QUESTION] e.g. *may I …* *let me …*	80
L Asserting that it is possible for the hearer to do something [POSSIBILITY] e.g. *you may …* *you can …*	12
M Referring to the speaker's opinion that something is preferable [PREFERENCE] e.g. *you had better …* *the best thing to do …*	15
N Referring explicitly to the act of requesting [PERFORMATIVE] e.g. *I was going to suggest …*	5
O Referring to a state of the world which needs to be changed [STATE] e.g. *There are (some scented rushes)*	5
P Naming the object requested [NAMING] e.g. *(the next slide) please*	14
Q Checking the availability of the desired object, etc [EXISTENCE] e.g. *is (Mrs Davy) there*	4
R Other (e.g. giving a justification for a request)	14
Total	465

necessary, particularly in view of the fact that finding reliable criteria for such a division in two languages is very difficult' (1985: 23). She concluded that 'it is therefore better simply to look for the expressions for the directive speech act in general, without attempting any subclassification' (p. 23).

Another problem, not discussed by Markkanen, is that it is difficult to know when we should assign a new illocutionary function to an indirect request and when a request is simply more tentative (polite), or direct, performed from a new perspective, etc.[7]

In the present work I shall distinguish between requestives, advisories and offers.

4.8.1 Requestives, advisories and offers

We are able to distinguish between types of request in terms of whether the future action is good for the hearer or for the speaker. In this work, strategies with a requestive function will therefore be subclassified into requestive and advisory (cf. Sperber and Wilson 1986: 251).

In Figure 4.1, I have grouped strategies into requestives and advisories. If the speech act is of the requestive type, the speaker does not believe that the action is beneficial to the hearer. Advisories (advice, suggestions, offers, etc), on the other hand, imply that the future action will be good for the hearer:

(6)   C you'd ^better 'buy a :flàt - **{^màdam#}#**
(8.2 739)

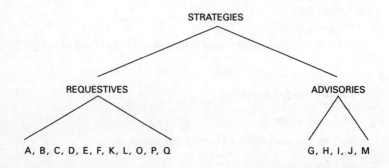

Figure 4.1 Classification of strategies into requestive and advisory (strategies N (performative) and R (other) have not been included)

(7)   b   I sug^gest that we 'ask Mr !Mŏore# .
           to ^stăte# .
           as . con^cisely as he cán# -
           ^whàt it 'is#
           that he ob^jĕcts 'to#
           ^in fóx'hunting# -
(5.6 17–22)

Edmondson and House make a similar distinction between suggests and requests:

> The Suggest as an illocution is analysed as the case in which a speaker communicates that he is in favour of a future action in H's own interest, while in the case of the Request, the future action to be performed by H was claimed to be in the interests of the speaker.
> (Edmondson and House 1981: 56)

According to Tsui (1994: 100), a distinction is also necessary between requests or suggestions and actions committing both the speaker and the hearer to a future action ('proposals'). In my analysis 'proposals' involving both the speaker and the hearer result from so-called defocalization strategies or impersonalization devices and are accounted for on the dimension of politeness or modification (see section 4.17).[8]

Why not is, for example, appropriate for polite suggestions. The implication is that the action might be beneficial for both the speaker and the hearer:

(8)   B   ^yèah# .
           ^wèll#
           ^why not ^why not !dŏ that#
(7.3 1359–61)

Related proposal phrases are *how about* and *what about*:

(9)   A   ^l=ook# .
           [ə] ^what about 'double glàzing# - -
(3.4 291–2)

The hearer is invited to share a view on the advantages of double glazing.

The following morphosyntactic pattern with *perhaps you'd like* has been analysed as a suggestion since it can be argued that it is in the hearer's interest to say what he wants:

(10)   A   ((and ^will you just 'come)) this wày#
           per^haps you'd 'like to 'tell us 'what you wànt#
(2.3 288–9)

The class of actions benefiting the hearer includes those carried out by the speaker ('offers'). Offers may be distinguished from requests because they are benefical to the hearer (i.e. they are 'advisories') and because they commit the speaker to the action. Compare:

(11)　B　*do you ^want a !lèmon#*
　　　c　but [ən ən]
　　　A　^[m̂]#
　　　c　until he
　　　A　^thânk you# -
(2.11 1216–20)

and

(12)　C　^can I hèlp you# .
　　　B　[əm] . hel^lò#
　　　　　I'd ^like to be 'put on your :màiling-'list
　　　　　pléase#
(8.2 13–15)

Do you want introduces an offer, because the action must be beneficial to the hearer. *I'd like to*, on the other hand, marks a request. However, as Leech points out, the difference between requests (impositives) and offers (commissives) goes deeper:

> In an impositive such as *Would you mind cleaning the windows?* there is implied a transfer of 'goods', or more often of 'services' from *h* to *s*; while in a commissive such as *Would you like me to clean the windows?* there is implied a transfer in the opposite direction.
> (Leech 1983: 129)

4.8.2　Explicit and implicit indirect requests

Why do speakers prefer forms like *can you, will you*, etc, either in a simple or modified form? Semantically, they 'realize the act by reference to contextual preconditions necessary for its performance, as conventionalized in a given language' (Blum-Kulka 1989: 47).

In example (13) the speaker directly states what he wants the hearer to do (the sincerity condition associated with requesting):

(13)　b　and I ^want [m?] 'Captain and 'Mrs Kǎy# .
　　　　　to ^witness 'my !sìgnature 'to it# .
(11.1 121–2)

In example (14), the speaker questions one of the preconditions of requesting (the hearer is able to do the action):

(14)　B　can ^you !put it in :lots of :well 'salted
　　　　　:wàter# -
　　　A　^yés# .
　　　　　^how mùch#
(7.2 515–16)

A reflection of the centrality of these strategies is that they occur in many languages. In the eight languages studied within the Cross-Cultural

Speech Act Realization Project (CCSARP) (Blum-Kulka 1989: 47), indirect requests referring to a small set of preconditions for a request were the most frequent type in all the languages.

To give an example from the CCSARP material, 82.4 per cent of the requests investigated in Australian English were realized by conventionalized indirect forms such as *can you, will you, can I, I want you to*, etc. Only 9.8 per cent of the examples in fact used a direct strategy.[9] The lowest figure was found for non-conventional indirect strategies or 'hints'. The same tendencies were represented in other languages (e.g. Hebrew, German, Danish) studied in the project.

Other requestive strategies reflect politeness conventions and cultural assumptions, which are more likely to be language-specific and are less conventionalized. As Mulder points out, 'in everyday conversation utterances that refer to all sorts of conditions and norms related with the desired act can function as a request' (1993) (see also Wierzbicka 1991: Chapter 6). Other types of strategy are more indirect, i.e. they 'leave the hearer uncertain as to the speaker's intentions, and (leave) the speaker the possibility to opt out' (Weizman 1989: 73). The strategy illustrated in example (15) is a pre-sequence or a pre-request since it serves to check whether a more general precondition for a request is fulfilled, such as whether a requested object exists or not:

(15)   B   ^you haven't 'got a[?] an ad:dress in Ni!gèria
            'for him#
(8.3.1128)

Example (15) implies that the speaker is not sure if the hearer has the address and therefore wants to check if this is the case before making the request (see Labov and Fanshel's 'rules for indirect requests' and their discussion of the example *Have you dusted yet*? (1977: 82)). Usually, pre-requests are not regarded as conventionalized. I agree with Tsui, however, that the use of a pre-request 'is a face-saving strategy that is so commonly employed that conventionalization occurs' (Tsui 1994: 111).

Schematically, we can distinguish between explicit requests which refer to the felicity conditions for the illocutionary function associated with the verb *request* and pre-requests (see Figure 4.2). Weizman (1989) distinguishes between conventional indirect requests and hints. On the other hand, Pufahl Bax (1986) regards all indirect requests as pre-requests, including forms like *can you*. There are, however, several arguments for distinguishing between two kinds of indirect request. First, we can distinguish between two types of indirect request on the basis of the responses that are acceptable to them (Tsui 1994: 112). As pointed out by Tsui, in sentences like example (5), the response must include a non-verbal compliance with the request. Pre-requests, on the other hand, are preliminary to a request and can be answered by *yes* without the non-verbal action of compliance. Secondly, pre-requests are recognizable by the fact that they may give rise

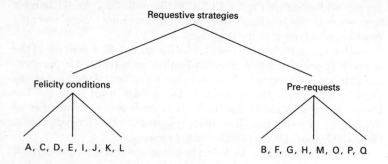

Figure 4.2 Classification of requestive strategies with regard to explicitness (strategies N (performative) and R (other) have not been included)

to misunderstandings. Such a situation can be illustrated by means of the following episode from Lewis Carroll's *Through the looking-glass*:

> 'Oh, please! There are some scented rushes!' Alice cried in a sudden transport of delight. 'There really are – and such beauties!'
> 'You needn't say "please" to me about 'em,' the sheep said, without looking up from her knitting. 'I didn't put 'em there, and I'm not going to take 'em away.'
> 'No, but I meant – please, may we wait and pick some?' Alice pleaded. 'If you don't mind stopping the boat for a minute.'
> (Lewis Carroll, *Through the looking-glass*, 1962: 256)

The illocutionary force of 'There are some scented rushes' may be that of a request, an assertion or a warning, etc. In such cases the interpretation is determined by what the hearer thinks the utterance means (or pretends to think that it means). A related argument is that the ambiguity of pre-requests may result in processing breakdown (or garden-path effects) (see section 4.5). When this happens, the hearer reverts and chooses a different path of interpretation.

4.9 Requests and politeness

On a deeper level, the way the speaker makes a request is motivated by his wish to be polite. Here are some examples of polite strategies:

- the use of a question instead of a declarative sentence
- the choice of a suggestion rather than a request
- the choice of modal auxiliary
- the choice of subject
- giving reasons for doing something rather than stating one's wishes abruptly
- softening the force of an impositive speech act

In order to account for such strategies the relation between requests and politeness must be explained. As we have seen in Chapters 1 and 2, the social point of a speech act can be to express a positive attitude to the hearer, such as the expression of gratitude ('convivial speech acts'). Convivial speech acts can be contrasted with other speech acts, such as quarrels or threats, which are inherently aggressive ('conflictive speech acts'). A request is not, in itself, aggressive like a threat, but can be potentially offensive or threatening because it impinges on the privacy of the individual who is requested to do something. As a result, we find a number of indirect requests of the form *can you* whose politeness is derived from 'the interactional balance between pragmatic clarity and apparent noncoerciveness achieved by these strategies' (Blum-Kulka 1987: 144).

In Leech's taxonomy, requests would be 'competitive' (Leech 1983: 104).[10] Competitive speech acts are discourteous and require politeness strategies of a negative kind which contribute to 'minimizing the impoliteness of impolite illocutions' (Leech 1983: 83). The politeness of indirect requests is derived from the need to make it easier for the hearer not to comply with the request and is associated with indirectness or tentativeness. Requests such as *can you answer the phone* or *will you answer the phone* are polite since the speaker leaves the hearer considerable freedom to choose whether or not to comply with the request. On the following scale of directness, the propositional content of the request is the same but the illocutions differ with regard to indirectness and politeness:

	more direct	less polite
[A] Answer the phone.		
[B] I want you to answer the phone.		
[C] Will you answer the phone?		
[D] Can you answer the phone?		
[E] Would you mind answering the phone?		
[F] Could you possibly answer the phone?		
etc.	less direct	more polite

(After Leech 1983: 108)

The imperative is the most direct alternative since the speaker's wishes are expressed without any hedging. Similarly, the explicit expression of the speaker's wants (*I want you to*) in [B] leaves the hearer little choice not to comply with the request and is therefore close to the directness end of the scale. The variants in [C]–[F] have been placed on the scale in the order of increasing indirectness and optionality (Leech 1983: 38). Since a question implicates that the addressee has a choice, the request is more indirect. In [E] and [F], the past tense form of the modal auxiliary marks increasing tentativeness as well as an increase in the degree of indirectness/politeness.[11]

The validity of ranking scales has been tested experimentally with interesting results. Mohan (1974) reported, for example, that the tested items which had interrogative form were rated as the most polite among a large number of requestive expressions. He also found that *you can* was considered more polite than *you will* since the addressee is given more option to refuse to carry out the request (Mohan's results are reported by Perkins (1983: 124). See also Clark and Schunk 1980; Fraser and Nolen 1981; and Blum-Kulka 1987). The scale explains the contribution of felicity conditions to indirectness and politeness.

The scale suggests, for example, that it is more polite to make a request by means of *could you* than by *I want you* because this strategy is more indirect. We can also explain that speakers use questions rather than declarative sentences, that *could you help me* is more polite than *I should like you to help me*.

Indirectness or politeness is a property which is distributed over the utterance and depends on sentence type, felicity conditions and the type of subject. Other strategies for making a request polite or indirect involve downtoners and hedges, disarming apologies and 'grounders'. Modified indirect requests can therefore also be analysed with regard to indirectness. Moreover, more indirectness and more politeness is expressed by combining different devices. This will be discussed later in this work (sections 4.15–4.17).

Leech was primarily interested in comparing requests with regard to politeness. Since I analyse requests as routines, I will classify requests and requestive strategies in terms of absolute politeness.

4.9.1 Assertive and tentative indirect requests

Politeness is an important feature of many requestive forms which can be identified with strategy type. As a result, we can describe the request forms in the material with regard to politeness. The most direct or assertive requests are those expressing the speaker's wishes directly, without considering the hearer. Requests are tentative if the hearer's wishes and options are considered. The labels are language-specific and refer to absolute politeness. Compare Edmondson and House:

> ... we must remember that these markers attach to utterances, considered independently of the specific contexts in which they might be used. In other words, an 'authoritative' (= assertive KA) utterance may not necessarily be perceived as 'authoritative' in particular circumstances.
> (Edmondson and House 1981: 91)

'Assertive' and 'tentative' can also be regarded as endpoints on a cline rather than binary features. Requests falling between the endpoints are said to be 'unmarked' (cf. Edmondson and House 1981: 91). In Table 4.2, I have given examples of request expressions which are 'assertive' or 'tentative'. *I would be grateful if you would, is it possible for you to* ... are associated with tentative requests since they contain several markers of indirectness. Markers in the form of a declarative sentence have been analysed as assertive. On the other hand, a simple *could you* or *would you*

Table 4.2: Subclassification of (some) request markers as assertive or tentative

[ASSERTIVE]	[UNMARKED]	[TENTATIVE]
I want you to	*can you*	*you haven't got*
I ask you to	*will you*	*is it possible for you to*
I want (need)	*could you*	*would you mind*
you must (have to)	*would you*	*if you would*
you had better		*I would be grateful if you would*
you should		

can be regarded as the unmarked way of making a request. Notice that *can you* and *could you* could only be distinguished on a scale of relative politeness according to this model.

4.9.2 Requests and style

As Edmondson and House (1981: 93) have pointed out, style is an additional factor distinguishing between types of request. 'Formal' indicates a relatively 'high' level of style, typical of certain settings, and refers to a marked choice in situations where the hearer has power over the speaker. 'Familiar' refers to stylistic features characteristic of informal language. Certain types of request involve formality, for example those referring to a hypothetical action (*if you would*).

The strategy in example (16) is typically used when the conversationalists do not know each other or in formal contexts (debate, public speaking, leaving messages on the answering machine). Consider:

(16)   CK   [ə:m] . ^would you be 'good e'nough to 'let me
           knów#
           ^when Mr 'Buckram 'will be a'vailable 'on the
           tĕlephone#
(9.3 1256–8)

Mitigated imperatives are, on the other hand, associated with familiarity and informal discourse:

(17)   B   and ^they _s=ay . [ə:] yès#
           and ^you say well !!come ón then#
           ^get úp# .
           ^you knów#
           it's ^your re'sponsibílity# .
(1.12 711–15)

CONVERSATIONAL ROUTINES IN ENGLISH

4.10 Continuation patterns

From a discourse perspective, a request can be viewed as the first part of
an adjacency pair. Requests with a fairly fixed continuation are illustrated
in examples (18) and (19):

(18)   B   +(- laughs) could ^you ^could you+ _ask him to
            !rĭng me#
       A   ^yès#
            *^cèrtainly# .
            ^yès#
(8.4 360–3)

(Situation: Request for action on the telephone)

(19)   B   I'd be ^most gràteful#
            if you could ^pass that òn#
       C   ^OḰ#
            I'll ^do my bést#
(9.1 64–6)

Some characteristic continuation patterns are illustrated in Table 4.3. In
many requests, the response may be far away or be completed by a 'follow-up' move. In situations which are less routinized, the hearer is free to
manoeuvre, to express reservations or to ask for further details before
responding. Houtkoop-Steenstra (1987) describes the structure of 'remote'
requests consisting of five turns, but in fact requests may be much longer
because of insertions and side-sequences (Jefferson 1972).

Example (20) illustrates a request which is not answered immediately:

(20)   A   ^well . [ə:m] !ring me ùp#
            a^bout . [ə:m - - ə:m] - - 'B mínor#

Table 4.3: Types of request responses in the LLC (both single
strategies and combinations of strategies have been included)

Types of request response	Number
yes (oh yes, yeah, yup, m)	23
combinations (*I will yes, yes OK, yeah right*, etc)	17
okay	14
all right	4
I will (I will do that, I will indeed)	4
(yes) certainly	2
of course	1
Total	65

```
B  ^yés#
A  "^and !if you arrange 'lunch with Jámie {or
   *^sómething#}#*
B  *^yes .* ((^rìght))#
A  ^and [əm] . send me a lìst#
B  ^yés#
   ^I'll . !dò that#
   *((O^Ḱ#))*
A  *^gòod#* -
```
(7.3 831–40)

Compliance with the request takes place in steps, and several different strategies are used (*yes; I'll do that, OK*). The exchange is closed by an evaluating 'follow-up' move from the requester.

Leech and Thomas (1990: 198f) describe illocutionary force as cumulative in the sense that participants assign value to utterances in the light of what has gone before. Each step is associated with partial acceptance:

(21) A Is that your car?
     B Yes.
     A That's the third time this week you've taken my particular space. I don't pay fifteen quid a year for you to keep taking my place.
     B Sorry, I didn't know it was gone.
     A What the hell's that got to do with it? And now you do know, perhaps you'd be good enough to move it?

Speaker A's first turn is a pre-request answered in the affirmative. In Speaker A's second turn, further justification is given for the request. The request comes in the third turn uttered by Speaker A.

A rejection of a request needs more planning and is less likely to be routinized than compliance. Negative responses were usually longer than affirmative ones and have special structural features such as pauses. Moreover, they may contain extra components such as apologies, 'disarmers', 'softeners' and accounts. Consider example (22) where the rejection of the request contains an apology and an account (see the discussion of the preference system in Chapter 3, section 3.11.1.3):

(22) B is ^Mrs Dávy there 'please# .
     A ^sŏrry#
       she's ^ỳnter'viewing this 'morning#
     B ^òh#
(9.1 700–3)

In the following example, the failure to comply with the request is marked by a pause followed by a hesitation signal (*well*); the response is hedged by 'the thing is that' and is followed by an account explaining why the request cannot be complied with:

(23) A are ^you in a hùrry#
         can I ^have this trans'ferred to my 'phone
         upstǎirs#
      B [ə:m] ^well the !thing is that [? ə] . it's ^not my
         phòne#
      A ^OǨ#
(8.4 109–12)

4.11 The grammatical analysis of requestive routines

As a result of conventionalization, indirect requests are to some extent
fixed. We need, however, to distinguish between idiomatization and
indirectness. Idiomatization implies that the meaning of the phrase cannot be derived compositionally from the meanings of its constituents. In
conventional indirect speech acts the indirect meaning has been conventionalized. We can, however, describe phrases which are grammatically
irregular as 'extra-grammatical idioms' (see Fillmore et al. 1988: 505).
Indirect requests modified by *please* are an example since they create problems if they are analysed in grammar.

It should be noted at the outset that not all requests containing *please* are
problematic. Imperatives modified by *please* (e.g. *hurry up please*) can easily
be generated by a phrase structure rule since the restrictions on *please* can
be accounted for by means of grammatical subcategorization. The problematic sentences are of the following type:

(24) Can you please pass the salt?
(fabricated example)

where preverbal *please* occurs in an indirect request in the form of a question. *Please* is also allowed in requests which have the form of permission
questions (*may I please*). There is, however, no possibility of using (preverbal) *please* in an ordinary question (see, for example, Sadock 1974:
88–91; Levinson 1983: 265f). If example (24) is grammatical, it is difficult
to 'block' the generation of the ungrammatical:

(25) *Why do you please pass the salt?

The generalization about *please* is that the phrase is allowed in conventionalized indirect requests (especially in the combination *(MODAL) you
please*), and also, although less frequently, in declarative sentences with a
requestive function:

(26) A *well I'd ^like to 'come a!lòng#* .
         I would "^lǐke to +'do that 'please#+
(1.10 950–1)

(27)　A　so ^what I'd "!lǐke from him 'please#
　　　is an ^indi_cation _of as . !màny . to be^gǐn
　　　with#
(9.1 113–14)

In order to permit example (24) but not 'genuine' questions with *please*, Bach and Harnish (1979) have suggested that sentences such as *Can you please pass the salt?* or *Will you please pass the salt?* should be regarded as not fully grammatical, although they must be acceptable as evidenced by their currency:

> We suggest that sentences like / *Can you please pass the salt?* / and / *Will you please pass the salt?* / in which 'please' occurs, are not fully grammatical, although their recurrent use makes them seem perfectly acceptable; … we propose that / *Can you please pass the salt?* / and / *Will you please pass the salt?* / are not grammatical sentences and should not be generated by a grammar of English. Instead they are examples of the phenomenon of syntactic liberty, ungrammatical but usable sentences that are perfectly acceptable to fluent speakers.
> (Bach and Harnish 1979: 199)

A small fact about the syntactic distribution of *please* may indicate that we need to abandon the view that all indirect requests can be accounted for in terms of generative syntax, compositional semantics, pragmatic rules and principles. Instead, indirect requests are grammatical constructions or 'stems' with constrained conditions of use. As Wierzbicka puts it, ' "ungrammatical" sentences such as *Why don't you be quiet?* or *Would you please be quiet?* can be rehabilitated as fully grammatical encodings of language-specific "pragmatic" meanings' (Wierzbicka 1991: 452). This has consequences for how we describe the language user's competence:

> It has seemed to us that a large part of a language user's competence is to be described as a repertory of clusters of information, including, simultaneously, morphosyntactic patterns, semantic interpretation principles to which they are dedicated, and, in many cases, specific pragmatic functions in whose service they exist.
> (Fillmore et al. 1988: 534)

4.12　Describing request expressions

4.12.1　*Prosodic modification*

It is likely that a special prosodic profile makes it possible to recognize an indirect request just as much as the modal auxiliary, question form, negation, etc. The fall-rise tone of indirect requests is both a cue to illocutionary force and a mitigating device with downtoning function:[12]

(28)　B　could ^you 'give her a :mĕssage *for me#*
　　　C　*^cêrtainly#* .
(8.11. 862–3)

4.12.2 *Requests and discourse type*

As may be expected, requests were not equally frequent in all text types
(see Table 4.4). Text types can be analysed as interactional or transactional,
monologues or dialogues, formal or informal, institutionalized or not.
Requests occur, above all, in text types which involve some interaction
between the speaker and hearer, such as conversation face-to-face or on the
telephone. On the other hand, requests were practically missing in genres
which are monologic in nature (e.g. public speech, prepared commentary).

As shown in Table 4.4, the frequency of requests in the London-Lund
Corpus ranges from about 75 per 10,000 words in telephone calls to
slightly more than two in public and prepared speech. The large number
of requests on the telephone can be explained by the frequency of routinized situations on the telephone, such as asking to speak to a third person
or leaving a message and, above all, by the transactional goal (see section
4.18.2).

Table 4.4: Distribution of requests over different genres in the LLC
(the figures have been normalized to 10,000 words)

Type of conversation	Number	Number per 10,000 words
FACE (surreptitious)	165	9.7
FACE (non-surreptitious)	69	11.5
TELEPHONE	376	75.2
DISCUSSION	98	16.3
PUBLIC	16	2.6
PREPARED	18	2.6
Total	742[13]	117.9

In writing, requests seem to be frequent, above all, in business letters
(see Yli-Jokipii 1990).[14] The letters in the SEU corpus contained embedded
requests which were heavily modified, such as *We would be grateful if you
would* …, *I should very much appreciate it if you would* ….

(29) We would be grateful if you would retain the questionnaire …
(W 7–10)

(30) I would be grateful for any help you can give in establishing an
aetiological diagnosis for Mrs Name …
(W 7–11)

(31) I recognize that our research may not have been as exhaustive as
yours and I should very much appreciate it if you would let me
know the authorities upon which you were relying.
(W 7–11)

(32)   I shall be obliged if you will kindly call to see me and in the mean-
       time please do not embarrass us both by issuing any further
       cheques.
(W 7–11)

But there were also several examples of imperatives modified by *please*:

(33)   Please phone if there are any queries.
(W 7–10)

As indicated by these data, the form of requests differs in speech and writing. In an interesting study, Pufahl Bax (1986) has compared spoken and written instructions at a work-place. She found, for example, that the spoken requests had more modality markers ('downtoners') and polite prefaces and were less direct than the requests which were produced in writing. Similarly, in a study by Blum-Kulka et al., 'the trend was for written requests to be the most direct, and requests on the phone to be the least direct' (1985: 131).

4.13   Indirect requests and speech-act stems

When the notion speech-act frame was introduced by Coulmas (1979), the purpose was to describe routinized speech acts with regard to socio-linguistic, pragmatic and contextual factors. Here, I also use the notion speech-act frame to describe speech acts which are not completely fixed formally and pragmatically.[15] Fixedness is thus a relative rather than an absolute notion.

What is fixed about conventionalized indirect requests is not their form, since there is an enormous amount of related variants. *Can you help me, will you help me, do you think you can help me, you can help me* are similar although the relationship between them is not easy to describe either grammatically, functionally or pragmatically. On a fairly abstract level, they can be described as variants of a recurrent or basic 'stem': *MODAL you VP*. Requests in the form of a restricted number of morphosyntactic patterns can be generated from the stem according to certain principles or syntactic operations such as inflection, modification, reordering, embedding, ellipsis, expansion, and combination with other elements (Barkema 1992). By means of inflection[16] the MODAL constituent can, for example, be substituted for one of the modal auxiliaries *can, could, will, would*. There is, however, only a small set of modal auxiliaries which are permitted by the stem. On the other hand, the choice of VP is relatively unrestricted except for the selectional constraint that the verbal action must be controllable.

On a deeper level, stems can vary grammatically with regard to sentence form (e.g. whether they consist of a declarative or an interrogative sentence) and the choice of subject. Requests in the form of a single noun phrase (*next slide please*) have been analysed as elliptical imperatives, and conditional sentences (*I would be grateful if you would help me*) as variants of the declarative sentence.

Nattinger and DeCarrico have made the interesting proposal that 'the flexibility allowed within a particular frame [what I have called stem] may well account for why that frame, rather than another, has come to be one of the favored, conventional ones for a given indirect speech act' (1989: 126f). In order to account for the conventionalization of indirect requests we need to describe in as much detail as possible the variability permitted by the stem.[17] On the one hand, the stem MODAL you VP is characterized by a high degree of flexibility because of the large number of operations which can modify its form. On the other hand, requests introduced by *what about, how about* are completely frozen.

Another feature of the flexibility of the stem has to do with the number of variants which can actually be derived from it. The frequency of the permitted variants can be said to give a measurement of the productivity of the stem.

It should be stressed that it is not enough to describe how new variants of requests can be formed according to rules and by creative 'departure'. It is equally important to describe the new situations in which the variants are used with regard to setting, the social roles of the participants, etc. To begin with, however, we need to look in more detail at the stems.

4.14 Types of stem

Requestive expressions can be regarded as variants of a few extremely flexible and productive sentence stems. These can be added to, embedded, etc in order to 'build up' large and elaborate request patterns which are appropriate in the new situation. Because the stems are grammatically incomplete, they contrast with direct requests such as *hold on, stop it*, etc which have been routinized as whole utterances (see Bahns et al. 1986: 704f).[18]

The most interesting of the stems has a modal verb and a second-person subject and has the grammatical form of a declarative or an interrogative sentence:

A   you MODAL VP
            [Declarative sentence]
B   MODAL you VP
            [Interrogative sentence]

The purpose of this and the following sections is to investigate the frequencies of the different patterns which can be derived from the stem. The stems contain a number of gaps for downtoning devices and can be modified by 'external modifiers' giving support for the request.

To begin with, we can notice that about one-third of the requests in the London-Lund Corpus were modified in some way (271/742 or 36.5 per cent), and collocations of several modifiers in the same request were frequent.

A simple requestive strategy without modification is often enough, especially in routinized situations where no extra personal favour is involved. *Can you* is an example of a pattern which is normally used without modification for simple routinized requests:

(Situation: Male solicitor's clerk to female university secretary)
(34)   A [ə:] ^can you àsk 'her 'to [ə:m]# -
           ^to . !ring _her solìcitors# -
(9.1 286–7)

On the other hand, if the speaker asks for a major favour, if the hearer has no obligation to fulfil the requester's wishes, or if the persons do not know each other, a longer pattern may be used:

(Situation: Message left on the answering-machine)
(35)   AV it's ^nòt úrgent#
           but I ^would be 'grateful if you ((could)) 'give me
           a càll# .
(9.3 420–1)

(Situation: Male academic to female university secretary)
(36)   B so I was ^wondering if a :message could be
           :((given)) 'to Mr :Ssòames# -
           Mr ^Matthew Ssòames# -
(9.1a 8–9)

The pattern in example (36) is the result of strategies such as mitigation, defocalization, embedding (*I wonder if*), etc, representing different types of downtoning. In the following sections the different patterns will be described in more detail.

4.14.1 *Mitigated indirect requests in the form of declarative sentences*

Table 4.5 shows the patterns of requests based on assertions that were found in the London-Lund Corpus. The patterns include a number of constructions without a personal subject such as *it would be better, the best thing to do, perhaps one could*. Only a few patterns are recurrent (*perhaps you could, perhaps you would*). They can be described with regard to indirectness, style, setting, genre, and in terms of subfunctions such as advisory or requestive.

As a request *you can* is authoritative and definitive:

(Situation: Radio interview with male politician)
(37)   b ^ôoh#
           you can ^{lêave} :me ôut# .
           ^thank you very múch#
(6.3 62–4)

Table 4.5: Requestive markers derived from assertion-based sentence stem with a modal auxiliary in the LLC

Type of marker	Number of tokens
you can	8
I would be grateful if you could	6
I wonder if you could	6
if you could	6
you had better (you'd better, better)	6
you must	5
perhaps you could	4
you have to (you've got to)	4
perhaps you would	3
you might	2
perhaps you'd like to	2
perhaps we could (one could)	2
if you would	2
I wonder if you would (you'd)	2
you can perhaps	1
you can certainly	1
you can … can't you	1
you can just	1
you could	1
you couldn't	1
you could perhaps	1
you could . … if you want to	1
you could … couldn't you	1
you could always	1
perhaps it would be better	1
perhaps you'd better	1
you can perhaps	1
I think the best thing to do is	1
I would be grateful if you would	1
I should be glad if you would	1
I should be glad to	1
I should be interested to	1
I think it would be a good idea if you would	1
perhaps you could possibly	1
perhaps if you	1
we should be grateful if you can	1
you ought to	1
you should	1
I think you're entitled to	1
I think it would be a good idea if	1
I wondered if you could perhaps	1
I was wondering if you could	1
if you can	1
Total	87

In several examples, the meaning of *can* is closer to PERMISSION[19] than to POSSIBILITY:

(38) A [ə:m] ^you can certainly 'give me a :ring !bàck
        this 'afternóon#
        there ^mìght be sómething#
      B *^thànk you#;.*;
        ^rìght#
        ^ÒK#
(8.1 246–50)

You could as a request marker is tentative and introduces a polite sugges-tion:

(39) B *[ə ə]* ^Prudence and "Mò#
        are ^{théy 'present} at the móment#
        you could ^{àsk} thĕm#
(7.1 624–6)

You might is common in suggestions:

(40) B you ^might 'even 'pay a 'visit . ^if you ^if you
        - - (- - sighs) ^ŏh 'well#
        ^yèah# .
        ^ŎK# .
(7.2 152–4)

(41) d Frank I don't think Nancy – understood your
        references to – teaching alphabet – and all the
        rest of it . because . did you know what Frank was
        doing *((2 to 3 sylls))*
      c *IITU* ITA did you say
      d [m] so you might put her in the picture as
        regards your occupation . *((2 to 3 sylls))*
(2.4 54–6)

You can perhaps has the force of a suggestion (if the action is favourable to the hearer):

(42) a I'm ^ŏn the phone#
        ^so you can per!haps ring me :ùp#
      b *^[m̀]#*
(4.5 551–3)

Usually *perhaps* has a fixed initial position (see Blum-Kulka's (1989: 56) analysis of the Hebrew initial particle *ulay* with the meaning 'perhaps').[20] Such requests are characterized by politeness (tentativeness) and formal-ity. *Perhaps you would* (3 examples) and *perhaps you could* (4 examples) were the most frequent patterns, but other patterns also occur (as in example (45)):

(43) A [ə] . per^haps you could give :me a 'ring :bǎck#
      C ^yés#
(8.3 379–80)

(44)   per^haps you would 'give me a _telephone _call at
           !three [əu] f=ive# .
      BH ^one {five} :[əù] 'five# . ^thank yòu#
(9.3 735–7)

Example (45) has the function of suggestion or advice:

(45) BX per^haps it 'would be :bětter#
          if you ^put it :dǒwn# .
          [ə:] a^mòng [ði: ']# .
          [ə:m] - - - ^{lètters} and :sǒ on#
(9.3 1043–6)

If, as a request marker, has the pragmatic force of 'a polite concession towards the addressee, who is not expected to refuse the speaker's request' (Perkins, 1983: 124). Some of the request formulas which are tentative and formal are *if you would* (2 examples) and *if you could* (6 examples), and *if you can* (1 example):

(46) B ^if you'd col'lect them from :Mr !Gòrdon#
         +who ^will be 'going to+ [ði:] 'PLÀ meeting#
(9.1 722–3)

The routine phrase can be modified as in *if you could sweetly* or *if you could kindly*:

(Situation: Female university researcher to male administrator)
(47) A +if ^you could+ !sweetly 'put one in the pǒst#
      B ^yès#
         ^rîght# -
(8.4 508–10)

(Situation: Message left on the answering machine)
(48) CE ^if you _could 'very 'kindly 'leave a 'note on his
          dóor#
          to ex^pláin this# -
          ^thànks#
(9.3. 1152–4)

The pattern was used once for an offer (invitation):

(49) C *[ə:m]* . ^if you come 'over to !Tǔesday#
         if you **^want** to come up
      B **[mhm]**

(C to my :house and have a :còffee#
and ^or a . "^shèrry#
and ^have a !nàtter abóut it#
^[?]I'll be !very _willing to do "!thàt with 'you#
(8.2 479–84)

I wonder and the more polite *I wondered* (10 examples) were used as downtoners of the request (see Leech 1983: 118, 121):

(50)   B   good ^mǒrning#
             I ^wonder if you could 'put me on your
             :mâiling-list 'please {for ^prôperties#}#
(8.2 2–3)

(51)   w   I ^wonder if you'd :tell us fìrst# .
             ^what you your:self would !like to be [s] :see to
             be dóne {in this ^mátter#}# -
(5.3 8–9)

(52)   B   well I ^wondered if you could . per:haps give her
             a !mèssage 'for#
       C   ^yès#
          ^cèrtainly#
      (B ^Mr Ssòames# -
(9.1 31–4)

The progressive form of *wonder* in combination with the past tense adds to the tentativeness and politeness of the request:

(53)   B   so I was ^wondering if a :message could be
             :((given)) 'to Mr :Ssòames# -
             Mr ^Matthew Ssòames# -
(9.1 8–9)

Phrases like *I would be grateful if you could* are extremely tentative and formal. *Grateful* can itself have an intensifier (*very, most, extremely*):

(Situation: Message left by the caller on the answering machine)
(54)   AT   [ə:] ^I'd be !véry grǎteful# .
            ^if you would [ə:] . !get in tòuch [ə]# .
            ^with [ði] !clàssics depártment#
            [ə:] . at ^Cǎroline 'College# .
(9.3. 358–61)

(Situation: Message left by the caller on the answering machine)
(55)   AQ   ^I would be !gràteful#
            if you could ^telephone mé#
            this ^afternóon# .
            in con^nection 'with . Pro'fessor :{Wàrmleg's} .
            tỳpescript# .
(9.3 330–3)

I should be glad if you would is a tentative request marker:

(56)   BC   I should be ^glád# .
            [?] if you would ^ásk him to tèlephone 'me# .
(9.3 687–8)

In comparison *I should be glad to, I should be interested to* are more direct or assertive:

(57)   CH   [ə:] . ^in re!plỳ to your . nóte# -
            ^I should be !glad to 'see . [ði] :two
            stúdents# -
(9.3 1198–9)

(58)   A   [m?] ^I should be 'interested to 'hear your
            con!clùsions#
(7.3. 1151)

The illocutionary force marker *I think it would be a good idea if* is a more polite variant of *I think you should*:

(59)   C   ^well I don't knòw#
            I ^think [n] ^I . I ^think it'd be a 'good idèa if 'you#
            ^got in !tòuch with the 'porter's _lodge _to# -
            ^otherwise they 'might 'think they were a bòmb or
            'something#
(9.1 266–9)

I think it'd be a good idea if expresses advice, i.e. the belief that doing it is beneficial to the hearer (see Bach and Harnish 1979: 49). The utterance conveys a degree of imposition since the speaker intends that the addressee should take the speaker's belief as the reason for acting. The phrase is typically combined with a statement of the undesirable consequences of not carrying out the action ('otherwise they might think they were a bomb').

4.14.2   Want *and* need *statements*

A *want*-statement (5 examples) expresses the speaker's wishes directly. *I want you to* is direct and assertive as a request:

(Situation: Legal cross-examination; Speaker b is a male plaintiff)
(60)   b   I ^want you to 'witness my . 'signature to 'my
            wìll# .
(11.1 763)

The prosody is typically a fall tone. A more tentative correspondence is *I'd like you to* (15 examples):

(61)   A   and said . we've ^got a rather :mòre
            {e^laborate ma:chìne#}#

((that)) we'd ^like you to do ((a))
bro*chùre*
for#
(1.3 137–8)

The following requests are characterized by polite distancing since the agent is not mentioned explicitly (see section 4.17):

(62)   I'd like an enquìry to be máde #
for a new book for the lĭbrary#
(9.3 55–6)

(63)   AV [ə:] I'd ^like your 'help [ə:] in :trans'lating a
'small . :Latin !phrǎse# .
(9.3 409)

The speaker uses the agentless passive:

(Situation: Telephone call between business associates. Speaker B is a female university lecturer and Speaker C is a male estate agent)

(64)   C ^can I hèlp you# .
B [əm] . hel^lò#
I'd ^like to be 'put on your :màiling-'list
pléase#
(8.2 13–15)

In examples (65) and (66), the request is even more indirect since the hearer's permission is asked for:

(Situation: Radio discussion)
(65)   m ^n=ow# I would ^like if I :mǎy#
to ^turn to 'two pòints#
(5.6 910–12)

(Situation: Radio discussion)
(66)   m ^now I'd !like to 'carry 'on from thére#
^very brìefly if I máy# .^just to clárify#
^your 'own àttitudes# -
(5.6 355–8)

In examples (67) and (68) all reference to the hearer is absent:

(67)   A ^Ǐ want to 'speak to Mr "Chàllam#
in *"^room .* .
X *speaking*
A ^room five eight _[əù]#
(9.2 4–7)

I wanted to is more polite than *I want* on a scale of relative politeness:

(68)   B [ə:m] I ^wanted to 'speak to Pro'fessor :Hòkins'
_secretary#
(8.1 703)

In examples (69) and (70) the speaker makes the request in a maximally direct form by expressing his need (2 examples):

(Situation: Conversation between equals. Speaker b is a female language teacher and Speaker c is a male computer specialist)

(69)   b +^I+ need a !tòp up# -

      c ^ŎK#

         ^you top ùp#

(4.4 970–2)

(Situation: Message left on the answering machine)

(70)   AX [ə:m] . I ^need some informătion# .

        ^on the pro!cĕdure# .

        [ə:] . ^for !M'A exàminers# - - .

(9.3 510–12)

4.14.3 *Mitigated indirect requests in the form of interrogative sentences*

A large number of indirect requests have the form of *yes-no* questions containing one of the modal auxiliaries *can / could, will / would*. These can be described in terms of a sentence stem and constraints on its generative capacity. Table 4.6 captures what variants can be generated by 'inflection' and I have also shown some variants created by downtoning of the requestive stem. Of the examples, 104 had a question-form compared with the 87 examples which were assertion-based (see Table 4.5). Only two modal auxiliaries (*can/could, will/would*) occurred in the place of the modal auxiliary in the stem. As pointed out by Faerch and Kasper (1989: 228), other modal auxiliaries are either unacceptable or represent a marked choice, such as the formal *able to* in:[21]

(Situation: Message left on the answering machine)

(71)   BO [ə:m] . I'm ^sorry to impose . 'yet [ə] a :further

        [ə:m] 'task on Ma:lĭnda# -

        ^in the 'way of [ə:] "!bòok scróunging# .

        ^but I would be ex!tremely grăteful# .

        ^if !either to'day 'or :Mŏnday# .

        [ə:m] ^you would be !able 'to . :fĭnd 'for 'me#

        ^preferably at !Fŏyle's 'cut 'price# .

        and ^fàiling 'that# .

        at ^Dìllon's#

        ^where 'they 'have :àny 'sort of#

        ^cut príce# .

        the ^following vŏlumes#

        ^of . !Plŭtarch's# .

(9.3 821–32)

Depending on the choice of modal auxiliary in the stem and the type of modification, we can derive a number of morphosyntactic patterns, each

Table 4.6: Request markers derived from a stem in the form of hearer-oriented questions with a modal auxiliary in the LLC

Type of marker	Number of examples
could you	25
can you	20
would you	13
will you	10
could you ... please	6
could you please	3
would you like to	3
would you mind	2
would you ... please	2
do you think you could	2
can you ... please	1
please could you	1
could you possibly	1
could you kindly	1
could you sweetly	1
could you perhaps	1
could you just	1
could you not	1
couldn't you	1
will you please	1
will you just	1
would you care to	1
would you be good enough to	1
would you please	1
can't you	1
won't you	1
could you just	1
could you possibly	1
Total	104

of which needs to be described in terms of prosody, function, politeness, style, discourse type and situation.

4.14.3.1 *CAN/COULD YOU*

Can you was modified only in a single example (*can you VP please*). The phrase is typically used for minor favours in transactional settings such as telephone calls. There were 8 examples of the pattern *can you hold on* (*hang on*):

(72) A ^nò#
         ^he's !thĕre#
         but ^can !you !hold !ŏn#
      B ^yés#
(7.3 119–22)

Compare also:

(73) A [ə:] ^can you àsk 'her 'to [ə:m]# -
         ^to . !ring _her solìcitors# -
         ^Cŏrdham and 'Co# -
(9.1 286–8)

(Situation: Private telephone call. Speaker B is the sister of Speaker A)
(74) A but I'll ^[bil?] ^can you tell 'mum ((I'll)) be
         làte# – .
      B all ^rìght#
(7.3 1133–4)

(Situation: Male broker to female university teacher)
(75) A can you ^leave it with mé#
         ^I'll . !see if I can find !òut#
      B ^OƘ#
         ['m]
(8.1 297–300)

Could you was frequently modified by *please*. *Could you VP please* can, in
fact, be regarded as the preferred or unmarked way of making a request
because of the frequency of the phrase:

(76) B ^and ((!also)) could you :get some :chèese
         'please# -
      A I'll ^gèt some# .
         ^yés# .
(7.2 525–7)

(77) A *well* ^could you ex'plain 'what you 'mean in
         :sìmpler 'English Bárry#
(2.14 84)

(78) B ^so !could _you - "{get who'ever it ís} to :send
         them óff# .
         you ^know
(8.2 1075–7)

The phrase *could you ask him if he would mind* is tentative and formal:

(79) CC ^could you àsk him#
          ^if he would mínd . rìnging 'me# .
          be^tween . !{twèlve} and 'twelve : thȳrty# -
(9.3 1130–2)

The request can be further modified by the following *because*-clause:

(80) B **(- laughs)** ^anti-Se!mìtic a'gain#
      a yeah .
      B ^s=o#
         ^could you mèntion 'it to 'him#
         cos ^I've in'vited 'him as wèll#
      a yes - *OK*
      B *^OK̀#*
(7.1 1433–9)

Negation of the modality component (represented by *can't you*, *couldn't you* and *won't you*) was only found in isolated examples. In example (81), *can't you* suggests impatience because the addressee is not doing what the speaker thinks he ought to be doing:

(Situation: Speaker B is the sister of Speaker A, the requestee)
(81) B ^can't you 'do it this afternŏon#
         ^tell ((the)) 'prof you've :got you're ^bŭsy# -
(7.3 1113–14)

Similarly, *couldn't you just* implicates that the speaker is reproachful:

(Situation: Conversation between equals; Speaker B is a female teacher and Speaker C a male computer specialist)
(82) B *oh* ^dêar#
      C but ^couldn't you just swǎllow them#
         ((^whóle#))
(4.6 91–2)

Could you is both hedged and modified in the following example where the institutionalized setting requires formality:

(Situation: Message left on the answering machine)
(83) AS do you ^think you could 'possibly 'ring 'me at
          :eight 'four séven# .
          ^one 'two 'double [= əu]# .
          ex^t=ension# - - -
(9.3 351–3)

4.14.3.2 *WILL/WOULD YOU*

The simple *will you* is illustrated in examples (84) and (85):

(84) A ^will you say {thànk you} to :Bǎbcock for# .
         ^going to !gĕt you *. (({^fór me#}#))*
      B *^yès#
         ^OḰ#*
         ^OḰ#
(7.2 666–70)

(85) B **^tell us** ^Gordon !will you 'come *out of that
         létter#*
         ^tell us a
      c *no*
      (B _good film to 'go and 'see#
(2.10 585–6)

In both examples, *will you* is fairly direct and assertive. In comparison, *would* is tentative and suggests social distance and formality. The following two examples are taken from an interview with prospective undergraduates. The interviewer is responsible for the following requests:

(86) a [ə:] would you call in on . Miss Tannenbaum [ə:] do
         people have to see [ði:] . tutor to
(3.5 518)

(87) a well now [ə:] would you tell us about the argument
         - of the last paragraph . and . over the page -
(3.1 275)

In this context, *will you* would sound too peremptory. It is noteworthy that *would* occurred more frequently than *will* with the polite *please* (3 examples):

(Situation: Telephone conversation. Speaker A is a female administrator and Speaker B is a university secretary)
(88) A ^would !you tĕll him#
         (– laughs)
      B "^rîght#
         "^{Î} "wîll#
      A (- laughs)
(7.3 43–7)

(Situation: Legal cross-examination where Speaker a is the male counsel)
(89) a ^n=ow#
         (- coughs) - ^if !your - would you ^tùrn 'to# .
         [ði] ^last pàge# -
         [ði] - ^sècond 'page of thát 'please# - -
(11.1 806–9)

Would you can be expanded by means of *like, love, prefer, care to, mind, be good enough*:

(90) A you ^còuldn't very well 'say#
         ^well !you knów#
         ^would you mind :starting a:gă̆in#
         and . *^telling us*
(2.8 690–3)

The following phrase can be labelled formal and tentative:

(Situation: Conversation between disparates. Speaker A is a male administrator; Speaker C a female undergraduate)
(91)   A +^would you be+ _g=ood enough# .
            to *^have a 'look and 'let me knów# -
            ^write me a létter# .
            if it ^isn't thére#*
(3.3 375–8)

Would you like to may introduce a polite invitation (see section 4.20):

(92)   A would you ^like to come and mèet us#
(2.12 588)

4.14.3.3 REQUESTS IN THE FORM OF PERMISSION QUESTIONS

The permission question is paradigmatically flexible and can be described as a stem where the category MODAL can be replaced by a restricted number of modal auxiliaries:

C   MODAL + I + VP

The variation permitted is shown in Table 4.7. *May I* (*can I*) is used for fairly trivial requests of a routinized type. *Please* and *just* were frequent as modifiers, and many of the requests occurred in standard situations on the telephone:

Table 4.7: Requests in the form of permission questions in the LLC

Type of request marker	Number
let me[22]	20
may I	11
can I	10
could I	6
may I just	5
could I ... please	5
may I ... please	4
could I just	2
can I ... please	3
may I be permitted to	1
I wonder if I could	1
can we	1
can I just	1
Total	70

(93)   B   ^can I 'speak 'to !Jìm 'Johnstone pléase#
(9.1 133)

(94)   C   ^can I 'take a méssage 'please#
       A   ^{yès} plèase#
(9.2 275–6)

Another telephone phrase is illustrated in example (95):

(95)   A   [ə:] . ^may I 'leave my :tĕlephone 'number#
       C   ^ìf you wóuld#
           ^yés#
(8.3.376–8)

The permission question is also used to introduce new arguments, to interrupt another speaker, to ask for one's turn, to hold the floor, etc. In example (96), the speaker asks for permission to return to a previous topic:

(96)   tl   [kə] . ^can !I just come báck#
       f   ^yes Téd Leather#
       tl   with with a ^supplemèntary on thís#
            because ^this is a 'very im:portant :quèstion# .
(5.1 702–5)

In example (97), the permission question is used for a polite interruption:

(97)   j   can ^I . butt in 'here for !just a sécond#
           [f] ^cutting !rìght a'cross Géoffrey# .
           but . ^your 'wife is :hère Géoffrey# .
           and she's ^willing to 'come ín# .
           and ^talk wìth us {for a ^mìnute#}# .
(6.5 637–41)

Can we is not a permission question but a suggestion committing both the speaker and the hearer to an action:

(98)   j   ^*one sécond#*
           ^can we 'go báck a bit#
(6.5 680)

The following request is modified by *just* and followed by an explanation:

(99)   A   [? ə] . ^could I 'just get 'all this :dŏwn#
           be^cause
       B   ^yĕs O=K# .
           ^y=es#
       A   ^I've !never ((!hàd anything 'quite like
       A   'Sowerbarn befóre#))
(9.2 145–9)

I wonder if I could is tentative and formal:

(Situation: Radio interview where Speaker a is the interviewer)
(100)   a   I ^wonder if 'I could get you to _think alòud a
            a 'little#
            a^bout ['ði] . the :i'deal of a :social
            "!còntract#
            or "^còmpact# -
(6.3 429–31)

The request can be modified by *please*:

(101)   B   I ^wonder if I could 'speak to [bi] . 'Mr Pârker
            'please#
            ^or at !least 'leave him a mèssage#
            if he's ^not !thĕre#
(8.2 1188–90)

   Let me see in example (102) can be compared with *can I see* and has
therefore been included in Table 4.7. The illocutionary function conveyed
by the phrase is that of a suggestion:

(102)   A   +^let me sèe your 'beautiful+ 'camera# .
            ^I !haven't seen thóse#
            ^since **they** were . ^((óne))#
            ^since I !{làst} fiddled with it#
(2.10 281–4)

4.15   Lexical mitigating devices

As Stubbs points out (1983: 185), mitigation is a 'basic interactive dimension' of spoken language. By taking into account mitigation, we get a
detailed and fine-grained picture of what syntagmatic request patterns
there are.

   Mitigating elements or 'downtoners' (Holmes 1984) are elements which
do not themselves have illocutionary function but modify the speech act.
They belong to the interpersonal rather than the referential component of
language and they facilitate the cooperation between the partners in the
conversation by adding 'padding' to speech acts which can potentially
create conflicts by threatening the hearer's face. Mitigating strategies are
especially likely with speech acts such as requests, which are thought to
be competitive.

   Downtoners consist of lexical, grammatical, morphological and
prosodic devices which can cooccur in the same larger pattern. They
occur in stems and are not generated by grammatical rules. Functionally,
they can be subclassified as 'disclaimers'[23] (*if I may, if you've got time*),

'hedges' (*I think, I'm wondering if*), 'tag questions' (*right, would you*), 'consultative devices' (*do you think, you haven't got, would you mind*), 'disarmers' (*I am sorry but*), 'defocalizers' (*how about*), 'politeness markers' (*please, kindly, sweetly*), and 'minimizers' (*just*). Here also belong mood (e.g. the strategic use of an interrogative sentence to express politeness), the choice of subject, tense, aspect, modality, and negation when they have a downtoning function.

From Goffman's well-known discussion on 'face-work' (Goffman 1955; cf. Stubbs 1983: 176), it is easy to get the impression that mitigating signals are 'diffusely located in the flow of events in the encounter'. Their occurrence in particular speech acts and situations is, however, systematic and needs to be described. What makes downtoners so difficult to analyse is that we must describe both the patterns in which they occur and the situations in which they are used.

I think (7 examples) 'hedges', i.e. it 'expresses the speaker's tentativeness over the truth value of the matrix clause' (Quirk et al. 1985: 1114). It does not, however, precede all types of request (**I think you can get in touch with him*). On the other hand, it is frequent when the speaker suggests something, i.e. expresses an opinion that something is preferable or beneficial for the hearer (*I think it's better, I think it'd be a good idea if, I think that the best thing to do, I think you'd better*):

(103)   C   ^well I don't knòw#
            I ^think [n] ^I . I ^think it'd be a 'good idèa if
            'you# ^got in !tòuch with the 'porter's _lodge
            _to#-
(9.1 266–8)

(104)   A   ^wèll#
            I ^think the :bèst thing to dó#
            is ^probably to :come to [ði] 'main èntrance#
            in ^BЎre 'Street#
(8.3 988–91)

Do you think (3 examples) is a consultative device involving the hearer directly in the interaction (CCSARP coding manual, p. 283; Faerch and Kasper 1989: 234) that is only used with requests which have question form (e.g. *do you think you could (possibly), do you think it's possible*):

(105)   A   [ə:m] ^do you 'think you could :pùt this 'to
            him# -
            ^to to !sěnd me 'these#
        C   ^yes cèrtainly#
            ((^I wìll#))
(9.2 285–8)

(106)   AS   do you ^think you could 'possibly 'ring 'me at
               :eight 'four séven# .
               ^one 'two 'double [= əu]# .
(9.3 350–2)

Tag-questions qualify the imperative. The function of the tag is to
express intimacy and friendliness:

(107)   B   ^rĭght#
            ^sit down hére would you# - - -
(3.5b 552)

(108)   A   [ə:] ^come and 'sit ":hĕre 'will you#
(3.6 1911)

A performative verb can be regarded as a downtoning as well as an
illocutionary device, especially if the verb is itself mitigated:

(109)   A   ^what were you 'going to suggèst#
        B   ^no I was !going to sug'gest that we 'might 'look
            through Hàbi'tat#
            and ^see [s] if we can 'find her ánything *but
            [ə]#*
(7.2 155–7)

So-called 'content downtoners' (see Holmes 1984: 360) only attenuate
the propositional content of the request. *Little, a (little) bit (of)* signals that
the propositional content is uncertain and that the action requested is of
no great importance:

(110)   C   [ə:m] ^yês#
            ^let me 'just have a 'little 'look at my díary#
(8.2 1209)

Similarly, *and so on* (literally indicating a series) may have a softening
effect on the request:

(111)   BX   per^haps it 'would be :bĕtter#
             if you ^put it :dŏwn# .
             [ə:] a^mòng [ði: ']# .
             [ə:m] - - - ^{lètters} and :sŏ on#
(9.3 1043–6)

(112)   B   ^Jàcqueline#
            ^do 'try and 'find :whĕn and 'so on# -
(2.5 147–8)

The downtoning *please* is especially interesting since there are both
formal and situational constraints on its use in requests.

4.15.1   *Please*

Can you please is a request just as much as the simple *can you*, but *please* does not occur in all types of requestive stem. *Please* occurred, for example, in the patterns shown in Table 4.8.

   Please is especially frequent with imperatives. The large number of *please* after *could you* and after permission questions (*can I, may I, could I*) is also noteworthy. Since *please* is mainly used in situations in which formal politeness is needed, it is also frequent in some types of writing such as business letters and written notices. The following examples are taken from the SEU corpus:

(Situation: Business letter)
(113)   Could you please note that my address has changed.
(W 7–15)

(Situation: Printed notice)
(114)   And please note: Blessed are they who pay up and sign the
          Hash Book without being asked.
(W 13–4)

Also, there is some evidence from a study by Pufahl Bax that *please* is more important in writing than in speech. When Pufahl Bax examined requests with the function of assigning work in both speech and writing,

Table 4.8:   The distribution of *please* with different request markers

Type of request marker	Number of examples of *please*
imperatives	27[24]
could you	12[25]
NP (*a black coffee please*)	8
could I	5[26]
may I (we)	4
can I	3
I would (I'd) like to, I'd love to	3
let me	3
would you	3
is (NP) there	2
other patterns (*what initial please,* *black or white please*)	2
can you	1
I will have	1
will you	1
Total	75

she found that *please* was missing from the spoken data while half of the requests (directives) in her written corpus contained *please* (Pufahl Bax 1986: 688).

Please was frequent in telephone calls in the London-Lund Corpus (48 examples), especially in routinized situations. Fifteen examples occurred in discussion, and only 10 in (formal and informal) conversation. The phrase was, for example, used in the situations listed in Table 4.9.

Table 4.9: The use of *please* in requests made on the telephone

asking the other person to wait on the line	*hold on please*
	can you hold on please
	just a moment please
	one moment please
	hang on a minute please (2 examples)
	please hold
	could you hold the line please
asking to speak to a special person	*I wonder if I could speak to (…) please*
	I wanted to speak to (…) please
	is she there please
	could I speak to (…) please (4 examples)
	could I have (…) please
	can I speak to (…) (2 examples)
	Mrs X please
asking sb to call back	*please could you ask (…) to ring back*
	could you ring me and let me know please
	please could you ring
	could you please telephone
	would you please ring
	could you please ring me back
leaving a message	*will you please tell (…)*
	would you please talk to (…)
	please get an urgent message to (…)
asking for an extension, a special department, telephone number, etc	*principal's office please*
	Mrs X please
	extension (…) please
	the department of (…) please
	(telephone number) please
	could you put me through to (…)
other standard situations on the telephone	*what initial please*
	could you please give my apologies to (…)
	would you tell me if you got the message please
	can I take a message please

It is the operator's job to tell the caller to wait on the line, and the caller has the right to leave a message or ask somebody to call back. No extra politeness is therefore required besides *please*. Another routinized situation is accepting something to eat or drink:

(115) A +I'd ^lòve one of thóse please#+ .
          ^thànk you# .
(4.3 392–3)

(116) c whisky or
       A "^shèrry pléase#
(2.11 5–6)

When *please* occurs in less routinized situations, it conveys appeal or persuasion (8 examples):

(117) b ^nó#
          I ^think I'd 'like to a!vòid that if I *máy#*
       m *oh ^plèase* do#
          ^yès#
(5.6 171–4).

In example (117), *please* is not an illocutionary force marker. According to Markkanen, *please* is a shortened form of 'may it please you', 'if it pleases you' (Markkanen 1985: 89).

Please (with falling intonation) in the initial position can also convey irritation, rudeness, criticism. This is the case when it modifes a request not to do something or to stop doing something (see section 4.19):

(118) m ^plèase 'have the 'manners to lét me _finish# -
(5.6 379)

(119) b *oh ^plèase#*
          don't **^give us !any 'more quotàtions#**
(5.6 576–7)

Social and contextual constraints on *please* have also been noticed by Holmes (1983). In a study of teachers' directives in the classroom, Holmes found that *please* was relatively frequent as a softener when the teacher addressed the whole class (Holmes 1983: 101). In smaller group discussions where the social distance between the participants was reduced, *please* never occurred.

Downtoners have a variety of desirable or undesirable effects or implicatures which can be compared with the perlocutionary functions of speech acts. *Please*, for example, can be experienced as unfriendly or even rude:

> Excuse me a second, would you please? Funny how it's got ruder to say please than not, Jake thought to himself as the doctor began to turn slowly through a small leather-bound book on his desk.
> (Kingsley Amis, *Jake's thing*, 1978: 4)

4.15.2 *Just*

Just and *please* occur in different request patterns and in different social situations. On the one hand, *just* can be described as a restrictive subjunct which picks out a particular referent and contrasts it with another referent (Quirk et al. 1985: 604). But *just* can also be an attitude diminisher, i.e. a downtoning intensifier 'which seeks to imply that the force of the item concerned is limited' (Quirk et al. 1985: 598). If we choose this interpretation, the meaning of *just* is minimizing just like *perhaps, please, and so on,* etc. *Just* serves as a request marker in:

(120) A ((and ^will you just 'come)) this wày#
           per^haps you'd 'like to 'tell us 'what you wànt#
(2.3 288–9)

(121) B *^could* you just 'put them 'somewhere cárefully
           +'for me#+
(7.1 1467)

In addition, the minimizing or downtoning *just* was found in permission questions:

(122) b ++now ^may++ I 'just 'talk to 'Mr +Dánby
       m +^yes plèase do# -
           ^dò# - -
           ^yès please#+
(5.6 486–9)

In examples (123) and (124), however, it is difficult to know if *just* is minimizing or restrictive:

(123) AX I ^just want the !single . :page réference# .
           ^to 'his dis'cussion 'of :that :pàssage# .
           "^rìght# .
(9.3 504–6)

(124) B ^just a mò#
(8.4 766)

Just characteristically modifies imperatives and was unusual with forms such as *can you / could you* (see Table 4.10):

(125) D [ə:] ^Pàul# [ə: dzh] ^just 'tell us {brìefly} whàt# .
           [ə?] the ^main !dìfferences you 'feel be_tween [ə]#
           the ^teaching we 'do :hère#
           and the ^teaching you're 'doing at :Bèaton# -
(3.6 492–3)

(126) A +((^don't know 'when I shall))+ be ín 'but [əm]# -
           ^you just kéep it 'for me# -
(7.2 192–3)

The social effects of *just* are described by Wierzbicka, who writes that *'just* easily lends itself to mildly positive (reassuring, defensive, apologetic, even praising) interpretations' (Wierzbicka 1991: 351). In imperatives, however, its function is, above all, depreciatory, as pointed out by Lee:

> ... the speaker suggests that the action involved is a relatively unimportant one – that it will perhaps involve little effort on the (agent's) part, and that it has no significant consequences.
> (Lee 1987: 383)

Chafe, on the other hand, stresses that the effect of *just* is friendliness, enthusiasm and involvement (Chafe 1982).

I have discussed internal mitigation at some length in order to illustrate that there is a large number of devices which may contribute to the politeness of a request. As Blum-Kulka points out, such devices have been relatively neglected in comparison with indirectness:

> ... it is important to stress that levels of directness are only one dimension of linguistic variation available to speakers for softening the degree of coerciveness. The importance of the second dimension, namely the verbal and non-verbal means subsumed under mitigation, has been relatively neglected in the politeness literature.
> (Blum-Kulka 1990: 270)

4.16   Internal and external modifiers

Just, please, perhaps, if, etc, carry no propositional meaning of their own. Following Faerch and Kasper (1989: 222), we shall call them internal modifiers. They are fairly short and modify the request 'internally' as downtoning devices. For example:

> MODAL you VP (*please*)

Requests can also contain conversational moves giving 'support' (justification, explanation) for the request. When the request is modified by 'supportive' moves either before or after the stem, it is externally modified (Faerch and Kasper 1989: 22). External modifiers can have considerable length and are only loosely attached to the stem. They are probably less automatic and conventionalized than internal modifiers (see Faerch and Kasper 1989: 244).

There is probably no strict boundary between internal and external modifiers just as there is no fixed boundary between conventional requests or routines and non-conventional requests.

4.16.1   Requests and external modifiers

External modifiers are conversational moves made up of whole clauses or phrases which are normally placed before or after the request proper.

Table 4.10: The distribution of *just* with different types of request marker

Type of request marker	Number of examples with *just*
just + imperative (imperative + *just*)	13
may I just	8
let me just (*just let me*)	3
you just (*just you*) + imp	3
could you just	3
can I just	2
could I just	2
can you just	1
I just want to	1
will you just	1
other patterns	1
Total	38

Prosodically, they are separate tone units. Intuitively, there seem to be several types of external modifier, which all in some way prepare the ground for the request. They may provide justification for the following request, soften it, or are part of the speaker's strategy to control the hearer's actions. Since their main function is to signal that a request will follow, they can be described as pre-requests (Levinson 1983: 356f).

A grounder is a pre-request which may be taken as an explanation (reason, justification) for the request, as illustrated in:

(127)   d   Frank I don't think Nancy – understood your
          references to – teaching alphabet – and all the
          rest of it . because . did you know what Frank was
          doing *((2 to 3 sylls))*
    c   *IITU* ITA did you say
    d   [m] so you might put her in the picture as regards
          your occupation . *((2 to 3 sylls))*
(2.4 54–6)

In example (127), the grounder is separated from the proper request by an insertion sequence. Consider also the following example of a pre-request followed by a more explicit request:

(128)   B   ^there 'is ['ei] !packet of rìce# .
          ^in ['ði:] :cùpboard# .
          ^on I ^think on 'top of _where the !òther rice .
    A   ^yés#

(B 'is# -
   can ^you !put it in :lots of :well 'salted
   :wàter# -
A ^yés# .
   ^how mùch#

(7.2 511–16)

Example (129) illustrates a combination of external modifiers:

(129) A ^Cuthbert {Yòrk} is :awfully 'anxious to have a
          còpy {for the "^files 'here#}#
          and - ^I !feel awfully ":sĭlly#
          but the ^thing is I !don't seem to :hàve one#
          I ^wonder if [?] 'you could very _sweetly sĕnd
          us 'one# -

(8.4 483–6)

A compliment (*now this is very interesting*) is another way of preparing
the ground for a request which may not be popular:

(130) (a **yes** now this is very interesting because we
           haven't thought of this sort of .
       A ^I've got "!lots and "!lots *of :thĕm#*
       (a *intermed*iate ['] category may we borrow these
       A ^[ḿ]#

(2.2 160–3)

A 'disarmer' preceding a request minimizes the imposition on the
hearer's privacy:

(131) BO [ə:m] . I'm ^sorry to impose . 'yet [ə] a :further
           [ə:m] 'task on Ma:lĭnda# -
           ^in the 'way of [ə:] "!bòok scróunging# .
           ^but I would be ex!tremely grăteful# .
           ^if !either to'day 'or :Mŏnday# .
           [ə:m] ^you would be !able 'to . :fĭnd 'for 'me#
           ^preferably at !Fŏyle's 'cut 'price# .
           and ^fàiling 'that# .
           at ^Dìllon's#
           ^where 'they 'have :àny 'sort of#
           ^cut príce# .
           the ^following vŏlumes#
           ^of . !Plŭtarch's# .

(9.3 821–32)

(132) AV it's ^nòt úrgent#
           but I ^would be 'grateful if you ((could)) 'give me a càll# .

(9.3 420–1)

(133) b *^ăctually#* .
     I ^hardly 'like to :sày this#
     in ^view of your !rude re:mărks but [əm]# .
     ^could you give me an'other
(6.2 304)

A pre-request in the form of a question provides the hearer with the opportunity of finding an excuse for not complying with the request (Levinson 1983: 360–4). The function of the question is checking whether the hearer is willing and able to carry out the request:

(134) B [ə:m] – I[?] ^wonder if you could :hèlp me#
     ^could you 'tell me what [ði:] :starting
     :sălary#
     ^of a - a ^teacher 'coming . a ^qualified 'teacher
     from a 'college of 'edu!càtion [?] ís# .
(8 3 1145–7)

(135) A are ^you in a hùrry#
     can I ^have this trans'ferred to my 'phone
     upstăirs#
     B [ə:m] ^well the !thing is that [? ə] . it's ^not my
     phòne#
     A ^OǨ#
(8.4 109–12)

These devices are mainly 'face-saving'. Discourse markers such as *well, well now, the thing is, you know, what I'm leading up to* may also be used to hedge a request:

(136) a well now [ə:] would you tell us about the argument
     - of the last paragraph . and . over the page -
(3.1 275)

(137) a so really what I'm leading up to is saying if
     you can let us have ((your)) private letters [əm] we should be
     very grateful
     A ^yés#
(2.2 67–8)

(138) A ^wèll#
     I ^think the :bèst thing to dó#
     is ^probably to :come to [ði] 'main èntrance#
     in ^Bўre 'Street#
(8.3 988–91)

4.16.2 Combinations of modifiers

To be sure, little is known about the effect of combining politeness strategies. Perkins (1983: 121f) claims that one can make a rough assessment of the politeness potential of a sentence by counting the number of cooccurring modal expressions, and Holmes emphasizes how 'the skilful selection from amongst the vast range of linguistic and non-linguistic devices which are available to express affective meaning enables speakers to communicate their attitudes to their addressees very precisely ' (Holmes 1984: 350). Thus the following scale ranges from less to more polite requests (Perkins 1983: 121f):

Less polite	Stop writing.
	It's necessary for you to stop writing.
	It may be necessary for you to stop writing.
	It may possibly be necessary for you to stop writing.
	I imagine it may possibly be necessary for you to stop writing.
More polite	I would imagine it may possibly be necessary for you to stop writing.

The occurrence of several polite modifiers is illustrated by example (139):

(139)   B   ^I was :thìnking áctually#
            I ^((wouldn't)) . I would ^quite _like an
            oppor'tunity _to . you ^knów# .
            ^do a 'bit more :lìstening#
(9.1 477–9)

The request consists of the stem *I would like (an opportunity) to* and modifiers. The stem is embedded in *I was thinking*, which expresses the speaker's uncertainty. The polite effect of the clause is due to the tentativeness of the verb *think* and the modifying effect of the past tense and the progressive. *Actually* and *you know* are discourse markers with a polite, mitigating function, which are not, however, restricted to requests. Other noteworthy features are the circumlocution *do a bit more listening* and the use of *I would like an opportunity to* rather than the more abrupt *I would like to*. Finally, the adverbials *a bit* ('do a bit more listening') and *quite* ('I would quite like') have the effect of further downgrading the impact of the request on the hearer.

Such examples are characteristic of tentative and formal phrases which are appropriate in certain situations only. Example (139), which is taken from a telephone call among friends, shows that elaborate politeness characterized by modification of requests is also needed when people know each other well. Following Holmes (1990: 187), we can hypothesize that less certain relationships, that is, those between people who are neither strangers nor intimates, may also require mitigated requests. In Wolfson's bulge theory (1988) it is claimed that 'the two extremes of social distance – minimum and maximum – seem to call forth very similar behaviour, while relationships which are more toward the center show marked differences' (Wolfson 1988: 32; after Holmes 1990: 187).

4.17 Referential strategies

Referential strategies, i.e. strategies determining the reference of the subject in terms of the deictic categories speaker and hearer, can involve both a change of the perspective of the request and distancing from the hearer. It is the speaker's choice of referential strategy that determines if the speaker says *can I* or *can you*, *I would like to* or *would you like to*.

The pattern with a first person reference (found in 38.5 per cent of the examples) is illustrated in:

(140) A ^Ǐ want to 'speak to Mr "Chàllam#
            in *"^room .* .
       X *speaking*
       A ^room five eight _[əù]#
(9.2 4–7)

On the whole, a speaker-oriented strategy is characteristic of offers rather than of requests. A speaker-oriented request is illustrated in:

(141) A I would ^like to come 'back in the _after_noon if I
            !mǎy#
(1.10 950)

Roughly half of the requests (49.7 per cent) are instead hearer-oriented, as in:

(142) A [ə:] ^can you àsk 'her 'to [ə:m]# -
            ^to . !ring _her solìcitors# -
(9.1 286–7)

In some examples it is difficult to say if the perspective is that of the speaker or of the hearer:[27]

(143) AV it's ^nòt úrgent#
            but I ^would be 'grateful if you ((could)) 'give me a càll# .
(9.3 420–1)

A referential strategy, oriented to both the speaker and the hearer, is associated with suggestions:

(144) c we could ^stay in :bĕd 'later#
            in the ^mŏrning#
            ^còuldn't we# - -
(4.3 829–31)

The choice of reference is partly an automatic choice depending on the type of intended illocution. Referential strategies, however, can also have a mitigating or downtoning effect. By asking for permission to do something rather than asking the hearer to do it, the speaker indicates concern for the hearer's face-needs. Of special interest as mitigating devices are referential strategies which enable the speaker to create a distance to the hearer and to avoid responsibility for an act which may be experienced as threatening to the hearer's face. Such strategies, which Haverkate (1984: 79) calls defocalizing, are exemplified by impersonalizing devices such as *it is possible, it is a good idea, it would be better, the best thing to do, one could*:[28]

(145) A ^wèll#
          I ^think the :bèst thing to dó#
          is ^probably to :come to [ði] 'main èntrance#
          in ^B⌣ÿre 'Street#
(8.3 988–91)

(146) B ^but* . !if it 'would be 'possible to 'get them to
          go :ŭp#
(8.1 426)

It would be possible is more formal than *can you*. It is often softened by the 'consultative' *do you think*:

(147) CI [ə:m] . ^do you 'think it'd be :pòssible#
           to ^ask [?] :ěither 'Michael#
           ^or Pro'fessor :Fràncis# .
           [ə:m] - ^if the 'thing is . :òut yét# .
(9.3 1230–3)

The syntactic devices resulting from defocalization are related to House and Kasper's 'agent avoiders' (1981: 168). Thus a typical example is the agentless passive:

(148) B so I was ^wondering if a :message could be
          :((given)) to Mr :Ssòames# -
          Mr ^Matthew Ssòames# -
(9.la 8–9)

Other defocalizers are exemplified by *what about, how about, why not*:

(149) A ^l=ook# .
          [ə] ^what about 'double glàzing# - -
(3.4 291–2)

Defocalizers have the meaning suggestion or advice since they imply that the speaker has the hearer's benefit in mind:

(150) B ^yèah# .
       ^wèll#
       ^why not ^why not !dǒ that#
(7.3 1359–61)

Why not can be compared with the full form *why don't you*, which can also be described as a suggestion:

(151) B ((well)) I'm ^sǒrry about 'that# .
       ^why don't you 'do it hère# .
(7 3 1121–2)

Example (152) illustrates another type of defocalizing strategy. The elliptic imperative names the action to be performed rather than the performer:

(152)   ^next slìde ((pléase))
(2.8 934)

However, the elliptical request in example (152) seems to be motivated by the speaker's wish to be brief and efficient rather than by politeness or mitigation. (I return to a discussion of elliptical requests in section 4.19.)

4.18 Requests and pragmatic conventions

In a well-known analysis of indirect requests, Susan Ervin-Tripp discussed the interpretation of *Is Sybil there?* and *Can I speak to Sybil?*, which conventionally serve the function of bringing the desired person to the telephone:

> For instance, 'Is Sybil there?' (or the more general form 'Is X there' 'Is X in?', etc) is optimally a directive on the telephone when produced by the caller directly following the greeting. If it is a shout by a mother about her toddler, Sybil, who has disappeared upstairs, it is likely to be heard as an information request. (Ervin-Tripp 1976: 57f)

The relation between the linguistic form, the setting and the position in a larger discourse unit can be stated as a rule of interpretation:

> If a question contains *is (Name) there* or *can I speak to (Name)* and occurs at the beginning of the telephone call, it must be interpreted routinely as a request to be permitted to speak to the other person.
> (Houtkoop-Steenstra 1987: 65)

Another usage rule is needed to account for the interpretation of indirect requests in the classroom. According to Sinclair and Coulthard (1975: 32), the interrogative sentence *Can you play the piano, John?* is understood as a request or what they call command if the following conditions are fulfilled:

(i) it contains one of the modals *can, could, will, would* (and sometimes *be going to*);

(ii) if the subject of the clause is also the addressee;

(iii) the predicate describes an action which is physically possible at the time of the utterance.

Such usage or interpretation rules describe the meaning of requests on the basis of the discourse setting and form (see Holmes's 1983 discussion of teachers' directives).

The influence of the setting or discourse type on requests is clear and has been commented on in the discussion of the examples above. The largest problem, however, is constraining the information about the extra-linguistic situation in which a conventionalized indirect request occurs.

4.18.1 *Requests and the situation*

In any society a certain amount of conversational behaviour becomes fixed, i.e. 'participants know, so to speak, both where and who they are' because certain recurring features or parameters are set beforehand (House 1989: 107). Taking a clue from Bahns et al., we could say 'that it is not only the expression which is invariant and standardized, but it is also the situation, or . ... the situational frame that exhibits standardized recurring features' (Bahns et al. 1986: 695).

It is, however, difficult to know when a request is carried out as a matter of fact in a recurrent situation and when it involves planning on the basis of an assessment of the politeness required by the extralinguistic situation as well as the imposition involved in the request. One reason is that the conversationalists' role relationships are not fixed but depend on the setting. Depending on the role the speaker has at the moment, either more or less politeness may be required, as pointed out by Leech:

> Suppose a passenger *p* asks a driver *d* to stop the bus at a bus-stop. Very little politeness is required for this speech act, because it is the driver's job (*i.e.* his occupational duty) to let passengers get off at bus-stops. But now suppose that *p* asks *d* to stop the bus outside *p*'s house, where there is no bus-stop. In this case a great deal of politeness, as well as other redressive behaviour such [*sic*] apologizing and explaining, may be required. In both cases the amount of trouble or effort on the part of the driver is the same; but the imposition is far greater in the case where the driver is asked to do something 'as a personal favour' (Leech 1983: 129).

It is, however, not difficult to find examples illustrating that *can you, may I*, etc are bound to certain situations although there is not a simple relationship between routines and situational parameters. Blum-Kulka (1982: 46) observed that 'Can you ... , Could you tell me ... ' is the standard procedure in asking directions from a stranger in the street. And Gibbs (1985: 102) reported from a psycholinguistic experiment that the permission question ('may I') was frequently used in the context of buying stamps at the post office (26 per cent) but never in the situation of getting someone to fix a Xerox machine at the library.[29]

Gibbs concluded that the speaker prefers a routinized variant such as *can you* or *may I* when the request implies no extra effort or obstacles. Asking for stamps at the post office is an example of a situation in which the request is not associated with communicative difficulties because the legitimacy of the request is not in question. Similar examples of standardized requests from the London-Lund Corpus are also easy to find:

(153) C I'm ^sòrry#
           ^Doctor :Mărshall isn't ìn at the móment#
           ^can I 'take a méssage 'please#
       A ^{yès} plèase#
(9.2 273–6)

Asking the answerer to fetch the desired person is a standardized situation on the telephone, in which no extra politeness is required. Consequently, the request had a routinized form (*can/could I speak to, I want to speak to*, etc):

(154) A ^could I 'speak _to . 'Doctor :Màrshall 'please# .
       C [ə:m] . ^one mŏment 'please#
       A ^thank you *!very* mùch#
(9.2 268–70)

In simple, straightforward requests of this kind, language users follow the principle of being brief and efficient. The requests are normally short although they may contain modifiers like *just* or *please*, *do you think*, etc. They have a fixed form such as *can/could you (will/would you)* or the imperative.

(155) A [ə:m] ^do you 'think you could :pùt this 'to
           him# -
           ^to to !sĕnd me 'these#
       C ^yes cèrtainly#
           ((^I wĭll#))
(9.2 285–8)

(156) B *^could* you just 'put them 'somewhere
           cárefully
           +'for me#+
       a +put them+ safe . **yes** . I'll do that
(7.1 1467–8)

Such requests need not be 'supported' by a justification, but the speaker assumes that the hearer is able and willing to carry out the action in the immediate future.

There are a number of features which must be taken into account for the pragmatic description of indirect requests such as discourse setting and request type, style, politeness value, the social roles of the requester and requestee, etc.

4.18.2   Frames for requests

In routinized situations no extra politeness is needed, since people have certain rights and obligations and the requests do not involve any extra effort. This is illustrated by requests on the telephone, and requests for non-verbal goods (such as food). When the speaker asks for something trivial, or if the request can be characterized in terms of the obligation of the requestee to comply with the request (e.g. when the caller wants to leave a message on the telephone), the speaker uses a routinized form of a request which may be modified by *please*. In less stereotypic situations, such as asking a person to borrow money, or asking for information which is not easily available, the type of request would look different. Some frames for routines in recurrent situations are illustrated below.

FRAMES FOR ROUTINES IN RECURRENT SITUATIONS

A   *can you, could you*

Formal features

Function
requestive

Intonation
fall-rise tone

Continuation
okay, all right, certainly

Modification
please, just, do you think, etc

Politeness
ranging from less (*can you*) to more politeness (*could you*)

Style
unmarked (neither formal nor informal)

Situational features

Setting
at work, at home

Participants
(social roles) operator-caller
(personal roles) members of the same family

Types of requesting
asking for a small favour, asking for information, asking the caller to wait on the line on the telephone, asking someone to leave a message, asking to speak to a special person, asking for something in a shop, asking for food at table

B *I would like to, I want to*

Formal features	Situational features
Function requestive (order)	*Setting* at work, at home
Intonation fall tone	*Participants* (social roles) operator-caller, judges
Continuation okay, all right, certainly	and plaintiffs, secretaries and professors, business associates (personal roles) members of the same family
Modification please, if I may	*Types of requesting* asking for a favour, asking to speak
Politeness assertive	to another person on the telephone, asking for information
Style unmarked (neither formal nor informal)	

C *can I, may I*

Formal features	Situational features
Function (polite) request, suggestion, offer	*Setting* at work, at home
Intonation fall-rise tone	*Participants* (social roles) operator-caller
Continuation okay, all right, certainly	*Types of requesting* asking another person to wait on the
Modification just, please	line on the telephone, asking to speak to a special person, asking for something in a shop, asking for food at table, asking a business associate
Politeness tentative	for a favour, asking for permission to interrupt, to go back in the conversation, introduce an
Style unmarked (neither formal nor informal)	argument

4.19 Imperatives

In order to describe the function and situational constraints of indirect requests, it is necessary to make a comparison with direct requests, in particular with imperatives. Generally, the differences between imperatives and indirect requests have been emphasized rather than the similarities. There are, however, several reasons for including imperatives in the investigation here. An imperative can, for example, be used to make a polite request just like *can you* but under other conditions. Unlike what is usually thought, the imperative can be mitigated although there are constraints on what downtoners it cooccurs with. The imperative is, however, difficult to analyse since it occurs in both routinized and non-routinized situations, it can be polite or impolite, and its functions range from requests to offers.

If one compares *can you hand me the newspaper* and *hand me the newspaper*, they seem to have a different function. The imperative has the force of order or command and has a different illocution from *can you* (see Haverkate 1984). From a different perspective, imperatives are said to be less polite and be distinguished from the more polite indirect forms on one or several scales (see Leech 1983).

The existence of polite imperatives is often ignored or denied. It is therefore interesting to investigate imperatives in the London-Lund Corpus. As many of 288 examples (about one-third of the examples) consisted of imperatives.[30] It is true that one-fourth of these were what Weigel and Weigel (1985: 67) refer to as negative imperatives. For example, the imperative may ask the hearer to stop doing something or to not do something:

(157)   a   +you've got+ a damned good idea mate . now
           come on come off it
(7.1 1489)

(158)   C   ^shut ùp# .
           ^let me "thìnk# .
(8.2 207–8)

(159)   A   (- laughs) ^stop that ^stop that :heavy
           !brèathing# -
(8.4 209)

(160)   m   *^wait a mòment#*
(5.6 613)

(161)   b   ^don't interrúpt **'please#**
(5.6 820)

Though an effective means of achieving one's goal, a negative imperative signals the speaker's irritation or anger (i.e. it is intrinsically impolite) and may therefore create conflicts between the participants:

(162) (a *and* then leave it and for
    B   *^yès#*
    (a goodness sake don't write anything resembling an
       essay . *on* gobbets
(7.1 1713–15)

Besides, imperatives figure frequently in standard situations where they may occur alone or together with *please*:

(163) c [ə:] hang on a minute please -
(7.1 627)

The following examples have been analysed as elliptical imperatives. They only occur in routinized situations with *please* as an additional request marker:

(164) A the de^partment of _mathe!màtics 'please# .
(9.2 256)

(165) B ex^tension !two five èight *pléase#*
(8.1 336)

(166) C [ə:m] . ^one mŏment 'please#
(9.2 269)

(167) A ^just a mŏment 'please#
(8.2 931)

A special type of polite imperative is illustrated by mitigated imperatives such as *do sit down* or *you sit down*. Just as with indirect requests, however, there are many different types of mitigating device.

4.19.1 Imperatives and politeness

Polite imperatives are to be expected if the requested action is at a cost to the speaker and a benefit to the hearer. Consider the following scale of cost and benefit when the imperative mood is kept constant:

[1] Peel these potatoes.   more cost to H/ less benefit to S
[2] Hand me the newspaper.
[3] Sit down.
[4] Look at that.
[5] Enjoy your holiday.
[6] Have another sandwich.   more cost to S/more benefit to H
(After Leech 1983: 107)

[1] involves a fair amount of imposition (cost to H) and can be called an order. [2] implies less imposition because the task is associated with less effort. [3] and [4] are more like suggestions or advice, i.e. they are oriented to the hearer's benefit and leave the hearer the choice whether to act or

not, [5] is a well-wish and finally [6] is an offer. In the last examples the imposition is not felt to be heavy because the action benefits the hearer.

Thus offers can be performed more or less directly by an imperative (16 examples). The imperatives were of the following kind:

(168)   B   ^darling *!have some cherries#*
        d   *have a hand*ful
(2.10 1254–6)

(169)   A   ^have a 'bottle of 'Newcastle Bròwn#
(1.7 1191)

A closer look at the examples where the imperative is used as a request shows that a large number of the imperatives occurred in informal conversation or in telephone calls between close friends or members of the same family (see section 4.12.2).

(170)   B   ^go [? ə:?] ^use your lóaf# .
            [ə:] ^rìght#
            ^get your'self óff there#
            ^=and !tell 'Maureen that _we'll 'pay for a tàxi#
        A   ^yéah# -
            ^yeah I'll !dò that#
(7.2 449–54)

It is clear that speakers may use the imperative without sounding offensive if they know each other well:

(171)   A   well ^you _you know !have a wòrd with *'him#
(7.2 1215)

The account of politeness, which has been given earlier in this chapter, has stressed that it is polite to emphasize the distance to another individual by means of indirectness and to show respect for his personal autonomy by pragmatic elements such as hedges and downtoning adverbs. In order to explain why speakers use imperatives, we need to pay attention to the importance of stressing common ground and group membership in human interaction. This type of politeness has been described as solidarity politeness (Scollon and Scollon 1983: 167). Underlying solidarity politeness (corresponding to Brown and Levinson's 1978 positive politeness) is the assumption that there is little distance between the participants and no difference in power (Scollon and Scollon 1983: 167). According to Scollon and Scollon, if the relationship between the persons can be described by the configuration (-P(ower), -D(istance)), positive or solidarity politeness is the rule. This means that the speaker uses other mitigating strategies.

First we can notice that in 91 examples (about one-third of the examples), the imperative cooccurred with mitigation ('mitigated directness').[31] The imperative may, for example, cooccur with informal or affectionate address terms (*dear, man, mate*):

(172)   A   ^pass me 'my :hàndbag *déar#
        and I'll ^get out my 'old pair of glàsses# -
(2.14 163–4)

(173)   a   so I ^rang him ùp#
        and I said "^dèar 'Mr 'Trim#
        ^don't be twìt#
(5.11 913–15)

(174)   A   *^wéll#* .
        ^look áfter your'self dear 'Clive#
        +^and+ !get wéll 'soon#
(9.2 1152–4)

(175)   A   +O^Ǩ#+ -
        ^then be !!gòod then 'doctor#
(7.3 1293–4)

One possible intonation pattern is illustrated in example (172) with a rise tone on the address term (placed without a tone unit break after the imperative).

Another feature associated with polite imperatives is informality (e.g. informal vocabulary):

(176)   B   *you ^knów#;.*;
        ^give her the 'extra 'ten bòb#
(7.2 455–6)

(177)   a   *give* us all the griff
(7.1 1492)

Other politeness strategies are devices by means of which the speaker attracts the hearer's attention: *look, listen, hey* or an address term used to catch attention. An example is:

(178)   D   [ə:] ^Pàul#
        [ə: dʒ] ^just 'tell us {brìefly} whàt# .
        [ə?] the ^main !dìfferences you 'feel be_tween [ə]#
        the ^teaching we 'do :hère#
        and the ^teaching you're 'doing at :Bèaton# -
(3.6 39–43)

Just was found with or without other downtoners before an imperative (13 examples):

(179)   B   *^well 'just* 'do what_ever 'needs :dòing#
(7.2 431)

Politeness can also take the form of a combination of different downtoners. *Well, just* and *you know* frequently occurred together. The following combinations of mitigating elements occurred:

(180)   A   well ^you _you know !have a wòrd with *'him#
(7.2 1215)

(181)   A   well I ^[wəu] . !((won't)) - ^just 'do as you think
              fît#
              you ^knów#
(8.3 656–7)

Involvement can be expressed by hearer-oriented question tags (*right, all right, okay, would you, will you*):

(182)   B   ^rǐght#
              ^sit down hére would you# - - -
(3.5b 551–2)

(183)   C   *^and* then !come a'cross and 'see me on Sàturday#
              ^áll right#
(8.2 824–5)

The imperative also occurs with its own set of mitigating devices, namely *you* and *do*, which function as request markers just as much as the simple imperative. In this respect both *do* and *you* can be compared with *please* although they are found in less formal contexts.

4.19.1.1   DO + IMPERATIVE

Do (13 examples) occurs in invitations, offers and advice besides polite requests with the pragmatic value of persuasion, encouragement, appeal, urgency, friendliness. The intonation was normally the polite fall-rise tone or a fall tone:

(184)   b   - - ^how did you get on at _your ìnterview# .
              ^do tèll us#
(1.3 215–16)

(185)   B   ^anyway !dò carry ón Frank#
(2.4 1290)

Do may cooccur with the downtoning elements *I mean, you know, and so on* indicating familiarity:

(186)   b   oh well I mean do keep on ringing me you know
              I mean *(- - laughs)*
(7.1 1049)

(187)   B   ^Jàcqueline#
              ^do 'try and 'find :whĕn and 'so on# -
(2.5 147–8)

Do followed by the imperative introduces an invitation in:

(188) A ^do come *éarly#*
       B *((if)) ^that's* OǨ#
       A ^do come éarly#
          ^and we can !have a drìnk#
       B ^oh grèat# .
          ^yés#
(7.3 192–7)

Do is used when the speaker and hearer know each other well. In comparison, the initial *please* is more formal.

(189) BM ^please gét# an "^urgent 'message 'to . !\Mr
           Lárdner# ^if you 'possibly "càn# .
(9.3 790–2)

4.19.1.2 YOU + IMPERATIVE

You + imperative (6 examples) was typical of the informal style of conversation. The phrase may convey an admonitory or reassuring tone:

(190) A [ə:] . ^n=ow#
          ^just you ex'cuse me !twǒ 'minutes#
          while I ^try and find :out this [ə:] :fìgure#
(3.2 418–20)

(191) B ^oh you !take the gòod one#
          and ^leave !mè the 'old one#
          "^fáthead#
(7.2 443–5)

The *you*-imperative has a wide illocutionary potential indicated by the fact that it is used in invitations and offers, besides requests. In example (192), the imperative serves as an invitation:

(192) A well ^bòth of you come róund on Sàturday#
          and ((it'll)) be ^very nìce#
       B ^in the ěvening# -
       A is ^that what you'd !!líke#
          or ^êarlier if you wísh# -
          I ^feel . I ^don't know how you 'are about
          :èvenings thése days#
       B ^well (([ə])) they !have to be 'fairly early
          èvenings#
       A well ^come ěarly 'then#
          and . ^then you'll be 'able to go awày 'early and
          ((so on))# .
          +you ^knów#+
       B +((2 to 3 sylls))+ ^that'd be lòvely#
(8.4 603–13)

An invitation requires cooperation and negotiation, the use of routine as well as of planning, as shown in example (192). Before the invitation is accepted (*that'd be lovely*), the speaker and hearer discuss the time for the invitation ('would the hearer like to come in the evening, is an early evening preferable', etc). In example (193), the *you*-imperative has the force of an offer:

(193)   A   well ^you [tra] I ^mean !you trỳ a 'bottle ((of
            it))#
(1.7 1158)

But *you* is also found in discourse where clarity is more important than politeness (although this distinction is not always possible to account for in terms of different discourse types). The following example has the function of instruction as well as request:

(194)   A   ^nò#
            ^nò#
            you ^look on the bâck# .
            [ə:m . ðə] if ^you 'look . (. coughs)
        B   the the ^{thrèe} :little :brǒwn# .
            [ð] the ^scrěw things# .
        A   ^no nò#
            [ə: i əə:m] if ^you 'just '((turn)) ^you ^which
            'clock do you mèan#
            the *e^lèctric 'one#*
        B   *the e^lèctric#* .
            ^yéah#
        A   ^wèll#
            you ^look you ^unhóok it#
            +. [ə:m]+
(7.2 272–85)

Notice that the *you*-imperative frequently cooccurred with markers such as *just, well, OK, right*, tags, address terms, *I mean* stressing involvement and group membership:

(195)   B   well ^you keep trỳing#
            ^=and [ə:m]#
            ^I'll be in tòuch#
            all ^ríght#
        A   ^OḰ#
(8.1 269–73)

(196)   B   [j] you ^just cut 'out the !brèaks#
            and you ^get con_tinuous **!fílm#**
(1.7 1257–8)

4.20 Patterns expressing offers

As Hancher points out, there is something strange about the speech act of offering:

> To offer something to someone is both to try to direct that person's behavior, and also to commit oneself to a corresponding course of behavior. In offering you wine I am trying to get you to drink wine and also committing myself to provide you with wine to drink.
>
> (Hancher 1979: 6)

This fuzzy nature of the offer explains that a large number of strategies are used. The speaker may use a stem with a commissive rather than directive function. The stem (I (we) WILL VP) is very productive (12 examples):

(197) C and ^I [?ə] ^I 'said I was 'going off to 'have a
           'cup of téa#
           and he ^said "!òh#
           [ə]. ^I ^I'll 'buy you a 'cup of !tèa#
(2.7 791–3)

(198) (a ((before you)) sit down I'll get another glass
        B ^èxcellent Míke# - .
           you're ^on the !bǎll#
           ^òbviously#
        a **oh yes** -
(1.7 504–10)

(199) B ^oh well 'I'll bring a 'copy of mìne néxt
           'time#
        A *((^nò no* no nó no no no#
(2.10 548–9)

A permission question (*can I give you, what can I offer you, may I be permitted to, can we*) was found in offers in 7 examples:

(200) C [ə:] well ^I ^I'd ^can I 'give you the 'ones in the :sècond
           'batch#
           that [ə:] that ^I'd .
        ? *^yèah#
        ? ^plèase#*
(2.6 1027–30)

(201) A ^what can I òffer you# - .
           I ^said I !want the !Irish 'Press and the 'Irish
           Tìmes# .
(1.14 278–9)

In example (202), the permission question is negated:

(202)　c　^D=an#
　　　　^can I not 'get you a drìnk#
　　　D　^yes you mày#
　　　　^thànk you#
(4.4 854–7)

In example (203) the speaker's strategy is instead to ask if the hearer wants the speaker to do something (*shall I, shall we, should I*):

(203)　A　there are ^cúps# .
　　　　^něs'cafe# -
　　　B　shall we ^have a 'cup of cóffee# .
　　　A　^yes cèrtainly#
　　　　^yes !cèrtainly# .
　　　　^yès#
(1.8 1–6)

Other speaker-based routines expressing offers are *let me* and *let's* (3 examples). *Let's* suggests more politeness than *let me*. *Let me* is illustrated in:

(204)　B　*^let me se'lect a :ripe chèrry* for 'this#
　　　A　^oh of !course you càn't#
(2.10 1331–2)

On the whole, speakers seemed to prefer the strategy of asking what the hearer wanted (9 examples), which permits the hearer to reject the offer. Offers in the form of questions include *do you want, like, want, do you need*, etc:

(205)　A　+do you ^want+ a !cǐggie# *- - -*
(2.11 320)

(206)　B　^want any súgar# .
　　　A　^yěs 'please 'Brenda# -
　　　B　^óne# .
　　　A　^that's about rìght#
　　　　^yes !that's enóugh 'thank you# - - -
(1.8 43–7)

Will you, would you like to, won't you were used in offers and invitations (7 examples):

(Situation: Invitation)
(207)　b　+would you+ ^like Èric# to ^pop ǐn one 'day#
(4.4 441–2)

Have to and *must* (*ought to, should*), 4 examples in all, are used for offers (and invitations) where the polite norm is that the speaker should be persuasive if the action benefits the hearer. The pattern has the form of a declarative sentence:

190

(208) C [ð] the ^only 'thing is !thìs#
          ^that . !you will 'have to come :ŏver#
          and ^have a 'little ":nàtter wíth me#
(8.2 471–3)

An offer may be accompanied by a move where the speaker justifies the imposition. In example (209), the move comes after the offer:

(209) A I ^must lènd it to you#
          it ^might be . ìnteresting# .
          because it's "^certainly a :period :I knew
          !nòthing a'bout {what^èver#}# .
(2.3 326–8)

The phrase *if you can* (*if you wish, if you want*) is used for an offer if it is clear that the action benefits the hearer:

(210) B *^and [ə:]* !if you can ^if you can [ə: ? ə:]
          :wrìte to us#
          and ^ãsk us for some 'help#
          we'd be "^vĕry 'glad#
          to ^gìve it to you#
(3.1 562–5)

Several offers had a fixed form such as *you're welcome, I'm at your service, what can I offer you*:

(211) C *yes ^hĕre we 'are# - - -
          ^you are :wĕlcome to have thìs# -
          ((I ^xĕroxed you)) a !còpy#*
       A ^thanks 'very mùch# - -
          ^yès#
(2.14 167–71)

You're welcome to presents the action as favourable to the hearer at the same time as it involves some effort for the speaker.

Invitations and requests are related because of the element of imposition. Invitations, however, are also linked to offers since the action is beneficial to the hearer. Edmondson and House define 'an Invite' as follows: 'A wishes B to know that he is in favour of a future action to be performed by B, which he believes may involve costs to himself and benefits to B' (1981: 131f). Invitations differ from offers since they are more elaborate speech acts which have to be repeated and negotiated before they are responded to. In example (212), it is the time which has to be settled before the invitation is accepted (see Wolfson et al. 1983):

(212) A ^*come to :dìnner#*
          of ^còurse#
          but I ^mean !come èarly for dínner#

```
                    *[?j]*
        B   ^sort of {sèven} . *!fif*tèen#
            ^rather than èight#
        A   ^òh yes#
            by ^âll 'means#
            ^I mean you knów#
            any ^time between 'six and sèven réally#
            if you'd ^like to have a 'drink and ":plǎy a
            bit#
        B   ^oh that would be vè*ry nice#*
        A   *^how would* thàt be#
        B   ^that would be lòvely#
        A   ^gòod#
            ^lòvely#
        B   ^=OK# .
            ^see you thèn#
```

(8.4 614–31)

The speakers make an effort to come to an arrangement which is suitable
to both speakers. As a result, the response to the invitation is recycled
before the invitation is completed. Similarly, in example (213), the
response takes place in several steps:

```
(213)   B   [ə ?] ^by the wày#
            ^I for!got to tèll you#
            ^last nìght#
            ^that [ə:m] - - _Bill !Pòtterton#
            ^wants us to 'go round on :Sunday [i:]
            'afternòon# .
        A   ^OḰ#
            ^yès#
            *^that's !fîne#;.*;
            ^yès#
        B   *is ^thát all right#* .
            ^rìght#
```

(7.2 88–98)

The offer in example (214) is expressed less directly. The phrase is what
we have referred to above as a 'pre-sequence' (Levinson 1983: 345f) or a
'lead' (Wolfson et al. 1983), i.e. a question or statement setting the stage
and signalling to the hearer that an offer, invitation, request, etc will
follow.

```
(214)   a   [əm] - there is a drop of Oloroso *which you ((can
            have))*
        C   *^oh no nò#*
            ^that's tòo 'sweet#
```

^nò#
I'll ^have the ((2 sylls \1 syll 1 syll))#
^yès#
(1.9 74–9)

(215) B I've ^got some '[tob] . ^some . ^some – !fŭnny
          'coloured Tòblerone 'for you#
          "^{fròm} *!Swìtzerland#* .
       A *"^how "vèry* kind#
(7.3 205–7)

In example (215), it is clear both from the form of the offer and from the
response that Speaker B's utterance serves as an offer.
   The offer in example (216) is characterized by hedging:

(216) A well I ^did bring a :vŏlume 'of this 'diary#
          I mean I[?] I ^don't 'know whether as I :sày# .
          it ^ìs of 'any concérn [?] ^ínterest 'to
          you# - - -
          but ^this is :rêally [ə:m]# .
          has ^never 'left my 'sight be!fòre# .
(2.2 255–9)

In examples (217) and (218), the hearer responds to a pre-sequence,
which is then followed by a more direct offer:

(217) (A I've ^just 'boiled some !wàter#
           for having ^còffee#
           cos I ^haven't !hàd
       B *((3 to 4 sylls))*
       (A 'time for téa#
       A *would* you ^líke some#
       B *^yès#*
          ^yès#
(1.4 4–11)

(218) B ((^would you like)) a !ménthol#
          ^or '[ei] plàin# .
       A [ə:m] .
       B ^you can hâve a ménthol#
(2.11 287–90)

   Example (219) is what Wolfson et al. (1983) calls a 'pseudo-kernel lead',
a step toward the accomplishment of a social commitment.

(219) C *^rìght#;.*;
          [ð] the ^only 'thing is !thìs#
          ^that . !you will 'have to come :ŏver#
          and ^have a 'little ":nàtter wíth me#

      and
   B *^yèah#*
   C we'll *^have* to dis:cuss 'your fi:nàncial
      situ'ation#
      in ^more !dĕ'tail#
(8.2 470–7)

The offer contains a modal auxiliary expressing obligation (*have to*); time is left undefined, and no response is called for.

Offers are distinguished from requests by their continuation patterns. Offers for minor favours may have a fairly routinized continuation in which the speaker uses one of the following strategies:

Strategies accepting an offer	realization
A requesting the hearer to do something	*do, please, could you*
B accepting the offer	*yes, certainly right, OK*
C expressing appreciation	*excellent*
D expressing thanks	*thanks*
E expressing intention	*I will*

Routinized pairs of offer and response are illustrated by:

(220) A there are ^cúps# .
          ^nĕs'cafe# -
       B shall we ^have a 'cup of cóffee# .
       A ^yes cèrtainly#
          ^yes !cèrtainly# .
          ^yès#
       B ^Ĭ see#
(1.8.1–7)

(221) d have a cherry - cherry -
       B I ^wìll have a 'cherry áctually#
(2.10 1126)

Much 'gushing' is used in:

(222) C but . ^would you get . 'one of them to :bring you
          róund#
          and ^have a 'pint of béer with us 'just 'now#
          ((if you've)) ^tíme#
          ^that would be lôvely# .
          *^that would be lòvely#
          ^yès# .
          ^rìght# .
          ^that would be !very* ((nice))
       C *^yès# .
(1.9 520–8)

Like requests, offers have several response options which are less conventionalized. One polite strategy is to accept the offer unwillingly and reluctantly as in:

(223) a ***I**** see . (offers sherry)
       A [əm] . ^well a !věry little#
          ((because I ^really mŭst be getting 'home {in a
          ^móment#}#)) .
(2.2 829–31)

Hesitation (*well*) and qualification (*very little*) are associated with politeness towards the hearer.

A direct way of saying 'no' to an offer is *no thank you* (with rising intonation):

(224) b *((let's)) give you some more*
       (C 'something at :lŭnch-'time# - .
          ^and was !just _going to go 'off and :have a _cup
          of !tèa# .
          ^nò thánks# .
(2.7 783–5)

(225) B "^hàve 'one#
       d (– laughs) no thanks
       B ^líke one#
          - ^have one 'after dìnner per'haps#
       d *no I'll I'll I'll have a nasty* French one -
       B **^[m̂]#**
(2.10 539–44)

A refusal of the offer can also be more elaborate:

(226) C or ^is there a . swèeter 'sherry Málcolm# .
       a [əm] - there is a drop of Oloroso *which you ((can
          have))*
       C *^oh no nò#*
          ^that's tòo 'sweet#
          ^nò#
          I'll ^have the ((2 sylls \1 syll 1 syll))#
          ^yès#
(1.9 73–9)

4.21 Conclusion

Indirect speech acts make up a significant portion of language. An important question is therefore how they should be analysed. According to the traditional account in speech-act theory, there are pragmatic principles alongside the syntactic and semantic rules generating the sentence which make it possible for the hearer to infer the force or function of indirect speech acts.

Alternatively, indirect requests can be analysed as fixed elements or patterns which have become standardized and linked directly to certain communicative functions and situations. A possible reason for this is that they express cultural norms and values in that society, and that they are efficient strategies for solving problems in the communication, etc.

Indirect requests are not completely fixed, however, but are characterized by a high degree of situational and formal flexibility. What makes them useful in communication is that they have the conventional form of stems, which can be adapted to different situations just as much as the phrases of thanking and apologizing dealt with in the two preceding chapters.

In fact, as more and more conversational English is studied one can expect to discover that the constraints imposed by the situation on language are even greater than has been suggested here. This, in its turn, may result in a rejection of the view that syntax and pragmatics should be kept apart. According to Perkins, 'syntax is merely a nexus – a meeting point of semantics and pragmatics, and although it is amenable to formalization as an autonomous phenomenon, it should not be forgotten that the notion of autonomous syntax is a theoretical abstraction' (Perkins 1983: 161). Indirect requests are a good example that one should not account for all the permitted combinations or restrictions on the use of linguistic forms in syntax. Exactly how the interaction between pragmatics and syntax should be accounted for will probably continue to be a problem, and has ultimately do with how we regard the role of pragmatics in linguistics and draw the distinction between language competence and performance.

In a discourse perspective, the adaptation and specialization of grammatical structures for pragmatic functions can be seen as a natural process, at least if we regard the hearer's role in conversation as central. Lexicalization of pragmatic structures facilitates speech processing since lexical look-up is a simpler and quicker process than figuring out what the speaker means. The case of indirect requests indicates that politeness may be another reason for lexicalization.

In recent years, linguists have developed a rich conception of the lexicon, which contains not only words but also lexicalized and semi-lexicalized structures and idioms and presumably conventionalized indirect speech acts. Alternatively, 'stems' can be accommodated in a special phraseological component. This component may be characterized as encyclopedic since it must contain a wealth of pragmatic information about particular routines, presumably in the form of pragmatic frames as has been suggested here.

However, the problems of accounting for indirect requests are considerable. The distinction between conventionalized and non-conventionalized indirect speech acts is fuzzy, and the question whether we can give a unified account of indirect speech acts remains.

Another distinction which is fuzzy is the division between direct and indirect requests. In fact, (mitigated) imperatives correspond to strategies on a deeper level and are situationally constrained just as much as indirect requests. They therefore need to be described in terms of pragmatic and situational factors such as politeness, formality, setting, discourse type, etc. Wierzbicka (1991: 88) goes so far as suggesting that the distinction between direct and indirect speech acts should be abandoned, and that the different phenomena associated with these labels should be individually examined.

Notes

1 See Tsui (1994: 46) for discussion and for additional arguments against Levinson's claim.

2 For an early attempt to deal with the conventionalization of indirect speech acts, see, for example, Sadock (1974). Cf. also Bach and Harnish's discussion of standardization and illocutionary devices (1979).

3 Tsui (1994: 110) finds that the most satisfactory characterization of indirect speech acts is that offered by the ethnomethodologists. Since linguistic elements are assigned function retrospectively in situated discourse, the problem of functional indeterminacy does not arise. Like the ethnomethodologists, however, Tsui has little to say about the conventional linking between form and function in general.

4 Additional preparatory rules are needed for *order* and *command* (Searle 1969: 66).

5 One can add the preparatory rule that the hearer is willing to do the act (see Gordon and Lakoff 1971).

6 Imperatives have not been included, although they represent this strategy.

7 It is therefore important that the criteria established for illocutionary functions are systematic and explicit (as stressed in speech-act theory). Compare also Edmondson and House, 'It is no use introducing illocutions rather like a conjuror producing rabbits out of a hat, such that nobody knows where they come from, how many there might be left in, or whether, indeed, the whole procedure is an illusion' (1981: 48f).

8 Tsui (1994) analyses *why don't you, you'll have to* as suggestions or advice but *what about* and *the best thing to do* as 'proposals'. On the other hand, Edmondson and House (1981: 125) regard 'Suggest-for-you' and 'Suggest-for-us' as the same illocution.

9 The category of direct requests in the CCSARP project includes performatives ('I am asking you to clean up the mess') and obligation

statements ('you'll have to move that car'). (Cf. Blum-Kulka et al. 1989: 18.)

10   A similar view is expressed by Brown and Levinson (1978), who regard requests as face-threatening actions which give rise to redressive action involving indirectness and mitigation. The analysis is related to Goffman's view of requests as 'remedial' when the hearer's face is threatened: 'A request consists of asking licence of a potentially offended person to engage in what could be considered a violation of his rights. The actor shows that he is fully alive to the possible offensiveness of his proposed act and begs sufferance' (Goffman 1971: 145; quoted after Owen 1983: 21).

11   A similar scale can be postulated for declarative sentences with *can* being more indirect than *will* (see Leech 1983: 121). Compare:

you must VP	more direct
you will VP	
you can VP	
you could VP	less direct

12   A more extensive description of the prosody of indirect requests remains to be done.

13   Imperatives have been included.

14   See Yli-Jokipii: 'The BL [business letter] register is quite unique in the sense that no other type of written language contains such a simultaneous density and variety of requests as BLs [business letters] do' (1990: 184).

15   When I have the form of indirect requests in mind, I speak about stems; frame focuses on the situational and pragmatic constraints. I also use frame to describe the cluster of form, function and situation.

16   See Pawley and Syder (1983: 210) for the term inflection. Inflection, unlike the other operations affecting the stem, is obligatory.

17   We could easily measure the flexibility of the stem in terms of the number of operations, as suggested by Barkema (1992).

18   Bahns et al.'s examples are, however, mainly from the speech of second-language learners.

19   Edmondson and House (1981: 134) suggest that a 'Permit' always appears as a response to a request for permission.

20   Blum-Kulka's Hebrew examples are translated as *perhaps you will*. According to Blum-Kulka, they are associated with a high degree of coerciveness.

21   Another reason that *be able to* is unacceptable is that it is too explicit. According to Bach and Harnish, *are you able to* (or *you are able to*) somehow focuses 'the hearer's attention on the question (or statement) of his ability rather than on the action itself' (Bach and Harnish 1979: 187).

22   This pattern has been added for comparison although it is not, strictly speaking, a permission question.

23 See Holmes (1984: 359) and the references there.

24 Including examples such as *please do*.

25 Including *I wonder if you could (...) please* (1 example) and *please could you* (1 example)

26 Including *I wonder if I could* (1 example).

27 Similar examples have, however, been counted as hearer-oriented.

28 Called 'defocalizers' in the following discussion.

29 Gibbs's aim is to investigate what people actually say in certain stereotypic situations rather than to describe routine phrases (see Gibbs 1985).

30 The high number of imperatives is partly due to the fact that I have not analysed the functions of the imperatives in detail. Thus, the number includes imperatives with the function of attention-getters, well-wishes, etc.

31 Mitigated directness, a term coined by Blum-Kulka (1990) to describe modified directness, has been studied much less than conventional indirectness or mitigated indirectness. Blum-Kulka found it to be a characteristic feature of (polite) family discourse, which is supported by the results in this work.

CHAPTER FIVE

Discourse markers as conversational routines

Much talk has less to do with expressing propositional content than with structuring, repeating, emphasizing, mitigating and generally 'padding'. .... It is precisely such items which are of interest to the discourse analyst, since they are the items which indicate the underlying structure of the discourse or the underlying functions of individual utterances.
(Stubbs 1983: 178)

5.1 Introduction

In Chapters 2–4, I discussed 'speech-act routines', i.e. socially bound speech acts such as thanking, apologizing, requesting and offering. In this chapter I want to deal with routinized elements which contribute to the coherence of discourse in various ways. Coherence has been described in the framework of Halliday and Hasan (1976) basically in terms of devices marking grammatical and lexical cohesion. Some examples of explicit 'connectives' marking the logical connection between two utterances are:

(1)   He left early. *But* there was no train. [adversative]

(2)   He left early. *Therefore* he missed the train. [causal]

We also need to account for how *the point is, come to think of it, let me tell you something*, etc, which are fixed or semi-fixed phrases, contribute to cohesion and to coherence in the discourse. These and similar phrases have been discussed by Keller (1981) as conversational 'gambits' (see also Gülich 1970 – 'Gliederungssignale'; Stubbs 1983 – 'prefaces'; Moon 1992 – 'hyperpropositional expressions'). Generally, they introduce what the speaker is about to say but they may also serve a number of other functions. In order to signal that a message represents a personal viewpoint, the speaker may, for example, use the gambit *the way I look at it*. As Keller showed, such elements are frequent in language and fulfil a large number of different discourse-organizing and textual functions.

In works on discourse markers in general, such as Schiffrin (1987), Hölker (1988) and Gülich (1970), such 'explicit' discourse markers have been mentioned most of the time only in passing. Since they have the function of commenting on and organizing the message, they will be referred to here as metadiscursive discourse markers or simply as discourse markers.

In the present work discourse markers are analysed as conversational routines which can be more or less fixed. Generally speaking, much attention has been paid to discourse elements expressing logical relations between clauses, probably because these relations are so important in writing. In order to see what types of discourse(-structuring) markers there are in spoken language and how they are used, I have gone through the London-Lund Corpus looking for expressions and patterns which have discourse-organizing or commentary functions.

The first part of this chapter deals with the properties of discourse markers as a set, in particular how they can be analysed in terms of their metalinguistic function and the speaker's aim to be relevant. The main part of the study is an investigation of conversational routines as discourse markers or prefaces in the London-Lund Corpus, with the emphasis on the contextual (deictic), functional, textual and linguistic properties.

5.2 Coherence and discourse markers

Lately there has been considerable interest in how coherence is established in discourse and in the role of discourse markers in communication. Should they be regarded as a kind of cohesive marker similar to anaphoric nouns or adjectives, demonstrative pronouns, etc? Are they necessary in order to understand a text? What functions do they have? How are they related to other linguistic features of the text? It has been emphasized in many works in discourse analysis that coherence is not established by special markers within the text itself but that it is a feature of the text expected by the conversationalists:

> The reaction of some scholars to the question of 'coherence' is to search for cues to coherence within the text and this may indeed yield a descriptive account of the characteristics of some types of text. It ignores, however, the fact that human beings do not require formal textual markers before they are prepared to interpret a text. They naturally assume coherence, and interpret the text in the light of that assumption.
> (Brown and Yule 1983: 66)

It follows that 'it is critically important to distinguish between the "underlying semantic relation" ... and those formal realisations which are available to, but not necessarily utilised by, the speaker/writer in constructing what he wants to say' (Brown and Yule 1983: 198).

The speaker uses two types of cohesive device to mark how the text progresses. On the one hand, the speaker may tell the hearer explicitly what he is going to do or how the different parts of the text are structured in a metalinguistic statement as in the following fabricated example:

> I'll first discuss A, then B and I will conclude by considering the effects of C.

Such devices ('prefaces') are common especially in certain types of text. They are defined in relation to their position before a conversational move or a larger discourse unit. Some other examples are:

> *let me (begin by saying, just ask initially) this, may I ask this one question, I have this to say first of all ...*

Prefaces are used, for example, in discussions:

(3)   f   *I I ^just want to ask the audience one quèstion#*
            ^háve you gòt#
            a ^large !holiday !camp !hére#
     aud   (- yes)
(5.4 1300–3)

The speaker asks for permission before adding something:

(4)   g   ^may I just add *:one* "wòrd# .
          [əm] . ^I agrêe#
     f   *^Gémmel#*
     (g that ^life is lived . in the présent#
         and ^one . !works . for the fùture# -
(5.2 480–4)

The 'preface' in example (5) is used strategically to bring the discussion back to a preceding topic:

(5)   a   ^let me !bring you . [k] !quickly 'back to Èurope
         'Prime Mínister#
         [ði] . the "^tone of the 'speech 'Mr Càllaghan
         'made . {this ^wèek#}# .
         ^struck !many péople#
         ^[?]as . !notably 'more ac":cŏmmo'dating than his
         fîrst# -
         ^rene'gotiátion 'speech#
(6.3 878–82)

In addition there are story-prefaces (Schiffrin 1987: 16), joke-prefaces and topic-markers (Stubbs 1983: 183). As Stubbs (1983: 183f) has pointed out, prefaces are a characteristic feature of formal text types, such as committee meetings, where they have considerable length and internal structure. The following (hypothetical) example from Stubbs (1983: 185) shows the full form of a preface:

1 John –   2 er I think perhaps   3 it would be useful
4 before we go any further   5 if I sum up   6 some of the
things Harry was saying ...

Secondly, the speaker uses discourse markers. Although many markers are small, unimportant words, they have a not negligible role in the process of creating coherence and organizing discourse. They have many interesting contextual properties which account for their cohesiveness: they can refer backwards and forwards in the discourse context; they are oriented to the speaker and/or hearer; their function is metalinguistic rather than referential. These properties are shared by markers which are not completely fixed and can best be analysed as emergent markers.

5.3 Discourse markers characterized

It is with some hesitation that I speak about discourse markers since the term is difficult to define and has been used in many different ways. The notion discourse marker (discourse particle, etc) is sometimes used to describe 'small words' or expressions which are 'peculiar to spoken language' (Stenström 1990). Both Stenström (1990) and Altenberg (1990b) refer to particles such as *well, right, you know* as items which function at the discourse level.[1]

It has also been argued that connectives such as *and* or *but* are discourse items (see van Dijk 1977; Schiffrin 1987; Nølke 1990). Schiffrin, for example, proposed a 'discourse analysis' of the conjunctions *and, but* and *or* since they cannot be accounted for in sentence grammar (see Schiffrin 1987: Chapter 6). There is, however, little agreement about what the different types of discourse markers have in common. Thus Schiffrin groups together disparate elements such as *oh, well, and, but, or, so, you know*, etc, although she is pessimistic about establishing what makes these elements into a single set:

> Consider the many different items that I am grouping together as markers: *oh, well, and, but, or, so, because, now, then, I mean, y'know*. Are these items members of a single word class? Are they constituents in a discourse grammar? What methods would we use to discover such membership: co-occurrence restrictions, semantic and/or functional criteria? Are such methods appropriate for discourse? Is it possible to define so disparate a list of items in a way which will let us identify other elements as members of the same class?
> (Schiffrin 1987: 40)

My intention is to discuss a subgroup of markers which are placed as a kind of boundary in the discourse and show how they can be defined by syntactic, semantic, prosodic and functional criteria. These have also been referred to as 'speech-act adverbials' (Andersson 1975) or 'illocutionary adverbials' (see Mittwoch 1977; Nef and Nølke 1982) since most of them have the grammatical function of adverbials.

I want to start by giving a few examples of such discourse markers and how they are used.

(6) f [ə ?]if ^one were to 'take the "!ðil
        'revenues
        for 'instance#
        to come "^băck to that 'subject# .
        ^then [ði] . the !Scottish . De'velopment Ágency#
        might ^well be the "!strònger 'unit# .
        ^in !terms of a'vailable fi'nance for in'dustrial
        de!vèlopment#
        ? ((^rêal *'money#))*
(11.5 842–7)

Discourse markers have functions which must be described in terms of the larger discourse context. *To come back to that subject* signals that the speaker intends to 'jump back' in the conversation to a prior topic.

In example (7), *(now) as I say* focuses on the relevance of the upcoming message against the background of what is known or believed:

(7) b ^nòw#
        ^as I sây#
        ^èvery'body#
        ^has its !code of rúles# .
(5.6 807–10)

I regard markers like *to come back to what you said, now as I say, frankly speaking*, etc as discourse markers just as much as *well* or *right*. There is, however, a difference between one-word markers like *well, now, right*, etc and other markers in terms of explicitness. *Well*, for example, has no meaning, only a number of discourse functions. In 'complex' discourse markers, the literal meaning is not completely obliterated but can be scrutinized by the hearer; for someone who did not know the phrase it would still be possible to figure out what it means on the basis of its constituents.

Because of the semi-fixed and variable character of many of the markers it is difficult to make a list of discourse markers (see Bazzanella 1990). The markers enumerated below are the result of an investigation of the London-Lund Corpus. I have wanted to cast the net wide in order to collect not only completely fixed phrases, but also elements which are best regarded as emergent discourse markers. As a result, the markers range from completely fixed phrases like *in any case, by the way, after all* to semi-fixed phrases or stems. Common one-word particles like *well, right, okay, so* belonging to the set of discourse markers have been excluded since I am mainly interested in conversational routines. On the other hand, I have, for example, included *actually* since the marker is functionally similar to markers such as *in (actual) fact*.

As a first step in the analysis, I have found it helpful to group the discourse markers from the London-Lund Corpus into two functional classes, depending on whether they mark elements of the macro-structure or emerge in the flow of communication as cues to the relationship between adjacent utterances.[2] Taking a hint from Schiffrin (1987), who distinguishes between discourse markers functioning in the local and global discourse context, I shall refer to local and global discourse markers:[3]

Local markers	Global markers
actually	*again (again as I say, again with great respect), there again, again I say*
after all	
as a matter of fact	*briefly*
as far as I am (X is, you are) concerned; so far as X is concerned	*to begin (with), first of all, firstly, in the first place, secondly*
as far as I can gather (understand, see, could tell, know, remember), as far as we can see, as far as one could see, as far as memory goes; so far as I know (we know), so far as one could tell, so far as appeared	*going back to this*
	in other words
as I say, as you say, as you might say, as we say, as they say, as X has suggested, as I believe, as I said (before)	
as the case may be	*to put it another way*
basically	*to come back to that subject*
(but) let us face it	*to follow up that (statement)*
believe it or not, don't you believe it	
come to that, if it comes to that, when it comes down to it	*anyway*
essentially	*going back to*
if I may say so, if I might say so at this stage	*in a word*
if you ask me	*now you come to mention it*
in actual fact	*once again*
in any case	*or put it another way*
in fact	*tell you what*
far more important (seriously)	*to put you in the picture*
(quite) frankly	*wait till I tell you*
generally (speaking)	
the point is	
needless to say	
of course	
practically speaking	
strictly between us	
when you think	

We can recognize discourse markers on the basis of their metalinguistic function.

5.4   The metalinguistic function

There is a close connection between discourse markers and metalinguistic function, although not all metalinguistic expressions are discourse markers. It is therefore necessary to begin by discussing different language functions. Much in language has no referential function but metalinguistic or expressive or both. The following example (from writing) where the metalinguistic elements have been italicized is taken from Östman (1982: 171):

> Conventional dictionaries are *essentially* lists of *what might be called* lexical entries. … The conventional dictionary *can, for our purposes, be thought of* as an unordered set of lexical entries, … *We should not forget*, however, *as linguists*, that *most* adult native speakers of English are accustomed to thinking of word-forms as *relatively* stable written entries …
> [Perhaps *conventional, however,* and *are accustomed to* should also have been italicized]

The distinction between a referential function and other types of function goes back to Jakobson (1960):

1   expressive/emotive function
2   directive/conative/persuasive function
3   poetic
4   contact
5   metalinguistic
6   referential
7   contextual/situational
(Cf. Hymes 1968; and Stubbs 1983: 46)

In this fine-grained classification of language functions, where functions are derived from factors of the communication situation, the metalinguistic function focuses on the underlying linguistic code.

It is because certain words, phrases and clauses have the 'right meaning' that they can be used with a metalinguistic function. Reichenbach (1947: 58) suggests that metalinguistic terms comprise certain verbs (*tell, put it (to sb), ask, add, etc*), and nouns (*point, problem, fact, question, etc*). *Point* is what Francis (1986) calls an A-noun, i.e. the noun functions anaphorically as a cohesive device referring back to a preceding stretch of discourse and serving as a transition or a springboard to the message. Compare example (8), where *point* is anaphoric and *this* points forwards cataphorically to the following message:

(8)   d   'good 'you sníffing# .
            the ^point is thìs#

^you 'have !nèver ex'perienced a húnt#
you've ^nèver 'seen a 'fox leave cóver#
you've ^nèver seen :hóunds - {^hunting a
!fóx#}# .

(5.6 537–42)

The metalinguistic function includes checking or controlling the communication channel since these are aspects of the communication itself (Stubbs 1983: 48). In a wide sense, the term metalinguistic (function) can be used to characterize speech acts in which the speaker adds a point or an argument, summarizes past talk, recapitulates, clarifies or reformulates an earlier utterance. The problem remains of delimiting the set of 'metalinguistic items' and of choosing an analysis which accounts for their discourse-organizing and deictic properties (see Weinreich 1966: 162; Schiffrin 1980, 1987). It is, however, clear from what we know about how discourse coherence is established that metalinguistic elements do not on their own create or build up structure.

As Tognini-Bonelli points out, the adjective *actual* or the adverb *actually* is not in the first place a cohesive element, but is inserted into the discourse structure by a process 'where each utterance makes reference to the preceding one and takes over from it the status of "state-of-the-text" ' (Tognini-Bonelli 1993: 202). The relationship between metalinguistic expressions and coherence is further developed in a relevance-theoretical framework in section 5.5 below.

I do not want to draw a distinction between discourse markers serving as cues to the interpretation and other cohesive elements which do not. *That* in the following example is, for example, a cohesive device referring to a specific antecedent which also functions as a signal to the hearer where to look for the interpretation:

(9)   f   [ə ?]if ^one were to 'take the "!ŏil 'revenues
for 'instance#
to come "^băck to that 'subject# .
^then [ŏi] . the !Scottish . De'velopment Ágency#
might ^well be the "!strònger 'unit# .
^in !terms of a'vailable fi'nance for in'dustrial
de!vèlopment#
? ((^rêal *'money#))*

(11.5 842–7)

Discourse markers, however, have a unique position as metalinguistic elements because they are placed in a special 'discourse marker slot' which is external to the proposition proper in the underlying syntactic phrase-marker. The discussion of the elements in this slot and their properties will occupy a large part of this chapter (see in particular section 5.7.1).

5.5 Relevance theory and communication

What I want to do in this section is to give a deeper explanation for the use and properties of discourse markers. A relevance-theoretical approach can explain how certain elements arise in the communication situation as 'props', disclosing the speaker's communicative intentions and guiding the hearer's interpretation of the discourse. More generally, relevance theory accounts for what cohesive devices are doing and for how coherence relations between discourse units are created.

What is expressed by what is said in an utterance is generally underspecifed so that the hearer must make inferences or guesses about what the speaker has intended to say. As early as 1924, Jespersen wrote 'only bores want to express everything, but even bores find it impossible to express everything' (Jespersen 1968/1924); quoted by Andersson 1975). It is, however, only recently that one has begun seriously to ask how communication can be successful if so much information is implicit only (see Grice 1975). What inferences are needed to interpret what is said, and what are the general principles guiding the hearer's interpretation?

According to relevance theory (Sperber and Wilson 1986), the message conveyed by an utterance is clarified with reference to the context in which it is inserted. An important feature of the theory is that context is not defined in terms of the physical context or the co-text only, but in terms of the speakers' and hearers' assumptions, i.e. their beliefs and knowledge. The following paired examples, quoted from Jucker (1993: 440),[4] illustrate how the interpretation of an utterance depends on a number of background assumptions associated with its position in the larger discourse context:

(10)   The road was icy. She slipped.

(11)   She slipped. The road was icy.

In example (10), 'she slipped' is most naturally interpreted as a result ('Therefore she slipped'); in example (11), the same utterance must be an explanation because of the background assumed by the first sentence in the pair ('The reason is that the road was icy'). It follows from this that hearers have to reconstruct the context in which the speaker's contribution is most relevant in order to interpret the message.

Relevance is not a new concept. In Grice's well-known theory (1975), relevance is formulated as a maxim ('be relevant') which is on a par with other maxims, which together make up the so-called cooperative principle and gives rise to implicatures. In Sperber and Wilson's model (1986), the speakers' wish to be relevant is, however, the main key to understanding communication and to utterance interpretation.

According to Sperber and Wilson, the relevance of an utterance depends on its contextual effects. The contextual effects of the information may, for example, be to strengthen common assumptions, to change a mistaken belief or to add something which provides evidence for a new assumption. As stated above, the contribution of an utterance to the discourse depends on the surrounding context.

In order to explain that the hearer chooses a single interpretation for an utterance, the principle of relevance is needed. According to this principle, each utterance comes 'with a guarantee of its own optimal relevance'. The principle is counterbalanced by the demand that the information should be easy to process for the hearer. The interplay between the two principles accounts for the fact that the interpretation of an utterance which yields maximal contextual effects may still not be the most accessible one when the effort of processing the information is considered.

Attention must now be paid to what discourse markers are doing and why they have certain functions.

5.5.1 The interpretation of discourse markers in relevance theory

In a relevance-theoretical framework, the main function of discourse markers is to serve as signposts, echoing a term used by Jucker (1993: 438) to describe the function of *well*; they are signals by means of which speakers display their understanding of the preceding speaker as well as indicate how the following utterance (or larger discourse unit) should be processed by the hearer. There is nothing mysterious about the appearance of discourse markers in communication. As Blass points out, 'such expressions should naturally arise in a framework where the speaker is constantly anxious to spare the hearer processing effort and thus increase his willingness to go on listening' (Blass 1990: 84).

We are fortunate to have several descriptions of individual discourse markers in a relevance-theoretical model. According to Blakemore (1987), connectives like *after all*, *but*, etc, can be explained in terms of how they constrain or guide the hearer's search for relevance. *After all* serves, for example, as an instruction to the hearer to treat the proposition to which it is attached as an item of evidence for some previous conclusion (see Blakemore 1987: 84; Blass 1990: 129):

(Situation: The topic deals with the employment of social workers)
(12)   C   and [ə] ^after àll#
they're "^not very 'well !pǎid#
but I sup^pose . 'even at !thàt *'rate#
((we)) ^can't af'ford too :màny 'of them#*
(2.14 733–6)

Jucker (1993), in particular, has provided a useful discussion of discourse markers which also takes care of their multi-functionality. The following example shows how *well* constrains the discourse interpretation by signalling a change of focus to a new part of the discourse:

(13)   but if they wanted people around to talk to, then I would be very
        happy to stay, and got a letter back saying we have arranged for
        you to stay – *well* let's take the interview first
(Jucker 1993: 446)

Of course a description of all the uses of a 'difficult' particle like *well* may
still be extremely complex since all the different (local and global) functions
of the particle must be accounted for. However, although the functions of
well are disparate, they can be explained on the basis of the core meaning
of *well* (non-acceptance, dissonance) and the position of the particle in the
discourse marker slot and the operation of the relevance principle.

What I want to argue here is that expressions such as *actually*, *as I say*, *as
far as x is concerned*, *I mean* and many others function as cues or guides to
the hearer's interpretation, i.e. they come about as a result of the way in
which utterances are interpreted as having certain contextual effects.

In principle, all discourse markers can be accounted for in a relevance-
theoretical approach. Consider again the phrase *to come back to (that subject)*. From the hearer's point of view, the phrase functions as an
instruction to search 'backwards' for the topic introduced. On a deeper
level, the phrase may be seen as increasing 'the accessibility of assumptions which have passed out of short-term memory and are therefore too
costly to use directly in establishing the reference of proforms' (Blass 1990:
60).

To sum up, the overriding function of discourse markers is to integrate
utterances into the flow of conversation and to instruct the hearer how
their interpretation is affected by the context. In relevance-theoretical
terms a discourse marker may, for example, signal that 'the most immediately accessible context is not the most relevant one for the interpretation
of the impending utterance' (Jucker 1993: 435).

In particular, discourse markers accompany coherence breaks. Such
breaks are most clearly seen in the change of speakers and in topic shifts;
in addition, there are misunderstandings, digressions, false starts, self-
repairs, etc, disturbing the conversational flow, which need to be signalled. Speakers do not only use discourse markers to facilitate the
hearer's comprehension when a trouble spot emerges in the process of
communication. Discourse markers may be used whenever the speaker
wants to reduce the hearer's processing efforts by showing explicitly how
what is said is relevant.

Before closing this section, it should be emphasized that it is difficult to
explain the use of discourse markers on the basis of relevance theory
alone since there are a number of non-relevance-theoretical factors 'producing' discourse markers, such as the speaker's wish to be polite or to
modify illocutionary force. Consider *I mean*:

(14)   A and she con^tìnues to 'be mád#
           I mean she's ^one of these 'rather nìce péople#

who ^obviously go !ŏn being 'mad# .
till their ^dying !dày#
(2.14 982–5)

I mean signals that the following unit of talk is an explanation or clarification of what has been said. Another and perhaps stronger reason for *I mean* is that the discourse marker makes the assertion less intrusive. An additional factor inducing the use of *I mean* might be 'playing for time' under the pressure of on-line processing.

5.6 The approach to discourse markers in this work

In a footnote in their important work on relevance theory, Sperber and Wilson write:

> … just as the natural links between intonational structure and pragmatic interpretation may become grammaticalised, so a language might develop certain structures whose sole function was to guide the interpretation process by stipulating certain properties of context and contextual effects. Clearly, in a relevance-based framework the use of such structures might be highly cost-efficient. This approach seems to us a particularly promising area for future research.
> (Sperber and Wilson 1986: 263)

It may be hard to decide when the connection between meaning and form (context) has been conventionalized or routinized. In a relevance-theoretical perspective it can be expected that a large number of linguistic structures are recruited into discourse as more or less routinized markers since an overall tendency in communication is to make what is said easier to process.

In this work discourse markers will be regarded as 'grammatical idioms' or routines, that is as 'something a language user could fail to know while knowing everything else in language' (Fillmore et al. 1988: 504). There are, however, degrees of conventionalization, and discourse markers can be more or less fixed formally and functionally.

5.7 The linguistic properties of discourse markers

The complexity of discourse markers as a group has recently come into the limelight mainly thanks to Schiffrin's work (see also Andersson's 1975 work on speech-act adverbials discussed below). Schiffrin (1987: 328) mentions a number of factors allowing an element to be used as a discourse marker:

> (a marker) has to be syntactically detachable from a sentence (see section 5.7.1)

it has to be commonly used in initial position of an utterance (see section 5.7.3)

it has to have a range of prosodic contours, e.g. tonic stress followed by a pause, phonological reduction (see section 5.7.2)

it has to be able to operate at both local and global levels of discourse (see section 5.9)

These and other factors will be discussed in the following sections.

5.7.1 'The discourse marker slot'

A discourse marker is not identifiable from its form. This can be clarified by analysing cases where the same structure must be given two alternative grammatical analyses. Consider *if I may say so*:

(15)　w　^yès#
　　　　　but ^Mr Na!bàrro#
　　　　　^this is . *if I may say so* begging the !quèstion#
　　　　　because we
　　　　n　*(([o:]))*
　　　　(w *'^âll* a_gree {that ^we are looking for
　　　　　mèans#}# -
　　　　to . [m] to . ^stop the rise in the crìme#
(5.3 742–7)

If-clauses can have two different uses depending on their meaning. In example (15), *if I may say so* functions as a discourse marker, i.e. the phrase has the metalinguistic function of restricting the message to what the speaker thinks. In example (16), on the other hand, the *if*-clause expresses a condition which must be fulfilled in order for the main clause to be true and is part of a sentence complex:

(16)　If it starts raining, I will bring my umbrella

Consider also:

(17)　b　*[ə] before I forget about it in the chatter* . [ə:]
　　　　　you remember - the [ə:m] - what do you call it
　　　　　[ə:m] - - cricket commentary . there was a
　　　　　manuscript . of that .
　　　　C　^[ɪ́nhm]#
　　　　b　OK .
　　　　C　^[ɪ́nhm]#
　　　　b　and . it was all typed and we're proof-reading it
　　　　　and we can't find the manuscript we've hunted high
　　　　　and low . can you remember where you put it - - -
(7.1 10–14)

In example (17), the *before-* clause comments on the circumstances under which the utterance is produced and is a discourse marker. On the other hand, the following *before*-clause is a subordinate clause modifying the main clause:

(18)   a   be^fòre I 'go any fúrther#
            I ^wish to 'say !thìs# .
            I've ^said it be:fŏre# .
            but it ^is !strìctly 'germáne#
            to the ^prèsent 'case# -
            ^no one can :sit hère#
            as ^long as !Ì 'have 'sat# -

(12.3 853–9)

A work which I have found useful in order to describe such differences is Andersson's (1975) work on speech-act adverbials.[5] Andersson distinguishes between adverbials referring to what is said ('the dictum') and 'speech-act adverbials' focusing on various aspects of the communication situation. Speech-act adverbials include adverbial disjuncts such as *frankly, admittedly,* phrases like *to tell you frankly* and whole clauses (*if I may say so*) as well as interjections, expletives (*oh God*) and address terms (e.g. *darling*), which have in common that they refer to the relationship between the speaker and hearer. Speech-act adverbials are therefore a broader category than discourse markers. According to Andersson, speech-act adverbials occupy a special slot (here called the discourse marker slot) outside the sentence core, as illustrated in Figure 5.1. The tree in Figure 5.1 describes what Fillmore et al. call a grammatical construction since 'constructions ... need not be limited to a mother and daughters, but may span wider ranges of the sentential tree' (Fillmore et al. 1988: 501). Grammatical constructions are exemplified by expressions such as *let alone* or *the sooner, the better,* which can neither be generated by the grammar nor listed in a general phrasal lexicon of the language and treated as fixed expressions (see Fillmore et al. 1988: 511). In section 5.7.4, I discuss grammatical constructions (what I call stems) and their internal grammatical composition.

Andersson's model provides a good starting-point for describing discourse markers because it makes a clean division between the message itself (the propositional core) and lexical material (the speech-act adverbial or discourse marker) which does not belong to the utterance but only comments on it.[6] Even if there are many examples where the split is not as syntactically clear-cut as in Andersson's model, where speech-act adverbials do not enter into construction with the sentential core, the analysis seems to give a good description of discourse elements.

Words and phrases in 'the discourse marker slot' can be characterized on several linguistic levels. Semantically, they are non-truth-conditional, that is they 'have at least a component of meaning that resists truth-

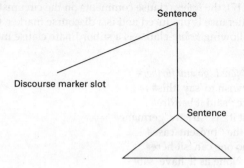

Figure 5.1 The discourse marker slot

conditional treatment' (Levinson 1983: 87f). Prosodically, they are recognized by a break between the marker and the host sentence, corrresponding to a tone unit boundary:

(19) B and . and ^after àll#
         there was ^always a :mǎid#
         to ^come and 'clear the 'damn _thing a_way in the
         :mǒrning# -
(1.13 434–6)

The distinction between speech-act adverbials (including discourse markers) and propositional elements can be shown by formal tests and operations. For example, speech-act adverbials cannot be the focus of a so-called cleft construction (*It is to come back to that subject that …). (See Quirk et al.'s 1985: 612 discussion of adverbial disjuncts.) Other formal criteria are, however, fuzzy or too general. To give an example, discourse markers may lose their prosodic autonomy and be integrated in the utterance without a tone unit boundary, as in example (20):

(20) (B ((^was)) – ^after all we !!are spècialists#
         . ^[ə:] and we ^cànnot _tackle#
         the ^broad fields
(1.2 1267–70)

Andersson's model is not restricted to finite clauses but we can also account for different types of to-clauses. Consider:

(21) a and there ^=is# .
         "^all the tìme# .
         through"^òut the _sixteenth _century# -
         ^this con"!tinuing "prèssure# - - -
         up^on her :sòurce of _income# -

or *to ^put it an:other way#* .
"^hér# .
"^rêlative _wealth# -
(12.2 465–72)

Grammatically, *to put it another way* is a 'dangling' verb phrase, which can be compared with other *to*-phrases:

(a) a *to*-phrase as an object clause (*I want to go there*)
(b) a *to*-phrase as a purpose clause (*He did it to be nice*)

Notice that purpose clauses can also be placed initially:

To study the mantis more closely, I transferrred some from the peach trees to a Kilner jar
(Quoted from Bäcklund 1990: 291)

Initial purpose clauses have been studied by Thompson (1985), who described them as text-organizing elements, naming a problem arising from inferencing from the preceding text (see Bäcklund 1990: 290).

The purpose clause can be distinguished from the discourse marker since it does not have a metalinguistic function. Grammatically, the purpose clause modifies the main clause, as shown in Figure 5.2.

Notice, finally, that sometimes the distinction between routines and expressions generated by grammatical rules is subtle. Whereas *the way I see it* is a discourse marker with the function of signalling the speaker's perspective (*the way I see it, you are wrong*), the longer form *the way in which I see this is different from the way other people see it* is a sentence generated by the grammar. Compare also the phrase *now you come to mention it*, which is a discourse marker characterized by its fixed form and function as a topic marker. On the other hand, there are fully grammatical sentences such as *now that I know you I would like to meet you more often*.

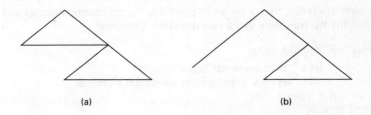

(a)   (b)

Figure 5.2   Phrase markers representing (a) *to* as a purpose clause and (b) a speech-act adverbial

5.7.2 Prosodic fixedness

Altenberg says about discourse markers that 'although their function is generally signalled both positionally and prosodically, the prosodic distinction is often the more important one' (1990b: 180). But even choice of tone may be important, as when it is possible to identify a functional class of discourse markers with a distinctive tone. Thus, according to Allerton and Cruttenden, 'validity-oriented adverbs like *basically*, *essentially*, *relatively*, *superficially* (as well as *actually* in some of its uses) require a fall-rise tone' (1974: 22).

(22)   B   ^cos they 'said they !couldn't 'keep a 'dossier on
        ĕvery'body#
        and ^have an inhĕritance 'thing# -
        and . and "^*băsically* you 'see#
        it ^would *[dis!tri]*
(1.13 954–7)

There was also some evidence in the material for a 'drop in the intonational contour at the end of the expression' with many discourse markers, although this was not as general as suggested by Keller (1981: 107).

(23)   tl   and ^*sĕcondly*#
        ^*let's be 'quite :clêar*# .
        ^Krupp is a !German cĭtizen#
        ^in Gĕrmany#
        ^which for !good or for íll#
        is a ^free and inde:pendent !còuntry# -
(5.1 714–19)

5.7.3 Positional fixedness

Since discourse markers are syntactically detached from the sentence as speech-act adverbials, they can appear initially, medially or finally. When they are placed initially, they call attention to something new or 'preface' a new utterance; they serve as responses to the preceding message and simplify the transition to the new utterance. Compare:

(24)   B   ^*tell you whât*#
        let's "^bòth leave our 'organizátions#
        and ^set up a 'management consùltant bu'reau#
   A,d   (laugh . *-*)
(2.11 1036–9)

There are degrees of positional fixedness, however, and many markers are inserted as a kind of 'afterthought' in different positional slots.

5.7.4 The grammatical analysis of discourse markers as stems

Viewed as external grammatical constituents, discourse markers are speech-act adverbials. Discourse markers also need to be described with regard to their internal grammatical structure and in terms of whether they are grammatical or ungrammatical. As in the previous chapters, I shall describe semi-fixed or irregular elements as (sentential, clausal or phrasal) stems. The stems are collocations where the recurrent part is a lexicalized pattern containing a grammatical slot, which can be filled with lexical material. Thus each stem is a 'mini-grammar', generating structures which would be difficult to describe in formal, autonomous grammar because of the constraints on their use. To give an example, *to put it another way* corresponds to a stem which can generate a number of other markers:

$$\left. \begin{array}{l} \text{to put it} \\ \text{putting it} \\ \text{put it} \\ \text{put} \end{array} \right\} \text{Manner adverbial}$$

The manner adverbial was realized as *this way*, *like this*, *another way*, *mildly*. Consider:

(25)   c   ((well)) it's ^most un!fòrtunate#
          ^ìsn't it# -
          ^putting it !mĭldly# .
          ^your clìent# -
          is ^sitting 'just behínd you# - - -
(11.1 268–72)

Notice also that since the stem contains a manner adverbial, it can be questioned by *how*:

(26)   a   but ^these are in:tàngibles# .
          and when in^tangibles m=eet – – ^how shall I pùt
          it# - -
          ^[ðì:]# .
          [ə:m . ðì] ^{{grìnding} - !{mìncing} ma:chìne}
          of :trèasury . fínance# -
          in^tangibles . disap:pèar# -
(11.2 318–22)

There is a large number of markers generated from the same stem, which can be further characterized with regard to function, prosody, position, etc. For example, the markers generated by the stem illustrated above have many features in common. The intonation is falling, and the marker is placed at an interactional boundary, indicating how the upcoming message should be interpreted against the background of contextual assumptions. Functionally, they form a subclass of phrases, signalling the point of view from which the upcoming message should be understood.

Consider also *generally speaking*. The morphosyntactic pattern cannot be derived by productive grammatical rules in any easy way. It is, however, not a unique pattern since we have also got *broadly speaking, frankly speaking*, etc. In other words, we have a stem:

ADVERBIAL speaking

Some evidence for the variability of the stem and restrictions on its generative capacity is provided by the London-Lund Corpus which contains *broadly speaking, practically speaking, strictly speaking, generally speaking* but not, for example, *frequently speaking* or *sincerely speaking*.

The grammatical patterns or stems can be varied, expanded, reduced, in a rule-bound way, to fit into new contexts and genres. Some of the stems, their realizations and associated functions are shown in Table 5.1. As shown by the potential realizations of the stem, we do not only have the phrase *to go back to*, but *go back to* can be substituted for *get back to* or for an *-ing* form (*going back to* ...). The phrase can also be embedded in *let us (let me)*. There is, however, a restricted number of verbs and constructions allowed by the stem associated with the function of resuming an earlier conversational topic.

Similarly, I would suggest that *to be frank, to be honest* correspond to a stem permitting only a few 'synonymous' adjectives. While *to be honest* is fully acceptable and idiomatic, *to be sincere* is not.

5.8   Contextual properties of discourse markers

Since so much of grammatical analysis has been carried out on the basis of decontextualized sentences, the embeddedness of language in the communicative context has tended to be neglected. In this chapter I have tried to remedy this by looking at elements which have come into language in order to carry out special metalinguistic functions. It has been argued that discourse markers are especially important because of their cohesive function. It should be clear from the preceding discussion that properties of the surrounding context are important when we describe and classify discourse markers. In particular, discourse markers can be characterized in terms of speaker and/or hearer-orientation.

5.8.1   *Discourse markers as deictic 'pointers' referring backwards and forwards in the discourse*

Cohesive devices in the form of discourse markers may point both backwards and forwards in the discourse. *Another thing* points backwards in the discourse context because the phrase presupposes that other aspects

Table 5.1: Discourse markers organized as stems

Stem	Realizations	Function
VP-ing / to VP / let's (let me) VP } back to	*going back to* / *to come back to* / *to get back to* / *let's go back to* / *let me bring you back to*	going back to an earlier topic, point in the discussion, etc
VP-ing / to VP } to	*switching to* / *to switch to*	switching to a new topic
to be ADJ	*to be honest* / *to be frank*	emphasizing the veracity of the message
I'll be ADJ	*I'll be frank* / *I'll be honest*	
to VP with	*to start with* / *to begin with*	listing
as far as I can VP	*as far as I can see,* *remember, know, tell*	restricting the perspective to what the speaker thinks, remembers, etc
as far as NP { am / are / is } concerned	*as far as I am concerned* / *as far as John is concerned*	restricting the perspective to a special individual
as NP say(s)	*as he says* / *as you say*	emphasis
if it VP / VP } to that	*if it comes to that* / *come to that*	envisaging a new perspective
far more ADJ	*far more important* / *far more serious*	emphasizing the seriousness or importance of the message
let's { VP / be ADJ }	*let's face it* / *let's be clear*	emphasizing the plain truth of the message
ADVL speaking	*generally speaking* / *frankly speaking* / *broadly speaking*	restricting the reliability of what is said

of the same topic have already been mentioned. The marker helps to remind the hearer of something which he might have forgotten unless the speaker had intervened:

(27)   C   an^ŏther 'thing 'Jock#
            ^[i ə:] ^in in in ^mў 'paper#
            in the ^Gŭardian#
            ^ànyway#
            it ^gives the !Uni'versity of the Áir 'programmes#
(2.5 1133–7)

The 'pointer' function can distinguish between discourse markers. *Well after all* points forwards to 'upcoming talk' (a new phase in the discourse, a new topic) and serves as a reminder of something which has been said before.

(28)   C   *well ^after !àll# -*
            it it's ^going :dŏwn#
            at the ^rate of [ə:] 'one or 'two per 'cent a
            !!mònth#
            ^ìsn't it#
            ^money nów# - -
(2.7 321–5)

(I'll) tell you what has typically the function to call the hearer's attention to something new or unexpected, a personal surprise, etc:

(29)   A   *I'll ^tell you whât#*
            we'll ^go éarly# -
(4.3 978–9)

Admittedly, markers do not fall neatly into categories depending on the direction in which they point. Still I have made an attempt to subclassify markers into different categories, depending on their pointing function, in Table 5.2.

5.8.2   Discourse markers and person deixis

Discourse markers refer to the speaker's attitude to the hearer and to the statement.

There is a whole range of phrases in which the speaker is 'understood'. Since these markers are, above all, 'flags' to the hearer, signalling the direction the discourse is taking, it is clear that the hearer is also implicit when a marker like *quite frankly* is used (cf. *I tell you quite frankly*).

(30)   C   [ə:m] . ^*quite frănkly#*
            we ^just 'sold the 'house :three 'doors dówn#
            for ^just over 'fourteen :òne#
(8.2 408–10)

Table 5.2: Discourse markers as 'pointers' backwards or forwards in the discourse context

Discourse markers pointing only backwards	Discourse markers pointing backwards and forwards	Discourse markers pointing only forwards
yes	*the point is*	*look*
oh	*(there) again*	*listen*
right	*far more important*	*guess who*
okay	*after all*	*now*
	as I said before	*let me put it to you*
	to come back to …	*wait till I tell you*
	or put it another way	
	before I go any further	
	well	
	the fact is	
	switching to …	
	talking about …	
	strictly speaking	
	I mean	
	another thing	

Note: Single-word discourse markers have been included for comparison.

A distinction can be made between markers which are primarily speaker-oriented, hearer-oriented or oriented to both the speaker and the hearer (see Table 5.3). Unlike, for example, Schiffrin (1987), I have included a category 'orientation to a third person', and I have classified discourse markers where no explicit reference to the speaker, hearer or third person needs to be made. In a relevance-theoretical perspective, a number of markers can have the function of restricting the validity of an assertion (*strictly speaking, between the two of us, let us face it*). The phrases are, however, subtly different since they centre on either the speaker or the hearer or the relation between the speaker and the hearer.

5.9 Functional properties of discourse markers

5.9.1 Global and local discourse markers

The distinction between global and local discourse markers can be considered basic. Global discourse markers comment on the relationship between larger discourse units. They accompany the introduction of new

Table 5.3: Classification of discourse markers according to deictic orientation

Speaker-orientation	Hearer-orientation	Orientation to speaker and hearer	Orientation to a third person	No speaker/hearer orientation
I mean	now you come to mention it	between the two of us	as X says as far as X is concerned	the fact is
to be fair I'll be frank		let us face it strictly between us		more important
I wanted to say something strictly speaking in my opinion		let's put it like this		

topics, serve a role in turn-taking and segment discourse into larger units; they mark the opening of conversation, order points in a discussion sequentially, etc. Local discourse markers signal intersentential connections and comment on the expectedness or validity of the new message; they underline its importance or simply facilitate the transition from one turn to another.

5.9.1.1 THE PRAGMATIC FUNCTIONS EXPRESSED BY 'LOCAL' DISCOURSE MARKERS

Discourse markers can be analysed according to the pragmatic relations between the sentences they connect or what relevance theorists refer to as contextual effects. There is a close relationship between local discourse markers and evidential function: if an element has evidential function, we can expect it to be used as a discourse marker. In Chafe (1986: 270f), *actually*, *normally*, *generally speaking* are analysed as evidentials, i.e. they comment on the mode or source of knowledge. *Actually* marks, for example, whether the following proposition is in line with expectations. A number of different uses of the discourse marker can be derived from this function. Consider:

(31)   A   and I ^thought !yés#
            ^that's fíne#
            ^don't 'like 'that 'coat 'very 'much ányway#
            (- laughs)
     a,A (- - - laugh)
     A   ^ăctually#

> to ^tell ((you)) the honest trúth#
> ^nothing had oc:cùrred to 'me 'by thén#
> at "^áll#

(2.12 629–37)

In example (32), *actually* signals how a speaker clarifies or sharpens a point recently made by means of a discourse marker:

(32)　A　so I ^went to the !School of Ap!plied Linguìstics#
　　　　　in ^Wìnchester# -
　　　d　[m]
　　　　A　^ǎctually#
　　　　　I ap^{plìed} to the 'British Côuncil#
　　　　　and ^failed to get :ìn# -

(2.4 1187–92)

The synonymous *in fact* is used in a similar way to correct or contradict a previous speaker:

(33)　B　^òh _no# .
　　　　　I have ^nêver said that# -
　　　　　in ^fáct {I ^wént#}#
　　　　　to ^gréat pàins#
　　　　　^I will be !perfectly frank with !!yòu# -
　　　　　I ^went to !gréat#
　　　　　^pǎins#
　　　　　^to . !pút it . abòut# -
　　　　　^quite públicly#
　　　　　^that !you were the óne#
　　　　　who in ^fact was sup:porting me in the inter!view
　　　　　_with - Professor !!Pìtt # - -

(2.1 142–52)

The effect of *in actual fact* in example (34) is to reinforce an earlier point in the discussion. Literally, it signals that the upcoming message conforms to the expectations generated by the preceding context:

(34)　1　you ^start off for instance by ob!jècting#
　　　　　to ^Wìlliams's _use#
　　　　　of the ^word . víolent# -
　　　　　for ^which you would substitute :sterner and more
　　　　　ro!bust méasures# -
　　　　　in ^actual fàct# .
　　　　　^medical téstimony#
　　　　　has ^said that - [ei] judicial :flǒgging# -
　　　　　[ə:] by ^cat o' nine táils# .
　　　　　and [ə] ^bìrching#
　　　　　which ^yòu advo_cate# .

223

is ^little . if :any . [ə] :less sevére# -
(5.3 119–29)

Other discourse marker functions which are 'evidential' in Chafe's terminology are as follows:

(a) restricting the validity or relevance of the upcoming message to a particular point of view

The following discourse markers allow the speaker to choose a perspective narrowing or broadening the knowledge basis against which a statement is made: *broadly speaking, practically speaking, generally speaking, essentially, strictly speaking.*

(35)   B   *^what 'kind of* ":càtegory# .
              ^of !nòvel {would you ^sày#}# -
              [ə:] ^*gènerally 'speaking#*
              ^Lord of the 'Flies be:longs tò# -
(3.1 406–9)

The following markers change the conversational perspective to something more important, serious, better, etc: *and far more important, better still, and far more seriously.*

(36)   h   and ^sècondly#
              and ^*far :mòre impórtant#*
              he was a ter^rific :lòver#
              a^mongst these dóur#
              ^Presbytérian :Scòts#
(5.1 509–13)

Expresssions which consider the seriousness or sincerity with which something is said or the relationship between speaker and hearer could also be regarded as evidentials since they present information not as categorically true but as true in a certain respect:

between you and me, confidentially, strictly between us, let's face it, I will be frank, let's be clear, to tell you the fact, honestly, quite frankly, to tell you frankly, to put it mildly, to tell you the (honest) truth, to tell you the fact, to be fair, to be frank, if I may say so, frankly speaking, seriously, I will be frank with you.

(37)   B   [ə:m] ^strĭctly be'tween 'us#
              I've ^still !gòt one# -
              ^so I can !stìll work at 'AC *on 'Sundays#
(2.4 494–6)

The markers show that the information in the following portion of the text is viewed under a special angle (as serious, as confidential, sincere, etc).

(b) bringing in old evidence
after all, come to think of it, as I say, as you know

(Situation: The topic deals with the employment of social workers)
(38)   C   and [ə] ^after àll#
           they're "^not very 'well !pǎid#
           but I sup^pose . 'even at !thàt *'rate#
           ((we)) ^can't af'ford too :màny 'of them#*
(2.14 733–6)

By means of *after all*, the speaker indicates that what is said is already
known to the hearer.

(c) restriction of the perspective to the speaker's point of view
*in my opinion, as far as I am concerned, the way I think about it, in my opinion,
to my knowledge, personally, my view is*

(39)   B   ^she 'put it in the :lòst book# -
           and as ^far as I 'know it's re:màined in the _lost
           book#;-;
(3.3 344–5)

(d) emphasising truth
the point is, the idea is, the fact is, the truth of the matter is[7]

(40)   a   ((but)) of course the ^truth of the :matter
           :ǐs# .
           that she "^wàs# .
           [ə] ^feeling :sèx _starved# .
           in ^nineteen 'sixty-thrèe# -
(12.3 277–80)

The effect of *the point is* is to reinforce an earlier point in the discussion:

(41)   (B the ^point ìs _you _see#
           that ^when we were :setting that kind of
           :quèstion#
           ((and ^Hart thinks)) we set it now in individual
           !sèntences#
           where there's ^little . !difficulty about :swapping
           over :swapping a!ròund# .
           you'll ^get your candidate will :punctuate :those
           things "!pèrfectly# -
(1.1 1176–81)

(e) reference to some authority as the source of information
As X says strengthens the reliability of the assertion as an authoritative
source for the information produced:

(42)   A   "^well . 'yes . as . as !Èlla 'says#
           she's ^had !kids - 'go 'thrǒugh 'that 'home# .
           that have had ^nothing but 'hate and re'jection
           from . :pěople# -
(2.13 1131–3)

5.9.1.2 FUNCTIONS OF GLOBAL DISCOURSE MARKERS

5.9.1.2.1 Discourse markers with global organizational tasks in the discourse
Discourse markers (and prefaces) are also used to guide the hearer to
global aspects of the text and to solve problems in the communication.
They are helpful when the speaker makes corrections, adds a point to the
discussion, inserts a comment or a digression, summarizes information,
recapitulates or clarifies a point.[8]

(a) adding a point or a fact
*another thing, another matter, two further points, the last thing I wanted to say;
just to add (…)*

(43) w ^just ^just to !àdd#
        a ^little 'bit to thís you 'see#
        I . I I ^think that - the "w=ay#
        that ^Gèoffrey's#
        been ^speaking about !yòu Máry#
        has been ^very !mùch# -
        ^of an !ĭdol# -

(6.5 960–6)

The speaker marks a segment of the discourse as the last point in the
discussion:

(44) B ^yès#
        the ^làst thing I wanted to sáy#
        was ^thîs#
        [ə:m] – "^în the _event#
        that the ^Ford does not come thrŏugh# .
        and ^în the _event#
        that the ^Nuffield says nŏ# - -
        ^you knòw#
        "^where does one !go from !thère# - - -

(2.1 814–22)

(b) listing
The speaker imposes some linear ordering on the structure of discourse.
Examples are *firstly, in the first place; secondly; to give an example, to begin with*:

(45) m ^wêll# .
        ^*firstly* I a:gree with the :questioner that
        wôrds#
        ^play an e!normous part in :raising us above the
        :ănimals# -

(5.2 658–60)

Firstly marks the first point in a series. At the same time the phrase creates
an expectation that further points will be made.

The next thing presupposes that the first point in a series has already been made:

(46)　a　and "^thèn of 'course#
　　　　the ^next !thing îs# .
　　　　that we've ^always re:lĩed in this 'college#
(11.2 261–3)

(c) repeating an argument or a point
again, there again, (but) again, then again, once again, as you know
Again marks the return to a previous statement:

(47)　A　*but ^there a:gǎin# -*
　　　　[ə:m] ^it's !Johnny's . younger 'brother Lènny# -
　　　　^who [?] ((would)) 'be :enu!rètic#
　　　　^the !nĭght#
(2.13 1200–3)

Again combines with the emphasizer *as I say* :

(48)　d　*but a^gàin as I sây#*
　　　　^this 'man _is ":d=angerous# .
　　　　^from !gong to gòng# - - .
(10.3 569–70)

(d) summing up
in a word, to cut a long story short, to be short, to sum up, briefly

(49)　A　(- - laughs) - (7 seconds untranscribable) - ^nò#
　　　　well [ə:] - ^ìn a wórd# - -
　　　　be^cause . they are !all psychólogists# - -
　　　　^=and# - -
　　　　d　well they must *do [s]*
　　　　A　*ex^peri'men*tal psychólogy#
(2.4 687–92)

(50)　a　^now - "!*brĭefly*#
　　　　these [ə:] ((2 sylls)) ^four members of 'staff at
　　　　the :mŏment# .
　　　　[ə] ^thrĕe of us#
　　　　^have òngoing re:s=earch#
(6.1 258–61)

(e) reformulating
in other words

(51)　(A in ^òther _words#
　　　　^sòmething l=ike# .
　　　　[ə:] a ^mĭnimum#
　　　　of ^let's say !twenty to :twenty-'five 'hours a

wèek#
(3.2 441–4)

5.9.1.2.2   *Global discourse markers with the function of organizing topics*
Discourse markers have an important role in the organization of topics in the discourse. Discourse markers are, for example, helpful if the speaker wants to abandon a topic which is under way and resume a previous one.

(a) renewing the topic
to get back to, going back to, to come back to, now let's go back to, may I take you back to, but I'd like to get back to

The transitional function can be marked in addition by a phrase such as *well now* or *anyway*:

(52)   A   ((oh well 8 to 10 sylls)) . ^àny'way# .
         [ə:m] . to ^*get 'back to :happier thìngs#* -
         [ə:m] . I ^thought abòut#
         [ə:] ^possibly 'getting you a re'search -as'sistant
         . -shìp# .
         ^in . Bìrmingham# .
(3.2 133–7)

(53)   A   *well* ^*nòw#* .
         ^*going 'back to Pete Bàskerdon#*
         ^this is anôther 'story# - - -
         ^Pete Báskerdon#
         ^is a !sàd 'man#
(3.14 941–5)

(b) bringing in a new (sub)topic
A new topic may be introduced by a marker of 'newsworthiness':
tell you what (who), guess who, guess when, believe it or not, wait till I tell you

(54)   B   ^*tell you whât#*
         let's "^bòth leave our 'organizátions#
         and ^set up a 'management consùltant bu'reau#
       A,d   (laugh . *-*)
(2.11 1036–9)

(55)   a   ^*tell you who I 'met yèsterday#* -
       b   ^whère#
       a   ^in 'Piccadìlly#
       b   ^whò#
       a   ^Miss Lòcke#
       b   ^did you *réally#*
       a   *^[m̀hm]#* -
(6.2 903–9)

Other discourse markers signal a switch to a new topic or subtopic (e.g. *switching to …* , *talking about …*).

(c) topic digression
A discourse marker may be needed when the speaker inserts information which can be seen as a digression in relation to the topic which is under way. The speaker uses an adverb (*incidentally*) or a fixed phrase (*by the way*), but he may also use a strategy which is only partly conventionalized (as in example (57)). Consider:

(56)   ^OǨ# –
         ^=and#
         [ə ?] ^by the wày#
         ^ I for!got to tèll you#
         ^last nìght#
         ^that [ə:m] - - _Bill !Pòtterton#
         ^wants us to 'go round on :Sunday [i:]
         'afternòon# .

(7.2 87–92)

(57)   a   *I was* ^going to s=ay#
             it ^looked like a "^bĭt like a phèasant in
             'flight# .
             ^certainly *((5 sylls . yes))*

(10.8 418–20)

Other semi-fixed phrases are:
I forgot to ask about … , *before I go any further, before I forget about it in the chatter, now you come to mention it, come to think of it*

(d) 'holding the floor'
The following preface is interpreted as a bid by the speaker to hold the conversational floor when interrupted by the hearer:

(58)   n   ^let me finish the point about Scòtland# -
             ^Scotland has a population of five mìllions# -
             ^England has a populátion#
             ^of – forty-two forty-'three mìllions#

(5.3 665–8)

5.10   Combinations in the discourse marker slot

In many cases the discourse marker slot is filled by a combination of discourse markers. Vicher and Sankoff (1989: 89), in their study of French pre-sentential turn openings, found, for example, that two-thirds of the turn openings in French conversations and debates they investigated had a particular opening consisting of a cluster of markers. The combinations found in the London-Lund Corpus were multi-word units making up a single tone unit (*there again*) which can be regarded as new discourse markers; we also find looser combinations of (local and global) discourse markers as well as interactional signals working together to facilitate and speed up the hearer's comprehension:

(59)　B　I ^don't sup'pose you :nèed 'Old 'English and
　　　　　　'Anglo-Sáxon#
　　　 A　^well !nò# .
　　　　　　^but ['m] you ^knòw#
　　　　　　*I "^dòn't#
　　　　　　have any ^lànguage#*
(1.5 25–9)

The first element in a series of markers is typically *yes, yeah*, etc, which signals receipt of information, or transition markers such as *well* or *I mean* (see Altenberg 1990a: 140). They are only preceded by hesitations and pause fillers as a reflection of the planning process. Global discourse markers are placed immediately before the message after local markers. Consider:

(60)　A　+[':m] . ^yès# .
　　　　　　I ^mean !I'm+ ^I 'wanted to :sày {^something
　　　　　　hère#}# .
　　　　　　that ^that ['m] . you ^knòw#
　　　　　　we "^{do "!lìve {in the ^mìddle#}#} of one of the
　　　　　　"!grèatest#
　　　　　　^{lìbrary} !cŏmplexes in the# .
　　　　　　^not in the :cŏuntry#
　　　　　　but in the *^wôrld#*
(3.3 433–9)

[əm] is a vocalization marking hesitation or a planning pause. *Yes* is a response signal followed by *I mean* which marks the transition to the new message. The upcoming message is marked as a new topic by the prefatory *I wanted to say (something here)*. Notice that the interpersonal *you know* can be inserted between the preface and the message it introduces as a softener.

Again, in example (61) we find the sequence Response + Transition + Discourse marker. *Frankly* is interpreted 'locally' as having the effect of emphasis:

(61)　A　+^yès#+
　　　　　　well "^{frànkly} 'this is 'what I òften 'feel#
　　　　　　when ^people :talk a'bout :schools for .
　　　　　　au"!tĭstic 'children#
(2.14 640–2)

I have only briefly discussed the tendencies we find if we look at larger patterns in the discourse marker slot in the London-Lund Corpus. Like Fraser, I think, however, that there are certain preferred sequential patterns:

> There is clearly some preference among alternative order of occurrence, e.g., *Well, anyway, let's ...* rather than *Anyway, well, let's ...* .This being so, is there some systematic way to account for this?
> Fraser (1990: 395)

5.11 Discourse markers and cognitive frames

In my approach, the speaker's knowledge of discourse markers is organized as a cognitive frame, i.e. as a unit of information in the speaker's long-term memory (see the description of routinized speech acts in the preceding chapters). The frame associated with discourse markers gives information about grammatical patterns and prosody, position, contextual properties, global functions associated with topics or turns and point-making, as well as locally negotiated functions. Each phrase is furthermore more or less characteristic of certain text types, although I have not discussed this here. Consider, for example, a frame for the phrase *to come back to (...)* on the basis of data from the London-Lund Corpus.

FRAME FOR DISCOURSE MARKERS

A *to come back to*

Formal features	*Situational features*
Linguistic features	*Contextual properties*
(a) Sentence-external ('placed in the discourse marker slot')	forwards and backwards-looking; speaker-oriented
(b) Sentence stem *to*+INFINITIVE	*Global or local function* global e.g. changing topic in a debate
(c) Prosody: separate tone unit; fall-rise tone	*Contextual effect* speaker signals that he is going back to an earlier point in the discourse
(d) Position: mid (mobile)	

Discourse-specific features
mainly discussion

Frequency[9]

Also one-word elements like *actually* , which are not stems, can be associated with a frame or a cluster of grammatical, prosodic, contextual, functional and stylistic properties:

B *actually*

Formal features	**Situational features**
Linguistic features	*Contextual features*
(a) Sentence-external ('placed in the discourse marker slot')	backwards and forwards-looking; speaker orientation
(b) Grammatical category: adverb	*Global or local function* local
(c) Prosody: depending on function (see Aijmer 1987)	*Contextual effects* contradiction, reformulation,
(d) Position: front, mid, end (see Aijmer 1987)	clarification, emphasizing something expected
(e) Collocational properties *well actually*	
Frequency high (see Aijmer 1987)	

5.12   Conclusion

The areas of most interest in discourse analysis are non-truth-conditional phenomena and their discourse functions:

> The obvious areas of theoretical interest in discourse, as I see them and which I have covered, are the distinction between truth-conditional and non-truth-conditional phenomena; the distinction between descriptive and interpretive use; the different ways utterances may have contextual effects; and how linguistic form (words, syntax, etc.) constrains the hearer's processing. By researching these areas it should be possible to come nearer to the goal that most discourse analysts seem to have: to be able to explain the correlation between the structure of discourse and the communicative effects the speaker wants to achieve in the hearer. On a linguistic level, this new approach should lead to greater understanding of the relation between structure and function, and to greater insights into a variety of hitherto puzzling linguistic phenomena … .
> (Blass 1990: 260)

Relevance theory provides a general explanation of what non-truth-conditional elements are doing since it accounts for communication as dynamic interaction between speakers and hearers.

In the relevance-theoretical framework, conversational uptake changes the speaker's and hearer's common knowledge basis in specific ways constrained by the principle of relevance. Special discourse markers have the function of signalling the effect of context on the discourse. The speaker signals how the speaker's and hearer's knowledge is affected by the message, e.g. that the message supports that knowledge, contradicts it or that what is said is valid only with certain restrictions. The signalling of the reliability of what is said, the source of information, etc by means of markers (what Chafe 1986 calls evidentiality) is a condition for successful communication. However, this is not enough. The hearer, who could only interpret what is said on a sentence-to-sentence basis, would be seriously disadvantaged as a conversational partner. In the relevance-theoretical analysis we can also explain how the hearer is given sufficient clues to interpret the macro-structure of the discourse.

In this work, discourse markers have been treated as a distinct linguistic category which can be analysed as a cognitive frame. A key to understanding what features they have is that they are metalinguistic and placed in a special discourse marker slot.

The problem of how and why certain elements in language develop discourse-structuring or cohesive functions in a historical perspective has not been discussed in this chapter. Investigating this process, which involves 'delexification', phonological weakening and 'pragmatic enrichment' of content elements under certain conditions, is another study.[10]

Notes

1   Erman wants to distinguish between 'connective' and items typical of impromptu speech, 'It is true that pragmatic expressions may serve to connect pieces of discourse, and could in such contexts be called "connective", but since van Dijk uses the term mainly to cover conjunctions and the logical relations they impose, I think we ought to look for other terms to refer to items typical of spoken language and more specifically of impromptu speech' (Erman 1987: 7).

Östman (1982) distinguishes between connectives (conjunctions) and 'particles'. Of particular interest is his attempt to establish a class of prototypical discourse particles by means of explicit criteria.

2   It is common to try to make some functional distinctions between different types of marker. Chaudron and Richards (1986) distinguish between micro-markers and macro-markers, corresponding to the distinction between local and global markers (see section 5.9.1).

3   See section 5.9 for a more detailed discussion of the two classes of markers.

4   Originally taken from Blakemore (1987: 117).

5   In Banfield (1973: 14), the discourse marker slot is identified with a special expression node introduced by the base rules. Cf. also Espinal

(1991) for a discussion of the shortcomings of formal grammar to account for the properties of disjunct sentence constituents.

6   In Schiffrin's analysis discourse markers are brackets (1987: 36f). Brackets mark discourse units of different length or initiate a spate of activity. They are, however, not analysed syntactically.

7   These phrases are usually integrated in the clause. They can, however, be regarded as emergent discourse markers.

8   Discourse markers are notoriously difficult to subcategorize. Several different classification schemas have been proposed. See, for example, Stubbs (1983: 50 f) on markers monitoring classroom talk, Ball's 'dictionary' of link words (Ball 1986) and Keller (1981).

9   This feature could, of course, have been included for other conversational routines as well.

10 See, however, Tognini-Bonelli (1993: 210); Schiffrin (1987: 328); Brinton (1990).

References

Aijmer, K. 1987. Why is *actually* so popular in spoken English? In Tottie and Bäcklund, 1987, 119–31.

Aijmer, K. and **B. Altenberg** (eds). 1991. *English corpus linguistics: Studies in honour of Jan Svartvik.* London: Longman.

Aijmer, K. and **M. Olsson.** 1990. *Handbok i talad engelska.* Lund: Studentlitteratur. [In Swedish.]

Alexander, R. 1984. Fixed expressions in English: Reference books and the teacher. *English Language Teaching Journal* 38(2): 127–34.

Allerton, D.J. and **A. Cruttenden.** 1974. English sentence adverbials: Their syntax and their intonation in British English. *Lingua* 34: 1–30.

Allwood, J. 1987 (1976). *Linguistic communication as action and cooperation. A study in pragmatics.* Department of Linguistics, University of Göteborg.

Altenberg, B. 1987. *Prosodic patterns in spoken English. Studies in the correlation between prosody and grammar for text-to-speech conversion.* Lund Studies in English 76. Lund: Lund University Press.

Altenberg, B. 1990a. Speech as linear composition. In Caie et al. (eds) 1990, 133–43.

Altenberg, B. 1990b. Spoken English and the dictionary. In Svartvik (ed.) 1990, 193–211.

Altenberg, B. and **M. Eeg-Olofsson.** 1990. Phraseology in spoken English: Presentation of a project. In Aarts J. and W. Meijs (eds) *Theory and practice in corpus linguistics.* 1–26. Amsterdam: Rodopi.

Amis, K. 1978. *Jake's thing.* London: Hutchison.

Andersson, L.G. 1975. Talaktsadverbial. *Nysvenska studier.* 25–47. [In Swedish.]

Apte, M.L. 1976. 'Thank you' and South Asian languages: A comparative sociolinguistic study. *International Journal of the Sociology of Language* 3: 67–89.

Atkinson, J.M. and **J. Heritage** (eds). 1984. *Structures of social action. Studies in conversation analysis.* Cambridge: Cambridge University Press.

Bach, K. and **R.M. Harnish.** 1979. *Linguistic communication and speech acts.* Cambridge, Mass: The MIT Press.

Bäcklund, I. 1990. *To sum up.* Initial infinitives as cues to the reader. In Caie et al. (eds) 1990, 289–302.

Bahns, J., H. Burmeister and **T. Vogel.** 1986. The pragmatics of formulas in L2 learner speech: use and development. *Journal of Pragmatics* 10 (6): 693–723.

Ball, W.J. 1986. *Dictionary of link words in English discourse.* London: Macmillan.

Banfield, A. 1973. Narrative style and the grammar of direct and indirect speech. *Foundations of Language* 10: 1–39.

Barkema, H. 1992. Idiomaticity in English NPs. [Abstract.]

Bauer, L. 1978. On lexicalization (neither a lexicalist nor a transformationalist be). *Archivum Linguisticum* 9(1): 3–14.

Bazzanella, C. 1990. Phatic connectives as interactional cues in contemporary spoken Italian. *Journal of Pragmatics* 14: 629–47.

BBI combinatory dictionary of English: A guide to word combinations. 1986. Compiled by Benson, M., E. Benson and R. Ilson. Amsterdam/Philadelphia: John Benjamins.

Biber, D. 1988. *Variation across speech and writing.* Cambridge: Cambridge University Press.

Blakemore, D. 1987. *Semantic constraints on relevance.* Oxford: Blackwell.

Blass, R. 1990. *Relevance relations in discourse. A study with special reference to Sissala.* Cambridge: Cambridge University Press.

Blum-Kulka, S. 1982. Learning to say what you mean in a second language. A study of the speech act performance of learners of Hebrew as a second language. *Applied Linguistics* 3(1): 29–60.

Blum-Kulka, S. 1987. Indirectness and politeness in requests: Same or different? *Journal of Pragmatics* 11(2): 131–46.

Blum-Kulka, S. 1989. Playing it safe: The role of conventionality in indirectness. In Blum-Kulka et al. (eds) 1989, 37–70.

Blum-Kulka, S. 1990. You don't touch lettuce with your fingers: Parental politeness in family discourse. *Journal of Pragmatics* 14(2): 259–88.

Blum-Kulka, S., B. Danet and **R. Gherson.** 1985. The language of requesting in Israeli society. In Forgas, J.P. (ed.) *Language and social situations.* New York: Springer-Verlag, 113–39.

Blum-Kulka, S., J. House and **G. Kasper** (eds). 1989. *Cross-cultural pragmatics: Requests and apologies.* Norwood, NJ: Ablex.

Blum-Kulka, S., J. House and **G. Kasper.** 1989a. Investigating cross-cultural pragmatics: An introductory overview. In Blum-Kulka, House and Kasper (eds) 1989, 1–34.

Blum-Kulka, S. and **E.A. Levenston.** 1987. Lexical-grammatical pragmatic indicators. *Studies in Second Language Acquisition* 9(2): 155–70.

Bodman, J. and **M. Eisenstein.** 1988. May God increase your bounty: The expression of gratitude in English by native and non-native speakers. *Cross Currents* 1: 1–15.

Bohn, O.-S. 1986. Formulas, frame structures, and stereotypes in early syntactic development: Some new evidence from L2 acquisition. *Linguistics* 24: 185–202.

Bolinger, D. 1976. Meaning and memory. *Forum Linguisticum* 1(1): 1–14. Also published in Haydu, G.G. (ed.) 1979. *Experience forms. Their cultural and individual place and function.* The Hague: Mouton.

Borkin, A. and **S.M. Reinhart.** 1978. *Excuse me* and *I'm sorry. TESOL Quarterly* 12(1): 57–79.

Brinton, L. 1990. The development of discourse markers in English. In Fisiak (ed.) 1990, 45–71.

Brown, G. and **G. Yule.** 1983. *Discourse analysis.* Cambridge: Cambridge University Press.

Brown, P. and **S. Levinson.** 1978. Universals in language usage. Politeness phenomena. In Goody, E. (ed.) *Questions and politeness: Strategies in social interaction.* Cambridge: Cambridge University Press.

Bühler, K. 1965 (1934). *Spractheorie: Die Darstellungsfunktion der Sprache.* 2 Unveränderte Auflage. Stuttgart: Verlag von Gustav Fischer.

Caie, G., K. Haastrup, A. L. Jakobsen, J. E. Nielsen, J. Sevaldsen, H. Specht and A. Zettersten (eds). 1990. *Proceedings from the Fourth Nordic Conference for English Studies*. Department of English, University of Copenhagen.

Carroll, L. 1962. *Through the looking glass*. In *Alice's adventures in Wonderland and through the looking glass*. Harmondsworth: Penguin.

Carter, R. 1987. *Vocabulary. Applied linguistic perspectives*. London: Allen & Unwin.

Carter, R. and M. McCarthy (eds). 1988. *Vocabulary and language teaching*. London: Longman.

CCSARP coding manual. 1989. In Blum-Kulka et al. 1989, Appendix, 273–94.

Chafe, W. 1979. The flow of thought and the flow of language. In Givón, T. (ed.) *Syntax and semantics, 12: Discourse and syntax*. New York: Academic Press, 159–81.

Chafe, W. 1982. Integration and involvement in speaking, writing, and oral literature. In Tannen, D. (ed.) *Spoken and written language: Exploring orality and literacy*. Norwood, NJ: Ablex, 35–53.

Chafe, W. 1986. Evidentiality in English conversation and academic writing. In Chafe, W. and J. Nichols (eds) *Evidentiality: The linguistic coding of epistemology*. Norwood, NJ: Ablex, 261–72.

Chaudron, C. and J. Richards. 1986. The effect of discourse markers on the comprehension of lectures. *Applied Linguistics* 7: 113–27.

Chomsky, N. 1957. *Syntactic structure*. The Hague: Mouton.

Chomsky, N. 1959. Review of B.F. Skinner, *Verbal behavior*. *Language* 35: 26–58. [Reprinted in Fodor, J.A. and J.J. Katz (eds) *The structure of language*. Englewood Cliffs, NJ: Prentice-Hall, Inc.]

Chomsky, N. 1965. *Aspects of the theory of syntax*. Cambridge, Mass: The MIT Press.

Clark, H.H. 1979. Responding to indirect speech acts. *Cognitive Psychology* 11: 430–77.

Clark, H.H. and E.V. Clark. 1977. *Psychology and language: An introduction to psycholinguistics*. New York: Harcourt Jovanovich Brace, Inc.

Clark, H.H. and J.W. French. 1981. Telephone *goodbyes*. *Language in Society* 10(1): 1–19.

Clark, H.H. and P. Lucy. 1975. Understanding what is meant from what is said: A study of conversationally conveyed requests. *Journal of Verbal Learning and Verbal Behaviour* 14: 56–72.

Clark, H.H. and D. Schunk. 1980. Polite responses to polite requests. *Cognition* 8: 111–43.

Cohen, A.D. and E. Olshtain. 1981. Developing a measure of sociocultural competence. The case of apology. *Language Learning* 31(1): 113–34.

Cole, P. and J. Morgan (eds). 1975. *Syntax and semantics 3: Speech acts*. New York: Academic Press.

Collins COBUILD English language dictionary. 1987. London: Collins.

Coulmas, F. 1979. On the sociolinguistic relevance of routine formulae. *Journal of Pragmatics* 3(3/4): 239–66.

Coulmas, F. (ed.). 1981. *Conversational routine. Explorations in standardized communication situations and prepatterned speech*. The Hague: Mouton.

Coulmas, F. 1981a. Introduction: Conversational routine. In Coulmas (ed.) 1981, 1–17.

Coulmas, F. 1981b. 'Poison to your soul'. Thanks and apologies contrastively viewed. In Coulmas (ed.) 1981, 69–91.

Couper-Kuhlen, E. 1986. *An introduction to English prosody*. Tübingen: Niemeyer.

Cowie, A.P. 1988. Stable and creative aspects of vocabulary use. In Carter and McCarthy (eds) 1988, 126–40.

Crystal, C. 1969. *Prosodic systems and intonation in English*. Cambridge: Cambridge University Press.

Davidson, J. 1984. Subsequent versions of invitations, offers, requests, and proposals dealing with potential or actual rejections. In Atkinson, J.M. and J. Heritage (eds) *Structures of social action. Studies in conversation analysis*. Cambridge: Cambridge University Press, 102–28.

Davies, E. 1987. A contrastive approach to the analysis of politeness formulas. *Applied Linguistics* 8(1): 75–88.

Du Bois, J.W., S. Schuetze-Coburn and **S. Cumming.** 1989. Discourse transcription. A handbook. [Draft.]

Edmondson, W.J. 1981. On saying you're sorry. In Coulmas (ed.) 1981, 273–88.

Edmondson, W.J. and **J. House.** 1981. *Let's talk and talk about it: A pedagogic interactional grammar of English*. München: Urban & Schwarzenberg.

Eisenstein, M. and **J. Bodman.** 1986. I very appreciate: Expressions of gratitude by native and non-native speakers of American English. *Applied Linguistics* 7(2): 167–85.

Erman, B. 1987. *Pragmatic expressions in English: A study of 'you know', 'you see' and 'I mean' in face-to-face conversation*. Stockholm: Almqvist & Wiksell.

Ervin-Tripp, S. 1976. Is Sibyl there? The structure of American English directives. *Language in Society* 5: 25–66.

Espinal, M. T. 1991. The representation of disjunct constituents. *Language* 67: 726–62.

Faerch, C. and **G. Kasper.** 1989. Interlanguage request modification. In Blum-Kulka et al. (eds) 1989, 221–47.

Ferguson, Ch.A. 1981. The structure and use of politeness formulas. In Coulmas (ed.) 1981, 21–35.

Fillmore, Ch.J. 1984. Remarks on contrastive pragmatics. In Fisiak, J. (ed.) *Contrastive linguistics. Prospects and problems*. Berlin: Mouton de Gruyter.

Fillmore, Ch.J., P. Kay and **M.C. O'Connor.** 1988. Regularity and idiomaticity in grammatical constructions. *Language* 64(4): 501–38.

Fisiak, J. (ed.). 1990. *Historical linguistics and philology*. Berlin and New York: Mouton de Gruyter.

Fónagy, I. 1982. *Situation et signification*. Amsterdam/Philadelphia: John Benjamins.

Forgas, J.P. (ed.). 1985. *Language and social situations*. New York: Springer-Verlag.

Francis, G. 1986. *Anaphoric nouns*. Discourse Analysis Monograph No. 11. English Language Research, University of Birmingham.

Fraser, B. 1981. On apologizing. In Coulmas (ed.) 1981, 259–71.

Fraser, B. 1990. An approach to discourse markers. *Journal of Pragmatics* 3: 383–95.

Fraser, B. and **W. Nolen.** 1981. The association of deference with linguistic form. *International Journal of the Sociology of Language*, 27: 93–109.

Gibbs, R. 1985. Situational conventions and requests. In Forgas, J.P. (ed.) 1985, 97–110.

Gleason, J.B. and **S. Weintraub.** 1976. The acquisition of routines in child language. *Language in Society* 5: 129–36.

Goffman, E. 1955. On face-work: An analysis of ritual elements in social interaction. In Laver, J. and S. Hutcheson (eds) *Face-to-face communication*. Harmondsworth: Penguin, 319–46.

Goffman, E. 1971. *Relations in public. Microstudies of the public order*. Allen Lane. London: Penguin.

Goffman, E. 1976. The structure of remedial interchanges. In Harré, R. (ed.) *Life sentences. Aspects of the social role of language.* London: John Wiley and Sons, 66–74. [Reprinted from Goffman, E. 1971. *Relations in public. Microstudies of the public order.* Allen Lane. London: Penguin, 171–78.]

Gordon, D. and **G. Lakoff.** 1971. Conversational postulates. *Papers from the Seventh Regional Meeting of the Chicago Linguistic Society.* Chicago: Department of Linguistics, 63–84.

Green, G. 1975. How to get people to do things with words: The whimperative question. In Cole and Morgan (eds) 1975, 107–42.

Greenbaum, S. and **J. Svartvik.** 1990. The London-Lund Corpus of Spoken English. In Svartvik (ed.) 1990, 11–59.

Greif, E.B. and **J.B. Gleason.** 1980. Hi, thanks, and goodbye: More routine information. *Language in Society* 9: 159–66.

Grice, H.P. 1975. Logic and conversation. In Cole and Morgan (eds) 1975, 41–58.

Gu, Y. 1990. Politeness phenomena in modern Chinese. *Journal of Pragmatics* 14(2): 237–57.

Gülich, E. 1970. *Makrosyntax der Gliederungssignale im Gesprochenen Französich.* München: Wilhelm Fink.

Gülich, E. and **K. Henke.** 1979. Sprachlich Routine in der Alltagskommunikation. Überlegungen zu 'pragmatischen Idiomen' am Beispiel des Englischen und Französichen (I). *Die Neueren Sprachen* 78(6): 513–30.

Haggo, D. and **K. Kuiper.** 1983. Review of Coulmas, F. (ed). 1981. *Conversational routine.* The Hague: Mouton. *Linguistics* 21: 531–51.

Hakuta, K. 1974. Prefabricated patterns and the emergence of structure in second language acquisition. *Language Learning* 24(2): 287–97.

Halliday, M.A.K. and **R. Hasan.** 1976. *Cohesion in English.* London: Longman.

Hancher, M. 1979. The classification of cooperative illocutionary acts. *Language in Society* 8(1): 1–14.

Hatch, E. 1983. *Psycholinguistics: A second language perspective.* Rowley, Mass.: Newbury House.

Haverkate, H. 1984. *Speech acts, speakers and hearers. Reference and referential strategies in Spanish.* Amsterdam/Philadelphia: John Benjamins.

Heritage, J. 1984. A change-of-state token and aspects of its sequential placement. In Atkinson, J.M. and J. Heritage (eds) 1984, 299–346.

Hölker, K. 1988. *Zur analyse von Markern. Korrektur- und Schlussmarker des Französischen.* Stuttgart: Franz Steiner Verlag.

Holmes, J. 1983. The structure of teachers' directives. In Richards and Schmidt (eds) 1983, 89–117.

Holmes, J. 1984. Modifying illocutionary force. *Journal of Pragmatics* 8(3): 345–65.

Holmes, J. 1990. Apologies in New Zealand English. *Language in Society* 19(2): 155–99.

Holmes, J. and **D. Brown.** 1980. Teachers and students learning about compliments. In Hamnett, M. and R. Brislin (eds) *Research in culture learning: Language and conceptual studies.* Honolulu: East-West Culture Learning Institute, 78–88.

Hoppe-Graff, S., T. Herrmann, P. Winterhoff-Spurk and **R. Mangold.** 1985. Speech and situation: A general model for the process of speech production. In Forgas, J.P. (ed.), 1985, 81–95.

Hopper, P. 1991. On some principles of grammaticization. In Traugott and Heine (eds) 1991, Vol. I, 17–35.

Hopper R. 1989. Speech in telephone openings: Emergent interaction v. routines. *Western Journal of Speech Communication* 53: 178–94.

Horn, L. 1989. *A natural history of negation*. Chicago and London: The University of Chicago Press.

House, J. 1989. Politeness in English and German: The functions of *please* and *bitte*. In Blum-Kulka et al. (eds) 1989, 96–119.

House, J. and **G. Kasper.** 1981. Politeness markers in English and German. In Coulmas (ed.) 1981, 157–85.

Houtkoop-Steenstra, H. 1987. *Establishing agreement: An analysis of proposal-acceptance sequences*. Dordrecht: ICG Printing. [Dissertation.]

Hymes, D. 1968. The ethnography of speaking. In Fishman, J. (ed.) *Readings in the sociology of language*. The Hague: Mouton, 199–138.

Hymes, D. 1971. Sociolinguistics and the ethnography of speaking. In Ardener, E. (ed.) *Social anthropology and language*. London: Tavistock Publications, 47–95.

Jackendoff, R. 1975. Morphological and semantic regularities in the lexicon. *Language* 51(3): 693–71.

Jakobson, R. 1960. Closing statement: Linguistics and poetics. In Sebeok, T. (ed.) *Style in language*. Cambridge, Mass.: The MIT Press, 350–77.

Jefferson , G. 1972. Side sequences. In Sudnow, D. (ed.) *Studies in social interaction*. New York: Free Press, 294–338.

Jespersen, O. 1968 (1924). *The philosophy of grammar*. London: George Allen & Unwin.

Jucker, A. 1993. The discourse marker *well*. A relevance-theoretical account. *Journal of Pragmatics* 19(5): 435–53.

Karlsson, F. (ed.). 1983. *Papers from the Seventh Scandinavian Conference of Linguistics*, Hansaari, Finland, 17–19 December 1982. Helsinki University: Department of General Linguistics.

Karlsson, F. 1983a. Prototypes as models for linguistic structure. In Karlsson (ed.) 1983, 583–604.

Keller, E. 1981. Gambits. Conversational strategy signals. In Coulmas (ed.) 1981, 93–115.

Kennedy, G.D. 1990. Collocations: Where grammar and vocabulary teaching meet. In Anivan, S. (ed.) *Language teaching methodology for the nineties*. Singapore: RELC Anthology Series, 215–29.

Kiefer, F. 1983. Review of Fónagy, I. *Situation et signification*. *Journal of Pragmatics* 7(6): 742–6.

Kjellmer, G. 1987. Aspects of English collocations. In Meijs, W. (ed.) *Corpus linguistics and beyond*. Amsterdam: Rodopi, 133–40.

Kjellmer, G. 1991. A mint of phrases. In Aijmer and Altenberg (eds) 1991, 111–27.

Knowles, G. 1987. *Patterns of spoken English*. London: Longman.

Krashen, S. and **R. Scarcella.** 1978. On routines and patterns in language acquisition and performance. *Language Learning* 28(2): 283–300.

Kuiper, K. and **P. Austin.** 1990. They're off and racing now: The speech of the New Zealand race caller. In Bell, A. and J. Holmes (eds) *New Zealand ways of speaking English*. Clevedon: Multilingual Matters, 195–220.

Kuiper, K. and **D. Haggo.** 1984. Livestock auctions, oral poetry, and ordinary language. *Language in Society* 13: 205–34.

Labov, W. and **D. Fanshel.** 1977. *Therapeutic discourse*. New York: Academic Press.

Ladd, D.R. Jr. 1978. Stylized intonation. *Language* 54(3): 517–40.

Lakoff, G. 1987. *Women, fire, and dangerous things. What categories reveal about the mind.* Chicago and London: The University of Chicago Press.

Lakoff, R. 1975. *Language and woman's place.* New York: Harper & Row.

Lamb, S. 1992. Idioms, lexemes, and syntax. [Unpublished handout.]

Lee, D. 1987. The semantics of *just. Journal of Pragmatics* 11(3): 377–98.

Leech, G.N. 1983. *Principles of pragmatics.* London: Longman.

Leech, G.N. 1992. Corpora and theories of linguistic performance. In Svartvik, J. (ed.) *Directions in corpus linguistics. Proceedings of Nobel Symposium 82*, Stockholm, 4–8 August 1991. Berlin: Mouton, 105–22.

Leech, G.N. and **J. Coates.** 1980. Semantic indeterminacy and the modals. In Greenbaum, S., G.N. Leech and J. Svartvik (eds) *Studies in English linguistics.* London: Longman.

Leech, G.N. and **J. Thomas.** 1990. Language, meaning and context: pragmatics. In Collinge, N.E. (ed.) *An encyclopaedia of language.* London and New York: Routledge, 173–207.

Levinson, S. 1979. Activity types and language. *Linguistics* 17: 365–79.

Levinson, S. 1983. *Pragmatics.* Cambridge: Cambridge University Press.

Lindström, O. 1978. *Aspects of English intonation.* [New edition.] Surte: Minab.

Lüger, H.-H. 1983. Some aspects of ritual communication. *Journal of Pragmatics* 7(6): 695–711.

McLaughlin, M.L. 1984. *Conversation. How talk is organized.* Beverley Hills, CA: Sage.

Mair, C. 1994. Is *see* becoming a conjunction? The study of grammaticalisation as a meeting ground for corpus linguistics and grammatical theory. In Fries, U., G. Tottie and P. Schneider (eds) *Creating and using English language corpora. Papers from the Fourteenth International Conference on English Language Research on Computerized Corpora, Zürich 1993.* Amsterdam: Rodopi, 127–37.

Makkai, A. 1972. *Idiom structure in English.* The Hague: Mouton.

Makkai, A. 1992. Idiomaticity as the essence of language. [Unpublished handout.]

Manes, J. and **N. Wolfson.** 1981. The compliment formula. In Coulmas (ed.) 1981, 115–32.

Markkanen, R. 1985. *Cross-language studies in pragmatics.* Jyväskylä: University of Jyväskylä.

Mittwoch, A. 1977. How to refer to one's words: Speech act modifying adverbials and the performative analysis. *Journal of Linguistics* 13: 177–89.

Mohan, B.A. 1974. Principles, postulates, politeness. *Papers from the Tenth Regional Meeting of the Chicago Linguistic Society.* Chicago: Department of Linguistics, University of Chicago, 446–59.

Moon, R. 1992. Textual aspects of fixed expressions in learners' dictionaries. In Arnaud, P. and H. Béjoint (eds) *Vocabulary and applied linguistics.* London: Macmillan, 13–27.

Morgan, J.L. 1978. Two types of convention in indirect speech acts. In Cole, P. (ed.) *Syntax and semantics,* Vol. 9: *Pragmatics.* New York: Academic Press, 261–80.

Mulder, G. 1993. Indirect speech acts, direct speech acts and hints. Poster, 4th International Pragmatics Conference, Kobe, Japan, July 1993.

Nattinger, J.R. 1980. A lexical phrase grammar for ESL. *TESOL Quarterly* 14: 337–44.

Nattinger, J.R. and **J.S. DeCarrico.** 1989. Lexical phrases, speech acts and teaching conversation. In Nation, P. and R. Carter (eds). *Vocabulary acquisition. Aila Review* 6: 118–39.

Nattinger, J.R. and **J.S. DeCarrico**. 1992. *Lexical phrases and language teaching*. Oxford: Oxford University Press.

Nef, F. and **H. Nølke**. 1982. A propos des modalisateurs d'énonciation. *Revue Romane* XVII: 34–54.

Norrick, N.R. 1978. Expressive illocutionary acts. *Journal of Pragmatics* 2(3): 277- 91.

Norrick, N.R. 1985. *How proverbs mean. Semantic studies in English proverbs*. Berlin: Mouton.

Nølke, H. 1990. Pertinence et modalisateurs d'énonciation. *Cahiers de linguistique française* 11. Unité de linguistique française, Université de Génève.

Nølke, H. 1991. Contrastive pragmatic linguistics. In Lauridsen, K.M. and O. Lauridsen (eds) *Contrastive linguistics. Papers from the CL-symposion at the Aarhus School of Business, 28–30 August 1989*. Aarhus: Handelshøjskolen i Aarhus, 199–231.

Olshtain, E. and **A. Cohen**. 1983. Apology: A speech act set. In Wolfson, N. and E. Judd (eds) 1983, 18–36.

Östman, J.-O. 1982. The symbiotic relationship between pragmatic particles and impromptu speech. In Enkvist, N.E. (ed.) *Impromptu speech: A symposium*. Publications of the Research Institute of the Åbo Akademi Fondation. Åbo: Åbo Akademi.

Owen, M. 1983. *Apologies and remedial interchanges. A study of language use in social interaction*. Berlin: Mouton.

Oxford dictionary of current idiomatic English. 1975–83. Compiled by A.P. Cowie and R. Mackin. London: Oxford University Press.

Paul, I. 1989. Ritual und Ritualzitat. Die Stilisierung des Rituals durch den pastoralen Diskurs. In Hinnenkamp, V. and M. Selting, *Stil und Stilisierung. Arbeiten zur interpretativen Soziolinguistik*. Tübingen: Max Niemeyer Verlag.

Pawley, A. 1986. Lexicalization. In Tannen, D. and J.E. Alatis (eds) *GURT '85. Languages and linguistics: The interdependence of theory, data, and application*. Washington DC: Georgetown University Press, 98–120.

Pawley, A. and **F.H. Syder**. 1983. Two puzzles for linguistic theory: Nativelike selection and nativelike fluency. In Richards and Schmidt (eds) 1983, 191–226.

Perkins, M.R. 1983. *Modal expressions in English*. London: Frances Pinter.

Peters, A. 1983. *The units of language acquisition*. Cambridge: Cambridge University Press.

Pomerantz, A. 1984. Agreeing and disagreeing with assessments: Some features of preferred/dispreferred turn shapes. In Atkinson, J.M. and J. Heritage (eds) 1984, 57–102.

Pufahl Bax, I. 1986. How to assign work in an office. A comparison of spoken and written directives in American English. *Journal of Pragmatics* 10(6): 673–92.

Quirk, R., S. Greenbaum, G. Leech and **J. Svartvik**. 1985. *A comprehensive grammar of the English language*. London: Longman.

Reichenbach, H. 1947. *Elements of symbolic logic*. London: Macmillan.

Renouf, A. 1984. Corpus development at Birmingham University. In Aarts, J. and W. Meijs (eds) *Corpus linguistics: Recent developments in the use of computer corpora in English language research*. Amsterdam: Rodopi, 3–39.

Richards, J.C. and **R.W. Schmidt** (eds). 1983. *Language and communication*. London: Longman.

Richards, J.C. and **R.W. Schmidt**. 1983a. Conversational analysis. In Richards and Schmidt (eds) 1983, 117–54.

Rintell, E.M. and **C.J. Mitchell.** 1989. Studying requests and apologies: An inquiry into method. In Blum-Kulka et al. (eds) 1989, pp 248–72.

Sadock, J.M. 1974. *Toward a linguistic theory of speech acts.* New York: Academic Press.

Schegloff, E.A. and **H. Sacks.** 1973. Opening up closings. *Semiotica* 8: 289–327.

Schiffrin, D. 1980. Meta-talk: Organizational and evaluative brackets in discourse. In Zimmerman, D. and C. West (eds) *Language and social interaction.* Special edition of *Sociological Inquiry* 50: 99–236.

Schiffrin, D. 1987. *Discourse markers.* Cambridge: Cambridge University Press.

Scollon, R. and **S.B.K. Scollon.** 1983. Face in interethnic communication. In Richards and Schmidt (eds) 1983, 156–88.

Searle, J.R. 1969. *Speech acts. An essay in the philosophy of language.* Cambridge: Cambridge University Press.

Searle, J.R. 1975. Indirect speech acts. in Cole and Morgan (eds) 1975, 59–82.

Searle, J.R. 1976. A classification of illocutionary acts. *Language in Society* 5: 1–23.

Searle, J.R. 1979. *Expression and meaning.* Cambridge: Cambridge University Press.

Searle, J.R. 1979a. Indirect speech acts. In Searle 1979, 30–57. [Originally published in Cole and Morgan (eds) 1975.]

Severinson Eklundh, K. 1986. *Dialogue processes in computer-mediated communication. A study of letters in the COM system.* Linköping Studies in Arts and Science 6. Linköping: University of Linköping.

Severinson Eklundh, K. and **P. Linell.** 1983. The structure of a minimal communicative interaction. In Karlsson (ed.) 1983, 293–304.

Sinclair, J.McH. 1987. Collocation: A progress report. In Steele, R. and T. Threadgold (eds) *Language topics: Essays in honour of Michael Halliday,* 2: 319–31. Amsterdam/Philadelphia: John Benjamin.

Sinclair, J.McH. and **R.M. Coulthard.** 1975. *Towards an analysis of discourse. The English used by teachers and pupils.* Oxford: Oxford University Press.

Sinclair, J.McH. and **A. Renouf.** 1988. A lexical syllabus for language learning. In Carter and McCarthy (eds) 1988, 211–22.

Sorhus, H.B. 1976. To hear ourselves – Implications for teaching English as a second language. *English Language Teaching Journal* 31(3): 211–21.

Sperber, D. and **D. Wilson.** 1986. *Relevance. Communication and cognition.* Oxford: Blackwell.

Stenström, A.-B. 1984. *Questions and responses in English conversation.* Lund: Lund University Press.

Stenström, A.-B. 1990. Lexical items peculiar to spoken discourse. In Svartvik (ed.) 1990, 137–75.

Stenström, A.-B. 1994. *An introduction to spoken interaction.* London and New York: Longman.

Stubbs, M. 1983. *Discourse analysis. The sociolinguistic analysis of natural language.* Oxford: Blackwell.

Svartvik, J. (ed.). 1990. *The London-Lund Corpus of Spoken English: Description and research.* Lund Studies in English 82. Lund: Lund University Press.

Svartvik, J. (ed). 1992. Corpus linguistics comes of age. In Svartvik, J. (ed.) *Directions in corpus linguistics. Proceedings of Nobel Symposium '82* Stockholm, 4–8 August 1991. Berlin: Mouton, 7–13.

Svartvik, J. 1993. Lexis in English language corpora. *Zeitschrift für Anglistik und Amerikanistik* 41: 15–30. [Preprint paper for the Fifth Euralex International

Congress, University of Tampere, Finland, 4–9 August 1992.]

Svartvik, J. and **R. Quirk** (eds). 1980. *A corpus of English conversation.* Lund: CWK Gleerup.

Svartvik, J., M. Eeg-Olofsson, O. Forsheden, B. Oreström and **C. Thavenius.** 1982. *Survey of spoken English: Report on research 1975–81.* Lund: Lund University Press.

Tannen, D. and **P.C. Öztek.** 1981. Health to our mouths. Formulaic expressions in Turkish and Greek. In Coulmas (ed.) 1981, 37–54.

Thompson, S.A. 1985. Grammar and written discourse: Initial vs final purpose clauses in English. *Text* 5: 55–84.

Thompson, S.A. and **A. Mulac.** 1991. A quantitative perspective on the grammaticization of epistemic parentheticals in English. In Traugott and Heine (eds) 1991, Vol. II, 313–29.

Tognini-Bonelli, E. 1993. Interpretative nodes in discourse. *Actual* and *actually.* In Baker, M., G. Francis and E. Tognini-Bonelli (eds) *Text and technology. In honour of John Sinclair.* Amsterdam/Philadelphia: John Benjamin.

Tottie, G. and **I. Bäcklund** (eds). 1987. *English in speech and writing. A symposium.* Stockholm: Almqvist & Wiksell.

Traugott, E.C. 1982. From propositional to textual and expressive meanings: Some semantic-pragmatic aspects of grammaticalization. In Lehmann, W.P. and Y. Malkiel (eds) *Perspectives on historical linguistics.* Amsterdam/Philadelphia: John Benjamin, 245–71.

Traugott, E.C. and **B. Heine.** (eds). 1991. *Approaches to grammaticalization.* Vols I and II. Amsterdam/Philadelphia: John Benjamin.

Trosborg, A. 1987. Apology strategies in natives/nonnatives. *Journal of Pragmatics* 11(2): 147–69.

Tsui, A.B.M. 1989. Beyond the adjacency pair. *Language in Society* 18(4): 545–64.

Tsui, A.B.M. 1994. *English conversation.* Oxford: Oxford University Press.

van Dijk, T.A. 1977. *Text and context. Explorations in the semantics and pragmatics of discourse.* London: Longman.

van Dijk, T.A. 1981. *Studies in the pragmatics of discourse.* The Hague: Mouton.

Vicher, A. and **D. Sankoff.** 1989. The emergent syntax of pre-sentential turn openings. *Journal of Pragmatics* 13(1): 81–97.

Vollmer, H.J. and **E. Olshtain.** 1989. The language of apologies in German. In Blum-Kulka et al. (eds) 1989, 197–218.

Walters, J. 1981. Variation in requesting behavior of bilingual children. *International Journal of the Sociology of Language* 27: 77–92.

Watts, R. (n.d.) Indicating relevance: Cross-cultural differences in the use of discourse markers. [Unpublished.]

Weigel , M.M. and **R.M. Weigel.** 1985. Directive use in a migrant agricultural community: A test of Ervin-Tripp's hypotheses. *Language in Society* 14: 63–80.

Weinreich, U. 1966. On the semantic structure of language. In Greenberg, J. (ed.) *Universals of language.* Cambridge, Mass.: The MIT Press, 142–216.

Weinreich, U. 1980. Problems in the analysis of idioms. In Labov, W. and B. Weinreich (eds) *On semantics.* Philadelphia: University of Pennsylvania Press, 208–64.

Weizman, E. 1989. Requestive hints. In Blum-Kulka et al. (eds) 1989, 71–95.

Wierzbicka, A. 1987. Boys will be boys. *Language* 63(1): 95–114.

Wierzbicka, A. 1991. *Cross-cultural pragmatics. The semantics of human interaction.* Berlin/New York: Mouton de Gruyter.

Wilkins, D.A. 1976. *Notional syllabuses. A taxonomy and its relevance to foreign language curriculum development.* London: Oxford University Press.

Wittgenstein, L. 1967 *Philosophical investigations by Ludwig Wittgenstein,* translated by G.E.M. Anscombe. Oxford: Blackwell.

Wolfson, N. 1983. Rules of speaking. In Richards and Schmidt (eds) 1983, 61–87.

Wolfson, N. 1988. The bulge: A theory of speech behavior and social distance. In Fine, J. (ed.) *Second language discourse: A textbook of current research.* Norwood, NJ: Ablex, 21–40.

Wolfson, N. and **E. Judd** (eds). 1983. *Sociolinguistics and language acquisition.* Rowley, Mass.: Newbury House.

Wolfson, N., L. D'Amico-Reisner and **L. Huber.** 1983. How to arrange for social commitments in American English: The invitation. In Wolfson and Judd (eds) 1983, 116–28.

Wong Fillmore, L. 1979. Individual differences in second language acquisition. In Fillmore, C.J., D. Kempler and W.S.-Y. Wong (eds) *Individual differences in language ability and language behavior.* New York: Academic Press.

Yli-Jokipii. H. 1990. Identifying requests in business letters: A two-level approach. In Battarbee, K. and R. Hiltunen (eds) *Alarums and excursions. Working papers in English.* Publications of the Department of English. University of Turku. No. 9, Turku: 175–95.

Yorio, C.A. 1980. Conventionalized language forms and the development of communicative competence. *TESOL Quarterly* 14(4): 433–42.

Index